"Over 95 percent of companies i
size firms. Yet, there has been nc
the benefits of sustainability strategies until now. Norman Christopher has
filled this void that is a must read for any small to medium-size business
owner or business leader. Packed with relevant examples, lessons learned,
and pragmatic guidance, it helps senior managers see the benefits for their
function when they embrace sustainability. Perfect!"
—*Bob Willard, Author of* The Sustainability Advantage

"*Sustainability Demystified!* is an indispensable guide and tool for
businesses looking to implement sustainability practices today and in
their strategic planning. It translates 'Triple Bottom Line' practices into
performance in a way that your business can compete and win."
—*Rick Baker, President and CEO of the Grand Rapids Chamber of*
Commerce, addressing the beginning of the Sustainability Revolution!

"This book describes the finer points of sustainability and the required hard
work to get there. By implementing the best practices that are described,
businesses can improve the overall efficiency of their operations."
—*Mark Lindquist, President of Rapid-Line Manufacturing,*
Grand Rapids, Michigan

"The more of the mystery that we can take out of sustainability, the
more that can be accomplished. This practical guide will allow business
leaders who have achieved some level of sustainability to improve their
performance even more. Norman has also created a clear approach for
the manager new to sustainability and those that have already achieved
some level of success but wish to go further."
—*Mike Olthoff, President of Nichols Inc., Muskegon, Michigan*

"The United States Green Building Council's Leadership in Energy
and Environmental Design (LEED) has been and continues to be
very important to West Michigan and demonstrates our leadership
in the green building movement. Also, very important is the ongoing

performance of our LEED buildings, measuring and reporting the impact to a business economically, environmentally, and to the health of the people that work there. Norman has captured the best practices and examples that we so desperately need to share about sustainability to improve overall business performance."

—*Renae Hesselink,*
Past Chair of the West Michigan Chapter of the USGBC

"Norman has been a catalyst in the field of sustainability in West Michigan, bringing together leaders from the business, government, education, and non-profit sectors. He has played a central role in West Michigan's rise on the national stage of sustainability and earned the respect and accolades from our community. *Sustainability Demystified!* is a practical, hands-on approach to the application of the many principles of sustainability as they touch all aspects of business. Norman has done a wonderful job of articulating concepts and then providing practical applications to demonstrate the teaching."

—*Brad Thomas, President, Progressive AE*

"Before most of us could spell sustainability, Grand Valley State University, under Norman Christopher's leadership, was far advanced in practice. This seminal book—coming as it does early in the sustainability movement—will rapidly become a classic in the field. Read it and be inspired."

—*George Heartwell, Mayor, City of Grand Rapids Michigan*

"Sustainability, while crucial to future prosperity, has become an overused buzzword, meaning everything from waste reduction to poverty. In this excellent and practical guide, Norman Christopher really does demystify sustainability, making it something that companies can not only aspire to, but reduce to practice."

—*Stuart L. Hart, Cornell University, Author of Capitalism at the*
Crossroads

"This practical guide will show the small business owner the ability to view his or her business from a different and strategic set of eyes. The entrepreneur will be able to assess their business, develop a sustainability plan, and implement new strategies for their business operations. It will be exciting to see how companies will transform their businesses while adding to the bottom line."

—*Dante Villareal, Director,*
West Michigan Small Business Technology Development Center

"Sustainability has become a business imperative. Those companies that are not preparing for a more resource and carbon-constrained world will find themselves struggling to maintain their place in a global marketplace. *Sustainability Demystified!* provides a valuable "essentials guide" to forward thinking business owners interested in staying one step ahead of the competition in the growing green economy."

—*Peter Perez, Past Deputy Assistant Secretary,*
Office of Manufacturing, U.S. Department of Commerce,
Owner of Carter Products Company

"*Sustainability Demystified!* is a comprehensive practical toolbox that addresses all aspects of the sustainability 'Triple Bottom Line' in a succinct way. What sets Norman Christopher's book apart is the array of tools and best practices for small to medium-size businesses. The wealth of the author's knowledge has been put to great use and will be beneficial to all who read this book. I would strongly recommend using this book for a foundation course in any graduate program, especially in an MBA program or Executive MBA program. We plan to use it at our university."

—*Dr. Jaideep Motwani, Chair and Professor of Management,*
Seidman College of Business, Grand Valley State University

"Sustainability has in many ways become an overused "buzzword", masking a very serious subject that requires commitment on the part of companies, communities, and individuals. Sustainability and the 'Triple Bottom Line' are well on their way to becoming what "lean manufacturing practices" are already, an expected way of doing business. Yet many companies are still struggling with the pathway to sustainability. The book *Sustainability Demystified!* is an eminently practical guide to a complex subject, and should put many companies, particularly small to medium-size firms, well on their way to a pathway of understanding and implementing sustainable practices in their companies."

—*Birgit Klohs, President and CEO of the Right Place Inc.*

"*Sustainability Demystified!* introduces businesspeople, regardless of industry or sector, to sustainability business practices. Whether you work for a small or large company, in banking or retail, in Michigan or Texas, there are lessons that can be gained that can immediately be applied to your business."

—*Kyle Denning,*
Managing Partner of Sustainable Energy Financing LLC

SUSTAINABILITY DEMYSTIFIED!

SUSTAINABILITY DEMYSTIFIED!

A PRACTICAL GUIDE FOR BUSINESS LEADERS AND MANAGERS

NORMAN CHRISTOPHER

PRINCIPIA
MEDIA

TABLE OF CONTENTS

PREFACE

The notion of sustainability and sustainable development can be traced back to our Native American past as far as seven generations with the ancient Indian proverb that states: "Treat the earth well. It was not given to you by your parents. It was loaned to you by your children. We do not inherit the earth from our ancestors, we borrow it from our children."[1] Then, in 1987, the United Nations Brundtland Commission defined sustainability in broader terms as "meeting the needs of today without compromising the ability of future generations to meet their own needs."[2] Then and now, the key concepts of sustainability deal with an overall process of change whereby the consumption of resources, the purpose of financial investments, the use of various forms of capital, and the formation of working partnerships with community stakeholders are compatible with needs of the present as well as future generations. The "Triple Bottom Line" of sustainability addresses reduced environmental impact, improved social impact, and increased economic impact. These perspectives, along with the use of clean technologies, will all play important and ever increasing roles in this transformation.

The roots of the "Green Movement" at a national level can be traced from the 1950s through the 1970s. In 1962 author Rachel Carson published the book *Silent Spring*[3] which became a bellwether of the environmental movement by drawing significant attention to the chemical industry and its use of petroleum based chemicals and pesticides that caused harm to the natural environment. Also, at the time, was news of oil tanker spills which became more prevalent in the media with such incidents as the Torrey Canyon and the spill off the coast of England. Then, in the 1970s, the United States passed creative new environmental legislation such as the Clean Water Act, the Clean Air Act, the Endangered Species Act, and the National Environmental Policy Act. All of this legislation provided the platforms and foundations for our current environmental standards and regulations.

We have intentionally focused the discussion in this book on West Michigan, a distinct area within the state of Michigan which includes such municipalities as Grand Rapids, Kalamazoo, Muskegon, and Holland. This five county region contains a population of over 1.4 million and is the fastest growing region in the state of Michigan.

In West Michigan, sustainability has been embraced for decades by the furniture industry with companies such as Herman Miller, Steelcase, Haworth, and many others. At Herman Miller, for example, their founder D.J. De Pree in 1953 "developed a statement of corporate values that included the declaration that Herman Miller will be a good corporate neighbor by being a good steward of the environment."[4] Even before that time, D.J. De Pree established a number of best practices that were considered as both common sense and environmentally sensible. Several of these action steps included placing windows in all facilities and buildings to provide both natural light and ventilation. Another practice involved setting aside 50 percent of all corporate sites as green space.

These sustainable development best practices provided the groundwork for their leadership in environmental stewardship, as with the other companies within the furniture industry. Herman Miller started designing and constructing "green" buildings in the 1970s; formed their Environmental Quality Action Team (EQAT) in the late 1980s; and embraced the formation and start up of the

U.S. Green Building Council (USGBC) in the late 1990s. Today, the USGBC has set the bar for building performance standards with their Leading Environmental and Energy Design (LEED) certification and rating systems. Herman Miller and others have certified many of their buildings to LEED building performance standards for many years which has helped "walk the talk." In West Michigan there are now approximately 160 LEED certified building projects that total over 25 million square feet of building capacity. It is estimated that the capital cost of these building projects is nearly $3.8 billion, which has also provided many new jobs for the local industry and economy, as well as saving natural resources through energy and water conservation and efficiency measures.

For the last decade the furniture industry, as well as general manufacturing in West Michigan, has grown their development and support for environmental stewardship by institutionalizing sustainability and sustainable development best practices. The leadership of the furniture industry along with other companies such as Cascade Engineering, Amway Corporation, and the Kellogg Company; universities and colleges such as Grand Valley State University, Aquinas College, Grand Rapids Community College, and others; hospitals such as Metro Health, St. Mary's, and Spectrum Health; and cities and communities, such as Grand Rapids and Holland have all helped lay groundwork for others in the public, private and academic sectors in West Michigan to pursue, adopt, and embrace sustainable development practices in their planning and operations.

During the last decade Michigan has gone through a most difficult and trying period with the loss of nearly 800,000 jobs. For many years during this time frame, Michigan had one of the highest unemployment rates of all states in the U.S. Fortunately, as the country has emerged from its economic downturn, West Michigan and the Grand Rapids area have seen significant improvement. Today, businesses and organizations are more efficient and productive, and industries such as professional services, construction, healthcare, leisure and tourism, and manufacturing are beginning to hire employees.

During this time frame, there has been a transition away from older business models, which have been tweaked and refined for improvement over many years. Today, there has been a distinctive shift toward the transformation of new business and organizational models built on applied sustainable development best practices. New businesses in life sciences, medical devices, renewable energy, waste materials, energy efficiency, water purification, advanced batteries, biofuels, and others that are built on sustainable development best practices and clean technologies are now emerging in West Michigan.

Moving forward, organizations and businesses in West Michigan, both large and small, are learning that they can become more profitable, better environmental stewards, and more socially responsible by developing and applying sustainable best practices. What has caused this improvement and progress? Businesses and organizations are now thinking holistically, becoming more creative, getting to root causes, working with collaborators and partners, and building upon cost savings and efficiencies for the future.

"Out of clutter, find simplicity. From discord, find harmony. In the middle of difficulty, lies opportunity."

—*Albert Einstein*

"We are living in an interminable succession of absurdities imposed by the logic of short-term thinking."

—*Jacques Yves Cousteau*

INTRODUCTION

While this book uses West Michigan as its study area, it is useful for any business or organization no matter where the location. Many times larger organizations with the greater availability of resources have the opportunity to be an early adopter of business processes and best practices, such as with sustainable development. However, sustainable development best practices are not just for large corporations, businesses or enterprises. These best practices can be applied by small and medium-size businesses and family owned businesses as well with the same, or even improved, performance results. Additionally, sustainable development best practices are also being imbedded and applied within other organizational entities, such as nonprofit organizations, governmental municipalities, and academic institutions

This sustainable development best practices guide has been written for business entrepreneurs, owners, managers, and department heads. In essence, the utilization of the sustainable development best practices that are described will enable the business executive to make better decisions about their business, both for tactical decisions today as well as strategic decisions tomorrow.

The guide is organized into sections by the major functions and disciplines of a business including administration and management; design, engineering and technology; marketing and sales; operations and manufacturing; information technology; supply chain management; and finance and accounting. Each business function section contains those sustainable development best practices that can be applied in the respective functional business area to upgrade business processes and systems and improve overall business performance and results.

There are 24 applied sustainable development best practices covered in this guide. Each of the sustainable development best practices is reviewed and discussed in the same context. First, an introduction to the sustainable development best practice is provided. Next there is a description of the sustainability system, process, or technique to be used. Areas of business application for the specific sustainable development best practice are then reviewed. The applications are followed by expected results or anticipated benefits with the use of the sustainable development best practice. Each chapter includes a case study. Local case studies of Michigan and West Michigan companies were used wherever possible to help illustrate the growth of sustainable development best practices in the overall West Michigan business community. At the conclusion of each chapter is a call to action for the business owner or manager. This call to action includes 4-6 key questions that will help stimulate the business enterprise to take the next steps in the use of sustainable development best practices.

Sustainability Demystified!: A Practical Guide for Business Leaders, Managers, and Owners is an essential guide or reference handbook of sustainable best practices. It provides top executives or business managers with an overall look at sustainable development best practices in the context of the entire business enterprise. Business department managers can use the guide to study specific sustainable development best practices that can be applied and implemented in their particular area of responsibility. Others will find it helpful in understanding and implementing sustainable development best practices within the context of the environment or their respective areas of interest. It is hoped you will enjoy the sustainability journey, stay the course, and celebrate the successes!

References

1. http://www.ilhawaii.net/~stony/quotes.html, accessed June 2012.
2. www.unece.org/oes/nutshell/2004-2005/focus_sustainable_development.html, accessed August 2011.
3. R. Carson, *Silent Spring* (New York, NY: Houghton Mifflin Company, 1962).
4. http://www.smartfurniture.com/hermanmiller/environmental.html, accessed July 2012.

PART ONE

ADMINISTRATION AND MANAGEMENT

Administration and management are critical functional areas for businesses and organizations. Traditionally, areas such as planning, development, accounting, and human resources are considered the backbone of any enterprise. Organizations want to ensure business operations are well resourced and well staffed. Today, however, businesses need to look at other key processes and systems such as leadership in sustainability and improved decision making; tactical and strategic sustainability planning; social responsibility and corporate citizenship; sustainability audits and assessments; and internal sustainability performance reporting. All of these sustainable development areas will become incredibly important for administration and management in the future for overall improved decision making within the business organization or enterprise.

The major driving forces for this change include the need for businesses to:

- become more transparent and accountable for overall operations
- engage more with both internal shareholders and employees, as well as external stakeholders, regarding overall operations and community outreach
- collect, analyze, and report on increasing amounts of data and information about the organization
- help solve key systemic sustainability issues within the communities in which they serve

1. LEADERSHIP IN SUSTAINABILITY

Introduction

Business and organization leaders today are being faced with the need to make difficult, more informed, and better decisions for their enterprises. In the past, business leaders have relied primarily on analytical and rational skills to make such decisions. Leadership in sustainability requires that executives of today and tomorrow need to react and think differently in order to deal with systemic sustainability issues and opportunistic new business ventures.

Today and in the future, business leaders will need to develop both "soft" and "hard" skill sets in order to improve management flow capabilities, as well as make more informed decisions for their businesses and organizations.

The case studies in this chapter include Peter Wege and Steelcase; The Right Place, Inc; Grand Rapids Chamber of Commerce; and the West Michigan Sustainable Business Forum.

Description

Much has been said recently about "right" and "left" brain thinkers in the business world. A balanced management style that uses the "steady state" or left side of the brain including analytical, logical, rational, structured, and controlled thought processes in configuration with the "change" or right side of the brain including intuitive, open-ended, creative, connected, and multitask thought processes is needed to address and make dynamic marketplace decisions.

In 1997 John Elkington in his book *Cannibals with Forks: The Triple Bottom Line of the 21st Century Business* identified seven revolutions in thinking that were taking place:[1]

- Markets are seeing a paradigm shift from a compliance perspective to local, regional, and global competitiveness
- Values are shifting from "hard" to "soft" or from tangible to more intangible guiding principles
- Open transparency is becoming required from a more closed communications and reporting process and style
- Products are moving from characteristics to functionality using Design for Life (DfL), Life Cycle Analysis (LCA) and Design for the Environment (DfE) processes
- Time frames are shifting to longer-term perspectives from shorter and wider periods
- Corporate governance is now seen as being inclusive rather than exclusive
- Partnerships are becoming more symbiotic in nature rather than subversive

Also, there are a number of related guiding principles of sustainability thinking that are also being embraced in the marketplace today:[2]

- Understanding interdisciplinary system approaches
- Recognizing limits such as with the use of resources
- Protecting and restoring nature
- Transforming business as usual to a proactive entrepreneurial business model in order to meet the challenges of the new economy
- Practicing fairness among employees and suppliers
- Embracing creativity and innovation in business processes and operations
- Seeking longer-term solutions versus short-term gains

With these revolutions in thinking and guiding principles of sustainability, business leaders and managers can now draw upon a number of innovative sustainable development processes and systems from their management toolbox. These processes and techniques can improve business operations and include the following examples of proven sustainable developments best practices:[3]

- Carbon Management
- Design for the Environment (DfE)
- Design for Life (DfL)
- Design for Disassembly (DfD)
- Design for Sustainability (DfS)
- Eco-Efficiency
- Energy Audits and Assessments
- Environmental Management Systems
- Environmental Preferred Purchasing or Green Procurement
- Green and LEAN Management Systems
- Life Cycle Assessment and Management
- Life Cycle Analysis (LCA)
- Materials Stewardship
- Pollution Prevention
- Resource Recovery
- Waste Minimization
- Product Stewardship
- Responsible Care
- Standards and Certifications such as ISO 14001 and LEED
- Sustainable Supply Chain Management
- Sustainability "Triple Bottom Line" Sustainability Reporting
- Total Cost Accounting

Business leaders will also now need to be equipped with additional skill sets to be able to address complex business issues, new business development opportunities, and organizational leadership challenges. Some of these sustainable development skills include:

- Balanced "Triple Bottom Line" (TBL) lens approaches including social, environmental, and economic impact
- Holistic systems-oriented thinking
- Critical Path Analysis
- Creativity, innovation, and entrepreneurship
- Risk management
- Change management
- Empowerment
- Collaborations, partnerships, alliances, and networks
- Quantitative and qualitative performance measurements
- Intercultural capacity and understanding
- Integrity, openness, and transparency
- Creation of efficiencies and value
- Accountability and authenticity
- Solutions oriented problem solving and decision making

Some additional skill sets needed for leaders of today's business or enterprise also involve:[4]

- Rapid prototyping of products and services
- The ability to clarify issues, concerns, and complex problems
- Looking at the glass as half full of opportunities, not half empty with issues and concerns
- The capability to break down a problem and identify the components or parts that work and can be used
- Rallying and inspiring others around common platforms of mutual understanding
- The ability to seek and learn wisdom and knowledge

Application

For small- to medium-size businesses, commitment to sustainable development principles, processes, best practices, and skills starts first with the business owner, president, and executive management team. For many business owners, including family owned businesses, sustainability is a passion and journey for their company. These leaders wear sustainability on their sleeve and have become role models for other business leaders in their community. Examples of these sustainability leaders include:

- Yves Chouinard, Patagonia[5]
- Jeff Hollander, Seventh Generation[6]
- Ray Anderson, Interface[7]
- Tom Chappell, Tom's of Maine[8]
- Fred Keller, Cascade Engineering[9]
- Gary Hirschberg, Stonyfield Farms[10]
- Ben Cohen and Jerry Greenfield, Ben and Jerry's Ice Cream[11]

Leadership in sustainability is now being implemented in a similar fashion by many others including executive management, general management, directors, department heads, and employees in business operations and organizations today.

These sustainability leadership skills can be accessed and reinforced through web-based information; attending conferences, trade and professional organizations; benchmarking role models; profiling competitors and using business consultants.

So where does a company start with implementing leadership in sustainability? The first place that leadership in sustainability should be seen is in the company vision and mission statement. These vision and mission statements should be communicated and shared with internal company and business shareholders including employees, as well as other stakeholder partners in the community. Next, management should address their company and organizational culture and ideology. Sustainability should be evident in the organization's value and guiding principles including stewardship, service, accountability, transparency, and the building of trustful working relationships. Business owners, managers, and employees should walk the walk together in achieving sustainability goals and talk the same talk regarding sustainability discussions, conversations, and dialogue.

Results and Benefits

Business leaders who embrace sustainable development guiding principles, best practices processes and techniques, and use sustainability skills in their organizations can expect to see a number of proven and demonstrated benefits to their company and business: These results include:[12]

- Improved financial performance
- Reduced operating costs
- Production and process improvements
- Quality improvements
- Reduced liabilities and risks
- Enhanced brand image and reputation
- Improved access to capital
- Increased employee morale
- Better attraction and retention of employees
- Increased opportunity for creativity and innovation
- Increased opportunity for revenue growth, new market and business development potential, and price premiums
- Better supply chain management
- Improved customer relationships and customer loyalty
- Trustful working relationships, partnerships, and collaborations
- Reduced regulatory oversight

Chris Lazlo in his book, *Sustainability Value*, addresses "how the world's leading companies are doing well by doing good." The sustainable company is one that undergoes transformational change both internally and externally from the outside in and the inside out. This change can be seen in how the company is organized, how it engages with suppliers and customers, and what role it has in the community. Below are listed some of the features and characteristics of what a truly sustainable company and organization looks like:[13]

- Sustainability performance is fully integrated into the strategies and action plans of the company.
- All managers consider sustainability to be part of their daily job and overall responsibilities.
- Metrics reward managers for sustainability performance and progress.
- CEO and senior leadership demonstrate full support and "walk the talk."
- Sustainability targets are set and progress monitored. The targets are quantitative and qualitative and measured against milestones.
- New management tools are used such as: stakeholder engagement; environmental and social accounting; Design for the Environment (DfE); Life Cycle Assessment (LCA); green and sustainable product standards and certifications, balanced scorecards, and sustainability assessments.
- Broad and diverse relationships between company shareholder and community stakeholders, including partnerships with nongovernmental organizations (NGOs) are developed.
- Managers are able to uncover business opportunities that fully integrate environmental and social performance into core business platforms and overall economic performance.
- New elements of corporate culture include transparency, accountability, deep listening, integrity, innovation, inclusion, and empathy for example.

Case Studies

West Michigan has emerged as a recognized leader in applied sustainable development best practices across the public, private, and economic sectors over the last 10 years. But the roots of sustainability go deep and have been engrained in our area and culture for years. Peter Wege has been a well-recognized leader of Steelcase, one of the oldest companies in the region and the international segment leader in office systems furniture. In 1967 he formed the Wege Foundation which has been dedicated to environmental sustainability and stewardship. Mr. Wege defined the term "Economicology" and has written several books on this subject matter that advocated his philosophy that "a prosperous economy depends on a healthy ecology."[14] In West Michigan sustainability is more than the products and services it designs and offers. Sustainability is about making better decisions today so future generations can enjoy a better quality of life tomorrow. Sustainable development is also about generating short-term efficiencies, and long-term value for our businesses, organizations, and communities. Leadership in sustainability can be demonstrated in three key areas:

- Reducing environmental impact and improving environmental stewardship
- Creating greater and sustained economic impact
- Improving social impact and overall quality of life

Through the leadership across the public, private, and academic sectors, West Michigan has been able to achieve demonstrated performance and raise the bar on overall sustainable development, progress, and performance.

Some of these achievements include:

- Creating the West Michigan Sustainable Business Forum in 1994, the first of its kind in Michigan.[15]
- Offering a sustainable business degree that was among the first in the nation offered through Aquinas College.[16]

- Establishing national recognition in the design and construction of Leading Environmental and Energy Design (LEED) certified buildings. Grand Rapids has ranked #14 as a city in the total number of LEED certified building projects and #2 in LEED buildings per capita according the West Michigan Chapter of the U.S. Green Building Council.[17]
- Creating Local First in 2003, a group originally known as BALLE dedicated to the growth of local businesses in Grand Rapids.[18]
- Being recognized nationally for its sustainable businesses including Herman Miller, Steelcase, Haworth, Cascade Engineering, and many others.
- Having a nationally recognized trade association, The Business and Institutional Furniture Manufacturer's Association (BIFMA), that has developed and implemented the first voluntary furniture sustainability standard and rating system, the BIFMA e-3 standard.[19]
- Being recognized by the U.S. Chamber of Commerce and Siemens Corporation as having the most sustainable midsize city in the U.S., Grand Rapids, Michigan.[20]
- Developing a region-wide sustainability effort and movement through articles and stories that have appeared in the *Detroit Free Press*, the *Grand Rapids Press, Fast Company, Inc., I BIZ, Grand Rapids Business Journal, Business Review,* and other newspapers, journals, and trade publications.

The Right Place Inc. was formed in 1985 and is the preeminient regional nonprofit economic development organization in the West Michigan region. Birgit Klohs has been the President of this organization for many years and has exhibited great leadership for the organization and community at large. The mission of the Right Place is to retain and attract businesses to the West Michigan area and to improve the overall health and economic vitality of the region. One of the strategies of the organization has been to foster sustainable economic development through applied sustainable development best practices. Currently the focus is on the following emerging growth opportunities:[21]

- Life Sciences including medical devices and biotechnology
- Alternative and Renewable Energy technologies such as solar, wind, and biomass power generation sources
- Agribusiness and Food Processing
- Aerospace and Defense
- Advanced Manufacturing
- Sustainability

The Right Place has had a focus for many years on the clean technology and green manufacturing economy in West Michigan for consumer products, waste management, public transit, building materials, and food and farming. The results of their 2004-2008 strategic plan include $467 million in new capital investment; $228 million in new payroll; 8,366 in new and retained jobs; and 2,332 in companies assisted.

The Grand Rapids Chamber of Commerce has been connecting, serving, and helping West Michigan businesses grow for over 120 years. In recent years the Chamber has taken a leadership role assisting companies with applied sustainable development best practices. One notable example is the generation of a 78 item business sustainability checklist including the following areas:

- Waste prevention
- Recycling
- Purchasing
- Energy and water conservation
- Engaging stakeholders
- Transportation
- Operations

Additionally the Chamber has established the greater Grand Rapids Partnership for a Sustainable Community. This initiative was created to help support the City of Grand Rapids and the overall community with climate adaption and climate mitigation best practices. Once a company joins this partnership, the company is provided a carbon calculator to guide the business through various strategies to reduce overall GHG emissions and environmental impact, while reducing costs at the same time.

As mentioned, some of the leadership in sustainability can also be traced back to the mid 1990s when the West Michigan Sustainable Business Forum (WMSBF) was originally established. Bill Stough, President of the Sustainable Research Group (SRG), helped form this organization along with the West Michigan Environmental Action Council (WMEAC), Perrigo, Crystal Flash, Herman Miller, and several other key organizations. Today the WMSBF has an active membership of over 100 organizations. (www.wmsbf.org)

Bill Stough has also been instrumental in helping form other Michigan Sustainable Business Forums. These other organizations include the Northwest Michigan Sustainable Business Forum, the Southwest Michigan Sustainable Business Forum, the Saginaw Bay Sustainable Business Partnership, and the Southeast Michigan Sustainable Business Forum. The mission for all of the sustainable business forums in Michigan is to work together collaboratively, generate long-term financial success and growth for their membership, and support the triple bottom line of economic, social, and environmental performance. Specific goals and objectives deal with establishing a learning network for applied sustainable development best practices, coaching and mentoring member companies on sustainable processes and tools, developing broad based partnerships, generating awareness and understanding for sustainability guiding principles through varied programs and activities, and determining key success factors and performance measurements.

Call to Action

- What are the key attributes and guiding principles of sustainability leadership that your organization currently has in place?
- Where are the organizational gaps in sustainability leadership?
- Which departmental areas of your business can be used as role models for sustainability leadership within your organization?
- What are a few steps that management can take to encourage organizational leadership in sustainability across the organization?

References

1. J. Elkington, *Cannibals with Forks: The Triple Bottom Line of the 21st Century Business*, (Oxford, U.K. Capstone Publishing Company Ltd., 1997), www.johnelkington.com/TBL-elkington-chapter.pdf, Chapter 1, page 3, accessed August 2011.

2. Alan AtKisson, The Seven Principles of Sustainability, http://alanatkisson.wordpress.com/youtube-short-course/the-seven-principles-of-sustainability/, accessed August 2011.

3. PE International & Five Winds Consulting http://www.fivewinds.com/english/resources/publications.html, accessed August 2011.

4. B. Johansen, *Leaders Make the Future:Ten New Leadership Skills for an Uncertain World* (Berrett-Koehler Publishers, 2009), accessed March 2012.

5. Patagonia Inc., www.patagonia.com, accessed August 2011.

6. Seventh Generation Inc., http://www.seventhgeneration.com, accessed August 2011.

7. Interface Inc., http://www.interfaceglobal.com, accessed August 2011.

8. Tom's of Maine, www.tomsofmaine.com, accessed August 2011.

9. Cascade Engineering Inc., www.cascadeng.com, accessed August 2011.

10. Stonyfield Farms Inc., www.stonyfield.com, accessed August 2011.

11. Ben and Jerry's Homemade Inc., www.benjerry.com, accessed August 2011.

12. Adapted from Bob Willard's, www.sustainabilityadvantage.com/products/sustainadv.html, accessed August 2011.

13. C. Laszlo, *Sustainable Value: How the World's Leading Companies Are Doing Well by Doing Good*, (Stanford, CA: Stanford University Press, 2008), page 66-67.
14. Economicology, http://www.wegefoundation.com/news/1007cityhigh.html, accessed June 2012.
15. West Michigan Sustainable Business Forum, www.WMSBF.org, accessed August 2011.
16. Aquinas College, http://www.aquinas.edu/sb/, accessed August 2011.
17. US Green Building Council, www.usgbc.org, accessed August 2011.
18. Local First, www.localfirst.com, accessed August 2011.
19. The Business and Institutional Furniture Manufacturer Association, www.bifma.org, accessed 2011.
20. City of Grand Rapids, www.grcity.us, accessed March 2012.
21. The Right Place, Inc., www.rightpace.org, accessed July 2012.
22. Grand Rapids Chamber of Commerce, www.grandrapids.org/sustainability, accessed July 2012.

2. SUSTAINABILITY PLANNING AND DEVELOPMENT

Introduction

Drivers for Sustainable Development

In the recent past, businesses may have looked at sustainable development as an option or opportunity. Today, many enterprises now view sustainability as a necessity for their company and business operations.

What's changed and why is there such urgency?

Evidence of sustainable development can already be seen in the West Michigan marketplace in many areas and sectors.

- There are many encouraging signs of progress regarding sustainable development in West Michigan. Recently the City of Grand Rapids was recognized as the most sustainable community in the midsize city category in the U.S. by the U.S. Chamber of Commerce and Siemens Corporation. Many endorsing partners of the Greater Grand Rapids Community Sustainability Partnership ("CSP")[1] that represent the public, private and academic sectors and the West Michigan Sustainable Business Forum[2] are transparent in reporting their sustainable development progress through periodic sustainability indicator reports using performance metrics. Many of these sustainability indicator reports are available online.

- There are many examples of significant systemic sustainability issues and concerns in West Michigan where applied sustainable development can be implemented to improve existing and future conditions. Many of these significant problems relate to both social and environmental concerns. One example is removal of lead based paint used in older city homes. Lead has been shown to be toxic and exposure to small children can affect health as well as learning capabilities.

Today, the Healthy Homes Coalition of West Michigan[3] is a collaborative effort that works with other NGOs and the City of Grand Rapids to remove lead based paint from inner city homes. Other catastrophes such as the oil spill in the Kalamazoo River remind us of the need for improved environmental management systems.

- Independent research reports, such as those from consultants, NGOs, and colleges and universities help identify current sustainability risks and liabilities that need to be addressed. There have been a number of these reports issued on the overall banking industry regarding ethical and transparency issues concerning national and global financial institutions. The global debt crisis now impacts us regionally here in West Michigan and those living elsewhere. Fiscal sustainability standards are now being considered by the Global Accounting Standards Bureau as well as other banking reform standards.

- Other encouraging proactive approaches to sustainable development can also spur companies and their respective trade associations to raise the bar and set higher expectations regarding their "Triple Bottom Line" sustainability efforts. One such example is The Business and Institutional Furniture Manufacturer's Association (BIFMA).[4] This organization has recently established an industry-wide voluntary assessment standard and rating system for furniture products based on TBL applied sustainable development best practices. It is known as the BIFMA e-3 Furniture Sustainability Standard. A company can evaluate its product performance against the standard and then certify to level performance through third-party verification. Another example is Herman Miller's Perfect Vision 2020 goals where the company has set a variety of zero environmental impact goals to be accomplished by the year 2020.

- Another reason for immediate action in sustainable development can be seen in benchmarking peers, competitors, and other industries. One such example is Walmart[5] and their sustainability index rating system for sustainable supply chain partners. A standard questionnaire and survey is provided to all current suppliers in their supply chain. The focus is on TBL sustainable development and climate impact. Suppliers are rated on their responses and suggested areas of improvement are provided. Many businesses are reviewing this sustainability index to determine how they would fare as a supplier to Walmart, as well as wondering if and when such a sustainability index might become applicable to their industry.

The case study in this chapter is Cascade Engineering.

Description

As can be seen, there are a number of reasons why businesses should conduct sustainable development planning for their business operations and company.

- There are many expressed concerns from independent organizations about futuristic issues and problems such as the depletion of non-renewable resources, access to water, and potential governmental legislation relating to sustainability such as with climate change legislation, potential cap and trade, carbon tax, and other regulations. Management must make a decision on whether to be proactive about these issues or wait and become reactive to dynamic market change forces.
- Moreover, there are increasing issues, concerns, and opportunities being expressed by consumers about green and sustainable products. The Natural Marketing Institute (NMI) started tracking the Lifestyle of Health and Sustainability (LOHAS)[6] market at the consumer sales level and estimated sales at $300 billion in 2008. About one in five consumers today regularly purchase products in the LOHAS market and are most

concerned about product authentication and sustainability certifications. Product "green washing" has now become a key awareness for both suppliers and customers as labels are read for active and inactive ingredients, pre- and post-consumer waste content, overall nutrition information, etc.

Before beginning a sustainability plan for your organization or business, management needs to first establish competitive skills and capabilities through a strengths, weaknesses, opportunities, and threats analysis (SWOT), followed by a determination of core competencies. Only a few core competencies are needed for a business and organization to develop its mission, vision, and strategic intent around sustainable development. There are several tests for core competency. These include: the development of core platforms and products from the competencies that generate efficiencies and create value and benefits for customers; the difficulty for competitors to copy and emulate the competency in their operations; and the ability for the competency to be transferred and established in a different market.[7]

Michael Robert in his book, *Strategy Pure and Simple,* identified the strategic intent of business being in one of eleven key functional areas.[8]

Strategic Intent of a Business

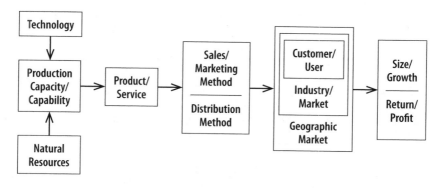

Source: Strategy Pure and Simple, adapted by Norman Christopher, 2012.

These core competency building blocks and platforms include: technology; production capability and capacity; natural resource base; product and service; sales and marketing channels; distribution mode; customer or user class; industry or geographic market segmentation; market growth and size; and financial return. Some examples include: telephone companies and their distribution method-driven strategy, General Motors and IBM for their product-driven strategies, and Lowes and Home Depot for their distribution modes.

Steps to Creating a Sustainability Plan

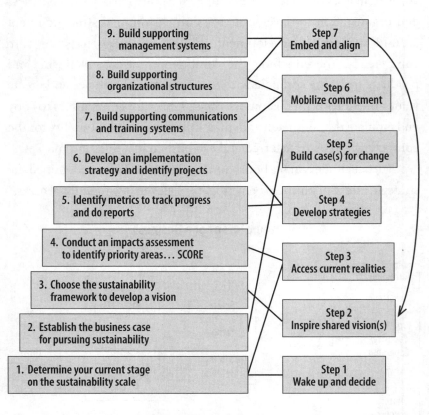

Source: Darcy Hitchcock and Marsha Willard, *The Step-by-Step Guide to Sustainability Planning* (Earthscan, 2008), adapted by Norman Christopher, 2012.

There are a number of steps to creating and implementing a successful sustainability plan based on strategic intent that a company can also take. Darcy Hitchcock and Marsha Willard in their book, *The Step-By-Step Guide to Sustainability Planning*, describe a sustainability planning process that businesses and organizations can follow.[9]

The keys to success in the development of this sustainability plan are as follows:

- Ensuring top management is committed to the overall planning process.
- Establishing a cross functional team with well-known respected team members, including employees where appropriate, to develop a sustainability vision.
- Empowering and recognizing the team for its work and efforts such as with sustainability assessments of core operations.
- Helping the sustainability planning team meet milestones and objectives that have been set in the process through metrics and performance indicators to track progress.
- Encouraging the team members to address challenging systemic sustainability issues and propose realistic goals and strategies for the sustainability journey.
- Supporting the team members in the use of creative, innovative, and entrepreneurial approaches and strategies including grassroots bottoms up input and feedback.
- Providing a supportive open structure and environment for conversations, dialogue, and the work to be accomplished.

There are also a number of strategic focus levels[10] that can be developed within the sustainability plan starting from a baseline compliance oriented risk management level that focuses on "protecting the license to operate" to an overall business context level that "changes the rules of the game." Patagonia[11] represents a company that has developed a sustainability culture and brand identity. Philips Electronics[12] represents a company that is trying to change the rules of the game by stopping the production of incandescent light bulbs and only producing compact fluorescent light bulbs (CFLs) in the future.

Levels of Strategic Focus   **Sources of Business Value**

6 → Changing the "rules of the game"
Business Context

5 → Developing a sustainability culture and brand identity. Becoming employer-of-choice
Brand Culture

4 → Addressing new markets driven by customer and societal needs
Market

3 → Creating product differentiation based on technical and environmental/social features
Product

2 → Reducing energy, waste, or other process costs
Process

1 → Compliance-oriented management of risks and protecting license to operate
Risks

Source: *The Sustainable Company: How to Create Lasting Value through Social and Environmental Performance* by Chris Laszlo (Island Press, 2003), adapted by Norman Christopher, 2012.

The sustainability plan for the organization can be developed to any one of these strategic focus levels. Targeted sustainability plan outcomes, however, will depend on specific knowledge and experience including understanding of sustainability guiding principles; how and where to implement sustainable development best practices; and management of overall expectations. For a company to achieve a business context level regarding sustainable development and to "change the rules of the game" will require a passionate leader and management team that is totally committed to increasing economic vitality, increasing social responsibility, and improving environmental stewardship.

Managing Expectations

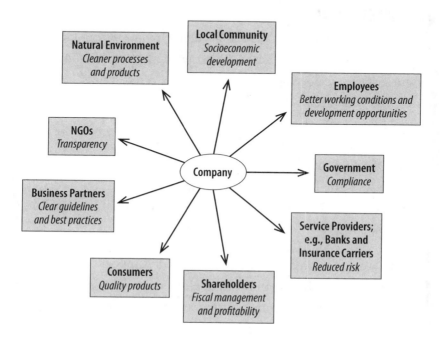

Source: http://www.ece.ucsb.edu/~roy/classnotes/eddw/report_developing_value.pdf, adapted by Norman Christopher, 2012.

SustainAbility, the International Finance Corporation, and the Ethos Institute issued a report in 2002 entitled "Developing Value: The Business Case for Sustainability in Emerging Countries." In that report it was recognized that a business or organization has many expectations to manage across the sustainability "Triple Bottom Line" besides shareholders, employees, customers, consumers, and service providers. Companies must now also manage expectations from the local community and its stakeholders including the local government, NGOs, as well as related social and environmental impact issues. Each of these shareholder and stakeholder groups, including business partners, may have different expectations for the business or enterprise.[13]

Application

Sustainable development planning can help guide and direct an organization or enterprise across its many integrated functional areas. These sustainable development best practices can be found in a:

- 3-5 year strategic plan
- 1 year tactical plan
- Operations, manufacturing, or facilities plan
- Departmental plan such as engineering, marketing, human resources, finance, and administration, etc.
- Personal Development Plan (PDP) or Personal Sustainability Plan (PSP)

In West Michigan there are several support and service organizations that have embraced applied sustainable development best practices in the planning and operations of other businesses and organizations. The West Michigan Strategic Alliance (www.wmsa. org) under the leadership of Jim Brooks was launched in 2000. The work of this organization has described West Michigan as a region in transition. One of their initial projects was the development of the Common Framework which was completed with a volunteer force of 250 from other partner organizations. The report embraced the guiding principles of sustainability including economic prosperity, environmental integrity, and social justice as a regional priority.

The Common Framework for the West Michigan region addressed such areas as:

- Environment
- Economic Development
- Tourism/Conventions/Entertainment/Sports

- Arts/Cultural Activities/History
- Education and Research
- Health and Human Services
- Land Use/Urbanization/Demographics
- Transportation/Logistics
- Infrastructure
- Governance

The priorities for the West Michigan region included:
- Developing a regional mindset
- Establishing a prosperous economy
- Strengthening community through diversity
- Providing for a sustainable environment
- Revitalizing urban centers
- Developing a tri-plex growth strategy

Examples of sustainability plans and goals are also readily available among a number of well-known companies today. Walmart in the early 2000s suffered from a number of issues including discrimination that negatively impacted the company's public relations and overall image. In 2005, Walmart set a number of sustainability goals to be accomplished by 2008 to improve overall community relations and help rebuild customer confidence. Moreover, Walmart employees were encouraged to develop a report on their own personal sustainability plans. The investments that Walmart has made as well as the overall impressive progress and results can be found on the Walmart website (www.walmartstores.com/sustainability). Walmart provides annual updates against targeted goals.

Results and Benefits

There are many benefits to sustainability planning for an organization or business. These benefits can be achieved by:

- Rallying the organization around sustainable development best practices, beginning the sustainability journey, and staying the course!
- Reducing organizational risks and liabilities
- Making better overall decisions for the organization
- Improving the "Triple Bottom Line" of social, environmental, and economic performance and impact
- Building or improving upon brand name and overall company recognition
- Transforming the organization to a new business portfolio based upon business capabilities and competencies
- Becoming a better corporate citizen and overall leader in the community

Sustainable development planning can now be accomplished by establishing specific goals or targets that can be quantified and qualified. These targets can be monitored and tracked using metrics and performance measurements to determine progress as well as met milestone targets. An example of a specific target for company or business might be to reduce overall energy consumption by 15 percent within a specific year. The same holds true for the amount of electricity used in kilowatt hours (kWh) or the amount of steam purchased in pounds (lbs). This target could be measured by determining the amount of energy consumed such as with natural gas in MMBTU's for baseline year as well as in the current year. Energy conservation and efficiency today is one of the most important priorities for any business or organization.

Case Study

A good example of a company that is transforming their business portfolio through sustainability planning is Cascade Engineering.[14]

Sustainability Planning—Cascade Engineering

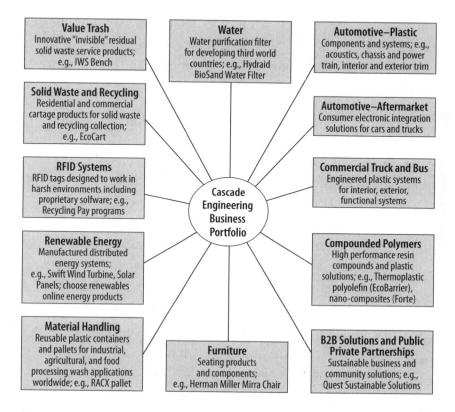

Source: Norman Christopher, 2012.

Cascade Engineering, through the inspirational leadership of its president and CEO Fred Keller, is using sustainable development best practices to transform their business portfolio as well as their overall organization. Cascade Engineering's knowledge, expertise and core competency in plastics and injection molding technology can be found in their automotive and furniture related polymers. Their compounded polymers business uses recycled plastic resins and materials that are compatible and cost-effective in the manufacture of cartage products for solid waste handling. Cascade's capabilities and competencies in precision parts manufacture and systems solutions have allowed the company to enter new markets such as renewable energy, sustainability consulting, and retail green and sustainable products and services. Moreover, Cascade Engineering uses an annual sustainability report that tracks progress and performance in social, economic, and environmental impact areas.

Call to Action

- Does your company have a well-articulated mission and vision for the organization that includes sustainable development and is clearly understood by employees, shareholders, and stakeholders?
- Does your business have a longer-term strategic plan in place (e.g., 3-5 years) that embeds sustainability within the organization?
- Does your company's tactical strategic plan encourage the use of sustainable development guiding principles and best practices?
- What are some of the key sustainability guiding principles that the company and business can leverage and build upon for its organizational planning?

References

1. Grand Rapids Community Sustainability Partnership, www.grpartners.org, accessed August 2011.
2. West Michigan Sustainable Business Forum, www.wmsbf.org, accessed August 2011.
3. Healthy Homes Coalition of West Michigan, www.healthyhomescoalition.org, accessed August 2011.
4. The Business and Institutional Furniture Manufacturer's Association, www.bifma.org, accessed August 2011.
5. Walmart Corporation, www.walmartstores.com, accessed August 2011.

6. Lifestyle of Health and Sustainability, www.lohas.com, accessed August 2011.

7. G. Hamel, and C.K. Prahalad, The Core Competence of the Corporation, *Harvard Business Review*, May/June 1990, page 1, www.hbr.org, accessed August 2011.

8. M. Robert, *Strategy Pure & Simple II: How Winning Companies Dominate Their Competitors* (New York, NY: McGraw Hill, 1998) page 66

9. M. Robert, page 66.

10. C. Laszlo, *Sustainable Value: How the World's Leading Companies Are Doing Well by Doing Good* (Stanford, CA: Stanford University Press, 2008) page 155, figure 10.4.

11. Patagonia Inc., www.patagonia.com, accessed August 2011.

12. Philips Electronics, www.philips.com/about/sustainability, accessed August 2011.

13. Developing Value: The Business Case for Sustainability in Emerging Markets, http://www.ece.ucsb.edu/~roy/classnotes/eddw/report_developing_value.pdf, accessed July 2012.

14. Cascade Engineering Inc., www.cascadeng.com, accessed August 2011.

3. SOCIAL RESPONSIBILITY AND CITIZENSHIP

Introduction

Companies today are being challenged with the need to be more socially responsible in their business operations. Many times these demands are being driven by the need for greater transparency and accountability within the organization. These requests today require more than just making philanthropic donations and having employees volunteer their time. Businesses need to look at their overall supply chain and know where their raw materials are purchased, component parts are manufactured, finished goods are produced, and under what labor, health, and safety conditions. Moving forward, businesses and organizations will be driven to be responsible corporate citizens and help find solutions to systemic social problems, such as poverty, and improved quality of life in their own communities. Businesses and organizations as corporate citizens have the responsibility to take leadership positions in their communities and act as good environmental stewards, social servants, and overall change agents. One area that both NGOs and businesses are gaining increased interest in is social entrepreneurship.

Case studies in this chapter include Wolverine Worldwide and the Kellogg Company.

Description

According to the World Wildlife Fund, the worldwide population currently uses over 1.3 times the Earth's resources in order to maintain its current lifestyle. And if China were to reach the consumption rate of the U.S., we would use the equivalent of two Earths.[1] The overall results of this consumption excess, environmental impact, and resultant degradation fall mostly upon the poor and marginalized.

World population grew to over 7 billion in April 2012 with approximately 3 billion living on less than $2 per day.[2]

Those living at the "Base of the Pyramid," or those 3-4 billion people that live on $3-5 per day, suffer many issues concerning access to basic needs and services. One billion people do not have access to clean drinking water according to the World Health Organization. Many others suffer from malnutrition, live in substandard housing conditions, cannot read, have no electricity, and do not have access to clean sanitation.[3] Some of these systemic sustainability issues can also be seen in West Michigan as well. There are a number of disturbing statistics that describe the need for improving literacy rates, reducing poverty, addressing homelessness, and improving education attainment levels in the greater Grand Rapids area.

Moreover, the results of a Millennium Poll and social sustainability survey showed that two-thirds of those surveyed wanted companies to go beyond their traditional role of making profits, paying taxes, employing people, and obeying the law. Business executives today, and especially those with multinational corporations, believe that companies that only focus on short-term profits and do not recognize their environmental and social impacts, will draw intense introspection and potential adversarial comment from stakeholders, shareholders, NGOs, and political advocacy groups.

How then can an organization become more socially responsible and an overall better corporate citizen? The first step that a company can make is in the area of social responsibility. Social responsibility is defined as "the obligation of an organization's management towards the welfare and interests of the society which provides it the environment and resources to survive and flourish and which is affected by the organization's actions and policies."[4]

There are many areas that a business or organization can focus on to foster social responsibility through donations, cash, in-kind, and volunteer contributions.[5]

Fostering Social Responsibility

- Education and Outreach:
  Tutoring of students within the Grand Rapids Public Schools (GRPS) system where approximately 25 percent of all students are in need of special education services.

- Access to Healthcare:
  Supporting community healthcare clinics (e.g., Cherry Street Health Services).

- Public Safety:
  Offering community education and awareness programs about company operations and products manufactured.

- Emergency Management:
  Supporting Community Emergency Response Team (CERT) programs and activities in Kent County.

- Arts, Culture, and Recreation:
  Volunteering at Frederik Meijer Gardens and Sculpture Park, ArtPrize, Friends of Grand Rapid's Parks, etc.

- Civic Vitality and Engagement:
  Assisting the City in the Grand River clean-up events and other civic programs and activities.

- Social Equity:
  Supporting diversity and inclusion programs (e.g., Grand Rapids Area Chamber of Commerce).

- Environmental Justice:
  Volunteering and supporting West Michigan Environmental Action Council programs and activities.

- Human Services:
  Partnering with the Heart of West Michigan United Way, Goodwill Industries of Greater Grand Rapids, etc.

- Affordable Housing:
  Volunteering and supporting Habitat for Humanity Kent County, Inner City Christian Federation (ICCF), Dwelling Place programs and activities, etc.

- Poverty and Homelessness:
  Serving at Mel Trotter Ministries, Guiding Light Mission, and other faith-based ministries.

- Educational Attainment:
  Providing reading, writing, and math basic skills to public school K-6 students such as Schools of Hope program, Kent County Literacy Council.

- Access to Healthy Food:
  Volunteering and supporting Kids Food Basket.

- Youth Development:
  Helping provide leadership and support for inner city scouting through Gerald R. Ford Council of Boy Scouts of America or Girl Scouts of Michigan Shore to Shore.

- Workforce Development:
  Supporting The Source, Pathways to Prosperity at Grand Rapids Community College, and other programs.

As can be seen, companies can improve their corporate and community social responsibility in a number of areas locally through donations, cash, in-kind, and volunteer contributions. Many of the respective NGOs and organizations in West Michigan need additional resources and support to meet the growing need for basic, life, and professional skills and services. Companies and enterprises can partner with organizations in the public sector to help provide these needed resources as well.

Corporate Citizenship

Once a company has started the sustainability journey and is recognized for its social responsibility initiatives, the organization then can become more engaged in the community through corporate citizenship. Corporate Citizenship is "recognition that a business has social, cultural, and environmental responsibilities to the community in which it operates as well as economic and financial obligations to its shareholders and community stakeholders."[6]

Companies that are good corporate citizens are leaders and change agents in their community and are willing to get at root cause analysis of systemic community issues through integrative interdisciplinary and transdisciplinary systems approaches across public, private, academic, and service sectors. Essentially, good corporate citizens walk the talk by applying sustainable development best practices in an open and transparent manner through collaborations and partnerships across the community. The key is to focus on one or two important community social impact issues and gain traction and support through a broad base of public, private, academic, and service sector partnerships and collaborations.

How then can a business look to become a better corporate citizen in their community?

Levels of Citizen Responsibility

	Personally Responsible Citizen	Participatory Citizen	Social-Justice Oriented Citizen
Description	• Acts responsibly in their community • Works and pays taxes • Picks up litter, recycles, and gives blood • Helps those in need, lends a hand during times of crisis • Obeys laws	• Active member of community organization and/or improvement efforts • Organizes community efforts to care for those in need, promotes economic development, helps clean up environment, etc. • Knows how government agencies work • Knows strategies for accomplishing collective tasks	• Critically accesses social, political, and economic structures • Explores strategies for change that address root causes of problems • Knows about social movements and how to effect systemic change • Seeks out and addresses areas of injustice
Action	• Contributes food to a food drive	• Helps organize a food drive	• Explores why people are hungry and acts to solve root causes
Core Assumptions	• To solve social problems and improve society, citizens must have good character, they must be honest, responsible law-abiding members of the community	• To solve social problems and improve society, citizens must take leadership positions within established systems and community structures	• To solve social problems and improve society, citizens must ask questions and change established systems and structures when they reproduce patterns of injustice over time

Source: Joel Westheimer, University of Ottawa and Joseph Kahne, Mills College. What Kind of Citizen?: The Politics of Educating for Democracy. American Educational Research Journal (Volume 41, Number 2, Summer 2004), Adapted.

As can be seen by the above chart and example,[7] personally responsible citizens feel obliged to help contribute to a local cause or NGO initiative and can do so by volunteering their time. Participatory citizens become more active and are willing to lead and organize a social cause of interest through personal commitment. Social-justice oriented citizens are those that want to go even further and explore root cause analysis and what causes systemic social problems and conditions in the first place. They are also willing to partner with others to help offer sustainable solutions to these systemic issues within their community.

Application

What are the ways an organization can become more socially responsible, demonstrate Corporate Citizenship, and make a significant contribution to their local communities?[8]

Organizations can:

- Embrace applied sustainable development best practices such as with Environmental Management Systems
- Exhibit leadership in helping address and solve systemic community issues such as with social justice concerns
- Help determine the future vision of the community and what the next generation will say about us
- Work collectively with others, and even the competition, in raising the bar on industry, market, and product regulations, compliance, and certification using sustainable development best practices
- Ensure products and services are manufactured sustainably, labeled appropriately and ethically, delivered efficiently, and do not exhibit "green washing"
- Create and influence positive internal and external change, through creativity, innovation, and entrepreneurship
- Measure success broader than financially including "Triple Bottom Line" sustainability indicator reporting including environmental and social impact as well
- Communicate success internally and externally through transparency and openness
- Partner with stakeholders by displaying integrity, accountability, and responsibility
- Allow stakeholders to play an important role in decision making through empowerment
- Endeavor to build system-wide solutions by sharing knowledge and using community capital

- Help build grassroots leadership by building social and cultural capital
- Generate efficiencies and savings and create value that can be rewarded for sustained positive economic impact

Results and Benefits

There are a number of demonstrated benefits to corporate social responsibility and corporate citizenship. A few of the most important attributes a company can have are:[10]

- Building brand reputation and overall public trust, goodwill, and positive reputation:
  Selecting appropriate socially responsible programs will open up a number of new business opportunities and partnerships.

- Attracting and retaining staff:
  Companies that have committed to Corporate Social Responsibility (CSR) programs have shown increased employee commitment, performance, and job satisfaction.

- Attracting customers:
  Companies with CSR programs can differentiate themselves from the competition and attract customers through innovative products that are environmentally and socially responsible.

- Attracting investors:
  Banks and financing institutions know that companies that practice CSR reflect sound and prudent management systems that can help make better business decisions for their organizations and communities.

- Encouraging professional and personal growth and development:

Companies that practice CSR also offer training and volunteer programs to help employees enhance their professional careers, as well as reach out to the community in needed areas of support.

- Reducing overall business costs and resource waste:
  Eco-efficiency programs such as energy conservation and waste minimization save money and resources. Socio-efficiency programs can save money and resources as well through shared knowledge and financial capital including in-kind contributions, volunteer time, efforts, expertise, and experience.

Case Studies

Wolverine Worldwide is a global supplier of high performing industrial and retail footwear and accessories. The company currently has approximately 12 well-known brands including Sebago, Hush Puppies, Patagonia, and Merrill, as well as others. Wolverine Worldwide has a culture that is built on environmental stewaredship, as well as strengthening the lives of families and children. The company sells products globally in over 190 countries and is a respected member of the global communities that they serve. The Wolverine Worldwide Foundation was founded in 1959 to contribute and support socially responsible activities in these countries. Currently the Foundation has supported more than 140 organizations worldwide, such as 1% for the Planet, Habitat for Humanity, and the Conservation Alliance. The company encourages employees to become social workers by volunteering their time in their respective communities.[9]

Wolverine Worldwide also has made great progress in reducing its environmental footprint as well by:

- Purchasing renewable energy credits that power its Michigan based headquarters

- Reengineering the footwear packaging that now uses 85 percent post-consumer recycled cardboard for boxes, 100 percent post-consumer recycled paper for packing tissues, biodegradable shoe forms and inserts, and soy-based inks
- Supporting environmental groups that focus on community education programs such as watershed activities in West Michigan including the Land Conservancy, the Blandford Nature Center, and Habitat for Humanity

Source: www.wolverineworldwide.com/about-us/causes/.

The Kellogg Company is a major global force with sales of approximately $13 billion in 2011. They are the world's leading producer of cereals and convenience foods with over 31,000 employees. Located in Battle Creek Michigan, Kellogg has established themselves as a responsible corporate citizen in West Michigan and the communities in which they serve.

Since 2008, Kellogg has been issuing an overall corporate responsibility report that provides sustainable development progress in four primary areas including:

- Marketplace
- Workplace
- Environment
- Community

The social performance sections deal primarily with the workplace and community. For the workplace, Kellogg has developed major programs in the following areas:

- Labor Standards
- Talent Management
- Diversity and Inclusion
- Employee Safety
- Employee Health, Wellness, and Benefits

In 2010, Kellogg reported the following progress in the key workplace areas:[11]

- "Significantly increased size of corporate safety staff in North America and also added safety professionals in other global regions.
- Refreshed our global workforce safety policies and implemented a strict mobile electronics use policy for our U.S. sales employees who drive Kellogg-owned vehicles.
- Established a new "total health management" program for all employees.
- Introduced a new diversity training program in Latin America that focuses on the inclusion of workers from all economic backgrounds.
- Were named one of "2011 Best Places to Work for LGBT Equality" by the Human Rights Campaign, the leading lesbian, gay, bisexual, and transgender civil rights organization in the United States.
- Contributed nearly $350,000 to diversity-related organizations, primarily to support scholarship programs that include diversity as a criterion.
- Launched a new leadership development program."

For the community, Kellogg has developed major programs in the following areas:

- Strategic Philanthropy
- Breakfast Programs
- Physical Fitness
- Community Development
- Disaster Relief

In 2010 Kellogg reported the following progress in key community areas:[12]

- "Donated $32 million in cash and products to charitable organizations worldwide.
- Continued to donate food to food banks and programs around the world.
- Contributed to breakfast programs that provided millions of morning meals to schoolchildren around the globe.
- Supported a downtown revitalization project in our headquarters city of Battle Creek, Michigan.
- Provided cash and/or product donations to assist with disaster relief efforts in Japan, Haiti, Chile, Australia, and other regions."

Call to Action

- In what areas and ways does your organization reach out to the community?
- Does the company encourage employees to volunteer their time in community activities?
- Who are the important organizations and NGOs that the company provides philanthropic donations and in kind contributions?
- Does the company act in a socially responsible manner and in what ways?
- How could the company become a better corporate citizen in the community?

References

1. Jeffrey Hollander, "The Responsibility Revolution," http://www.huffingtonpost.com/jeffrey-hollender/the-responsibility-revolu_b_476324.html, accessed August 2011.
2. One Shared World, (www.onesharedworld.com/facts/factsheet), accessed July 2011, Global Issues, www.globalissues.org, accessed November 2011.

3. Tom von Alten, *The World as 100 People,* http://fortboise.org/perspective. html, accessed August 2011.
4. www.businessdictionary.com, accessed August 2011.
5. Sustainable Community Frameworks, www.bygpub.com/books/tg2rw/ volunteer.
6. "Corporate Philanthropy: Unwavering Commitment and Focused Strategies in Stormy Times," http://www.mcf.org/system/article_ resources/0000/0168/givingforum_sp09_1_.pdf, accessed August 2011.
7. J. Westheimer, and J. Kahne, (2004). What Kind of Citizen? The Politics of Educating for Democracy, *American Educational Research Journal* 412. 237-269.
8. Adapted from Industry Canada. Industry Canada. (Online). 2010; (www. ic.gc.ca/eic/site/csr-rse.nsf/eng/h_r500100), accessed August 2011.
9. Wolverine World Wide, www.wolverineworldwide.com/about-us/causes/, accessed July 2012.
10. "Here's how my Business Benefited from Corporate Social Responsibility," www.findlaw.co.uk/law/small_business/business_operations/other_ business_operations_topics/real_life_examples/14003.html, accessed July 2012.
11. Workplace, http://kelloggcorporateresponsibility.com/workplace/, accessed August 2011.
12. Community, http://kelloggcorporateresponsibility.com/community/, accessed August 2011.

4. SUSTAINABILITY ASSESSMENT

Introduction

Sustainability assessments are critical to companies as they start their sustainability journey. These assessments are an important way for companies to gauge their readiness to implement sustainable development best practices. They can also be used to determine the business or organization's baseline data regarding operational, environmental, economic, and social performance. It is recommended that all businesses and organizations undertake a sustainability assessment before proceeding with the implementation of sustainable development best practices. These assessments vary in their depth of analysis and therefore can be used by organizations that are unfamiliar with sustainability, as well as those that have already started to implement sustainability practices within their organization.

The case study in this chapter is the West Michigan Sustainable Business Forum.

Description

Sustainability assessments, surveys, or audits can be completed by companies with different levels of awareness, understanding, and outcomes. Some assessments can be relatively simplistic and used as a "starter" for businesses to determine where they are in key areas of sustainable development. Other surveys are considered more in-depth. These audits might be appropriate for companies that have already begun their sustainability journey and want to examine their progress. There are also more comprehensive sustainability assessments for those companies that truly want to embed sustainable development best practices in their business and overall organization. A good example of these types of companies in West Michigan includes the furniture industry and The Business and Institutional Furniture Manufacturer's Association (www.bifma.org). Tier I suppliers such as Herman Miller, Steelcase, Haworth, and others have all adopted sustainable development best practices and are well along the way to embedding these practices across their supply chains. As a result Tier II and Tier III suppliers and businesses that provide components, products, assemblies, and parts to the Tier I furniture companies are being required to ensure that these products and furniture services meet "green" and sustainability standards and certifications.

The differences in these sustainability assessments really depend on the size of the business or organization that conducts the assessment, the access to resources to conduct the analysis, as well as the degree of familiarity with sustainable development best practices. However, in all cases these sustainability assessments or surveys should be comprehensive and cover all aspects of the "Triple Bottom Line" including, environmental, social, and economic impact areas. These sustainability surveys or audits will provide a business or organization an overall understanding of where they are and how to get started on their sustainability journey.

Application

If you are a smaller business or organization that is just getting started, you might consider conducting an "eco-audit" as an initial activity and determine the amount of:

1. Water consumed and discharged (e.g., gallons per month for specific uses such as for facility and building operations, landscaping, manufacturing processes, wastewater and sewer discharges, etc.)

2. Electricity used (e.g., kWh per month for specific end uses such as heating and lighting for buildings, operations, and facilities; industrial processes and equipment, etc.)
3. Natural gas consumed (e.g., MM BTUs per month for specific end uses such as heating for buildings, operations, and facilities; industrial processes and equipment, etc.)
4. Amount of steam purchased (e.g., lbs. per month for facilities and operations)
5. Fuel consumed by type (e.g., gallons per month for specific end uses such as building operations, auxiliary equipment, fleet vehicles, etc.)
6. Waste generated (e.g., tons per month of specific landfill waste such as food, paper, cardboard, metal, electronic, packaging, food, etc.)
7. Toxic and hazardous toxic wastes generated (e.g., gallons per month such as liquids, solvents, solids, i.e., paint that must be incinerated and cannot be land filled, etc.)
8. Air emissions generated (e.g., per month such as those required by the EPA for toxic release inventory (TRI).)

An eco-audit provides the business a basic framework regarding their overall environmental impact or environmental footprint as well. It will also identify areas where improvements in environmental stewardship can take place. Key areas of an eco-audit include electricity, natural gas, waste, etc. Key measurements include the consumption amounts of electricity, steam, and natural gas used for lighting, heating, and processing, etc.; water consumption such as for building operations and process use; waste sent to the landfill such as packaging, etc.; types, sources, and amounts of raw materials used, etc.; fuel consumption such as for building operations and fleet vehicles, etc: hazardous and toxic waste generated such as with paint and solvents; toxic air emissions; the amount of goods and services consumed that do not meet environmentally preferred purchasing (EPP) standards and requirements. All of the key environmental impact areas such as electricity, natural gas, waste, steam and fuel can also be easily converted to metric tons of carbon dioxide equivalents (MT CO_2E), so that the business can also determine a preliminary greenhouse gas emission inventory and climate impact analysis at the same time. Therefore, an eco-audit is a good way for most businesses and organizations to get started, determine their baseline data, and find out where they stand regarding key environmental impact areas:

Darcy Hitchcock and Marsha Willard in their book *The Business Guide to Sustainability* developed a Sustainability Competency and Opportunity Rating Evaluation (SCORE) in the following functional or departmental areas for a business:[1]

- Design
- Environmental Affairs
- Facilities
- Finance and Accounting
- Human Resources
- Internal
- Marketing and Public Relations
- Operations
- Purchasing
- Senior Management

Each functional area or department can take this self-assessment and rate their area based on self-evaluation. If the SCORE is less than one, you are considered "lagging" and falling behind others and the competition who are implementing sustainable development best practices. Developing a compelling business case for management for pursuing sustainable development best practices may be the next stage. "Low hanging" opportunistic projects should be framed out and key sustainable development projects pursued with management approval.

If the SCORE is between 1 and 3, you are considered "learning" sustainable development and progress is being made, but continual improvements must be established. Benchmarking other key competitors and companies in sustainable development best practices should be undertaken. If your SCORE is above 3, you are considered "leading." Your business or organization is benchmarking higher standards regarding sustainable development best practices and probably "raising the bar" internally with new self-imposed targets. Exceptional leaders are "braving new frontiers" with transparency, openness, responsibility, and accountability, as well as sharing progress and lessons learned about sustainable development best practices with other stakeholders.

Results and Benefits

There are many benefits to conducting an internal sustainability assessment, survey, or audit. The World Business Council on Sustainable Development has highlighted some of these advantages.[2]

- Establishment of business or organization baseline data regarding the status of sustainable development that can be analyzed and monitored such as electricity, natural gas, water consumption; toxic and industrial waste generated; air emissions generated, etc.
- Identification of environmental risks or liabilities that may have adverse effects upon the business or organization, as well as the environment.
- Determination of sustainable development best practice gaps that may require immediate attention by the business or organization. Some of these gaps may include areas such as social responsibility and environmental risk management.

- Desire to generate a future new business model and sustainability plan for the organization to help ensure sustained growth.
- Ability to help motivate employees to seek "continuous improvement" for their own performance as well as for their respective department and the overall organization.
- Identification of sustainability "champions" within the organization that will help lead transformational change within their departments.

Case Study

The West Michigan Sustainable Business Forum (WMSBF) is an organization that is comprised primarily of businesses as well as other organizations and enterprises that support and embrace sustainable development best practices. The WMSBF has developed an extensive sustainability Self-Assessment Guide (SAG) for businesses and organizations. For functional areas, specific responses can be answered by very little, little, some extent, greater extent, very great extent, and N/A to obtain an overview of the sustainability assessment for the company. The following represents four to five example questions for each business area from the SAG that can be used for the company or organization. The full Self-Assessment Guide can be downloaded from their website:[3]

A. Governance

- Has management made a commitment to sustainability?
- Has the company defined sustainability and the "Triple Bottom Line" as it relates to the business?
- Does the company have a measurable sustainability plan that is monitored and tracked?
- Is sustainability training made available for staff and employees?

B. Environmental Management

- Does the company have a formal Environmental Management System (EMS) in place?
- Does the company seek continuous improvement for its operations through periodic EMS audits?
- Are employees trained in environmental procedures and policies?
- Does the company allocate environmental costs and savings to the department that generated them?

C. Social Responsibility

- Does the company have a written Corporate Social Responsibility (CSR) policy or statement?
- Is social responsibility training available for staff and employees?
- Are social responsibility activities communicated in a transparent manner to shareholders and stakeholders?
- Does the company offer professional development and volunteering opportunities?

D. Product

- Does the company utilize the Design for the Environment (DfE) or Design for Life (DfL) process for product development?
- Are Life Cycle Analysis (LCA) and "cradle to cradle" processes an integral part of product design?
- Does the company use locally manufactured materials for product development?
- Are raw material specifications based on recycled and bio-based renewable materials?
- Are products and materials evaluated for their upstream and downstream environmental impact?

E. Facilities

- Does the company measure energy consumption, energy reduction, and savings from energy conservation projects and overall operations?
- Does the company measure water consumption, water reduction, and savings from water conservation projects and facilities services?
- Do facilities meet green building standards such as Green Globe or LEED building standards?
- Does the company formally track greenhouse gas (GHG) and carbon dioxide (CO_2) emissions and have a program in place to reduce the overall carbon footprint?

F. Purchasing

- Does the company have an environmentally preferred purchasing policy in place?
- Does the company monitor and track the purchase of green and locally manufactured products and raw materials?
- Does the company have a plan in place to reduce resource depletion?
- Does purchasing actively substantiate green and sustainability product and marketing claims and certifications from vendors and suppliers?
- Does the company educate its supply chain partners in green purchasing and sustainable procurement practices?

G. Operations

- Does the company have an operations plan in place to reduce overall environmental impact?
- Does the company have a formalized Pollution Prevention plan in place?
- Does the company leverage energy efficiency and waste minimization best practices?

- Has the company limited its exposure to hazardous and toxic materials and shifted to bio-based renewable materials based on green chemistry?

H. Packaging

- Has the company developed and implemented environmentally preferred and sustainable packaging guidelines?
- Does the company use recycled and reused packaging materials and supplies for inbound raw materials and outbound finished products?
- Does the company promote bulk, reusable, returnable containers and pallets for distribution and logistics?
- Does the company substantiate green marketing claims on product labels as well as proper disposal methods?

I. Delivery and Installation

- Does the company have policies and procedures in place to optimize transportation methods, reduce fuel use, and minimize transportation emissions?
- Does the company participate in formal transportation efficiency programs?
- Has the company implemented anti-idling policies?
- Has the company optimized distribution and logistics policies and procedures to minimize handling and repackaging of products?

J. Marketing and Sales

- Does the company track and monitor customer needs and wants for new green and sustainability products?
- Does the company have a performance goal target for the development and sales of new green and sustainability products?

- Are the company's marketing and promotional materials printed on recycled paper and use biodegradable ink?
- Does the company promote products that are manufactured from sustainable sources or raw materials that can be recycled and returned after use?

As can be seen, this thorough in-depth sustainability self-assessment will help companies determine their baseline sustainability performance and identify future opportunistic project areas with attractive returns.

Call to Action

- In what areas does the company conduct ongoing sustainability audits or assessments?
- Have the assessments or audits shown areas where the company needs to be in compliance or improve upon regulatory requirements?
- What are the company strengths in sustainability the organization can build upon?
- What are the most important weaknesses in sustainability TBL impact that the organization needs to address in the near future?

References

1. Darcy Hitchcock and Marsha Willard, *The Business Guide to Sustainability: Practical Strategies and Tools for Organizations* (Routledge, August 2009, 2nd Edition), 31-33.
2. World Business Council Sustainable Development, www.wbcsd.org, accessed August 2011.
3. West Michigan Sustainable Business Forum, Self-Assessment Guide to Environmental Sustainable Commerce, www.wmsbf.org/index.php/documents/cat_view/85-operations-and-accountability?limit=8&limitstart=0&order=name&dir=DESC, accessed July 2011.

5. INTERNAL SUSTAINABILITY PERFORMANCE AND PROGRESS

Introduction

Businesses and organizations today are increasingly aware of the need to utilize sustainable development best practices that will enable the creation of short-term efficiencies and long-term value for their enterprises. Moreover, business leaders are also challenged by new reporting requirements that are being requested from customers and suppliers to ensure transparency and provide timely and accurate reporting of sustainability progress and overall business performance.

Business leaders are most familiar with standardized financial accounting and reporting principles such as required audited annual financial statements, including cash flow and profit and loss statements. There are also a number of industry recognized financial performance metrics that businesses use currently for fiscal decision making. These metrics can be applied for the evaluation of capital projects as well as overall company performance and include: return on investment (ROI); return on assets (ROA); return on equity (ROE); return on capital employed (ROCE), and others. However, many of these financial reports are representative only of internal operations and company performance. Today, many suppliers, customers, company shareholders, and community stakeholders are now requiring disclosure of additional business information. Much of this data and information can be provided in the form of a sustainability report that can be used both internally and externally by the company for its business operations and community engagement.

The case study in this chapter is Gazelle Sports.

Description

This evolution in financial and company reporting has been occurring since the 1980s. In 1992 Robert Kaplan and David Norton published the book *The Balanced Scorecard*, after writing several published articles.[1] The "Balanced Scorecard" is a set of strategic business performance management tools that focus on 4 key areas including:

- Financial: "To succeed financially, how should we appear to our shareholders?"
- Customer: "To achieve our vision, how should we appear to our customers?"
- Internal Business Processes: "To satisfy our shareholders and customers, what business processes must we excel at?"
- Learning and Growth: "To achieve our vision, how will we sustain our ability to change and improve?"[2]

A modified balanced scorecard can also be developed to align more with sustainable development best practices. This type of report or dashboard might be developed in the following areas and track:

- Customers: new product sales from "green" products; percent of sales from new products developed using the DfE process; number of customer complaints; number of product warranty claims, etc.
- Finance and Operations: consumption of electricity, natural gas, water, and fuel; overall resource conservation; productivity improvements; avoided waste to the landfill; percent recycled raw materials used; percent improvement in gross margin, etc.
- Employees: turnover and retention rates; training hours per employee; health and wellness program participation; professional development, etc.
- Community: company cash and in-kind philanthropic contributions; amount of volunteering hours; partnerships

and support for specific organizations such as the United Way, Goodwill Industries, and others.

Balanced Scorecard reporting has enabled organizations to monitor specific sustainability goals that have been established, track progress against these targeted outcomes, while creating ongoing organizational efficiencies. Some of this information and metrics used might be considered for internal use only by the business because of the confidentiality of the information.

Today, many companies have also begun to develop and establish "Triple Bottom Line" (TBL) sustainability reports. TBL sustainability reporting is becoming a standardized reporting process for many international, global, and multinational companies and organizations. Many of the well-known global companies such as Nike, Johnson and Johnson, Proctor & Gamble, Baxter International, General Electric, Dow Chemical, Dupont, Walmart, and others all issue annual sustainability reports based on the "Triple Bottom Line." Global commerce has raised the questions about fair trade issues, the use of child labor, poor and unsafe working conditions, employee health concerns, and poor quality products that use toxic materials, etc. Transparent sustainability reporting addresses these issues and concerns, in many cases, depending upon the reporting format and standard used. Sustainability Reporting will be discussed in more depth in a later chapter.

Application

The Balanced Scorecard has become a very effective tool for companies to develop both financial and non-financial performance measurements. The Balanced Scorecard reporting process has also become quite sophisticated and developed into a model of performance reporting for many businesses. "It articulates the links between inputs (human and physical), processes, and lagging outcomes, and focuses on the importance of managing these components, to achieve the organizations strategic priorities."[3]

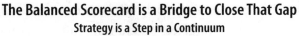

The Balanced Scorecard is a Bridge to Close That Gap
Strategy is a Step in a Continuum

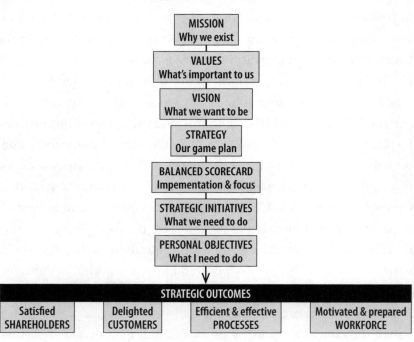

Source: The Balanced Scorecard Collaborative, adapted by Norman Christopher, 2012.

The Balanced Scorecard has gained in popularity over the years due to its relevance and the capability to "bridge the gap" between the organization's mission, vision, and overall strategy and the organization's specific strategic initiatives and desired strategic outcomes.

Specific performance measurements and metrics are usually developed in major areas such as:

- Satisfied shareholders
- Delighted customers

- Efficient and effective processes
- Motivated and prepared workforce

Depending on the specific performance measurements that are used, Balanced Scorecards based on applied sustainable development best practices can be used for both internal and external reporting to help create long-term value for the organization or business.

Results and Benefits

Companies and businesses that embrace and embed applied sustainable development best practices have been shown to yield a profit increase of up to approximately 40 percent for large enterprises and up to approximately 65 percent for small-to medium-size enterprises (SME). Bob Willard, author of *The Sustainability Advantage*, and *The Next Sustainability Wave*[5] has been tracking business performance over the last few years with the successful use of sustainable development and best practices.

Improved Business Performance

Area	Large Enterprise	Small to Medium Enterprise
Reduced recruiting costs	-1%	-1%
Reduced attrition costs	-2%	-2%
Increased employer productivity	+10%	+6%
Eco-efficiencies generated: savings in energy, water, materials, waste handling	N/A	-10%
Eco-efficiencies generated in manufacturing	-5%	N/A
Eco-efficiencies generated at commercial sites	-20%	N/A

Area	Large Enterprise	Small to Medium Enterprise
Increased revenue - market share	+5%	+5%
Lower insurance and financing costs	-5%	-5%
Profit Increase	+38%	+66%

Source: Bob Willard, Sustainability Advantage - adapted.

Overall profit increase can be achieved through a compounded effect on both the "top" and "bottom" line. SME businesses can achieve dramatic improvements through reduced recruiting and turnover costs; lower insurance and borrowing costs; and numerous eco-efficiencies such as savings in energy, water, waste generated, and materials used. These "bottom" line savings can add up significantly to an overall reduction in expenses. "Top" line growth is generated through employee productivity, increased revenues, and overall market share. As can be seen, by employing applied sustainable development best practices throughout the organization, bottom line business improvement and profit increase can be realized. These best practices will not necessarily increase individual business operation costs but will result in overall cost savings. Moreover, the pursuit of sustainable development best practices is seen as the "right thing to do" by investors, owners, management, employees, and, most importantly, by customers in today's marketplace.

As for measuring sustainable development best practices and improving overall business performance, it is suggested that a "Starter" TBL sustainability report with key performance measurements be developed.

The "Starter" sustainability report can either be generated or established by selecting a balanced number of corresponding key performance measurements that cover the TBL of sustainability including environmental stewardship, economic vitality, and social responsibility. These external reports are usually generated and reported with openness and transparency on an annual basis.

Some business owners have also chosen to develop an ongoing monthly internal "dashboard" report using specific sustainability indicators and performance measurements for key managers. Due to the sensitivity of some of the performance indicators used, the dashboard report might only be shared with the executive management team, as well as with board members and advisors, and not necessarily reported to external stakeholders or the community at large.

Case Study

Gazelle Sports in Grand Rapids opened for business in December 1985. Recently the company has been experiencing double-digit growth, expanding the Grand Rapids store by doubling its size and growing into other locations including Holland, Kalamazoo, and Grandville. In 2010 company sales grew 18.5 percent.[6]

The company has been following a "Balanced Scorecard" approach to maximize its performance:

Satisfied Shareholders

- Business owners focus on the mission of bringing passion for running and walking to customers.
- Mission and values of the company are driven by lifestyle choices.
- Willingness of owners to stay focused; e.g., "Can't meet everyone's need and that is okay."

Delighted Customers

- Supporting customers as they work toward their individual fitness goals. "Give them more than they expect."

- Providing customers with access to a great deal of information providing exceptional learning.
- Trust when speaking to a sales associate.

Establishing Efficient and Effective Processes
- Growing institutional sales division
- Organizing running camps
- Instituting strong fiscal controls through Plante Moran
- Hiring a HR Manager, as the 145 employee work force has grown rapidly

Motivated and Prepared Work Force
- Integrating a high level of training, more than anyone else in the industry.
- Providing ongoing weekly training programs that establish credibility for the consumer.
- Creating a positive culture through phenomenal products, a motivated staff, a passion about what they can do, and helping customers with their training needs.

In 2011, Gazelle Sports was recognized as one of the top 50 Best Running Stores in America by the trade and consumer publications *Running Insight* and *Competitor* magazine. The company was cited for its positive work environment, employee product knowledge, and community involvement.

Call to Action
- Does the company manage its business using a "Balanced Scorecard" or internal dashboard report? If so, how often are these scorecards and dashboard reports monitored and reviewed?

- What are the key performance measurements, indicators, or metrics that the company uses to measure its business as well as monitor company performance?
- What are the ways in which the company can improve upon efficiencies, cost savings, and productivity within business operations?
- List the top 5-10 highest priority eco-efficiency opportunities within business operations such as energy, water, waste, and overall material resource requirements?
- In what ways can the organization improve upon and measure "satisfied shareholders," "delighted customers," and "motivated employees?"
- What are the "efficient and effective" processes that the company put in place to optimize business performance?

References

1. Robert S. Kaplan and David P. Norton, "Using the Balanced Scorecard as a Strategic Management System," *Harvard Business Review* January-February 1996: page 76.
2. What is the Balanced Scorecard?, http://www.balancedscorecard.org/BSCResources/aboutthebalancedScoreCard/tabid/55/default.aspx, accessed July 2011.
3. M.A. Abernethy, M.H. Horne, A.M. Lillis, M.A. Malina, F.H. Selto, A Multi-Method Approach to Building Causal Performance Maps from Expert Knowledge, 2005, page 136.
4. Bod Garrison and Scott W. Goodspeed, Building and Implementing a Balanced Scorecard and Strategy Map at Riphey County Memorial Hospital September 2009, Slide 9.
5. Bob Willard, *The Next Sustainability Wave,* (New Society Publishers, 2005), page 38.
6. Run like a Gazelle: Retailer Gazelle Sports Hitting its Stride amid Expansion, Sales Growth, www.mibiz.com/news/small-biz/18185-run-like-a-gazelle, accessed July 2011.

PART TWO

DESIGN AND ENGINEERING

As we look toward the role of design and engineering in companies and organizations today, this function looks significantly different than in the past. Traditionally product development cycles were long and quite predictable. In fact, many times just redesigning an existing product with a few more features and benefits using the same core technology platform was good enough to ensure success and a profitable return. Many times these products were made with petroleum based chemicals and were produced in linear processes. Volume and outputs were driven toward mass production manufacturing. Tweaking of products, systems, and processes were a primary focus area for design and engineering. In essence the "older" economy was a "slower" economy. Hence, designing, manufacturing, and selling a product that met a specification and application standard was all that was needed.

Today, however, design and engineering departments have become a beehive of activity in retooling companies, their products, and their operations. The successful and sustainable company of tomorrow will be built upon processes and systems that can deal with shorter and more volatile development cycles, continuous improvement processes, highly differentiated products, fragmented market segments, and disruptive technologies. Design and engineering must also address a new dynamic change force that is being driven by the marketplace. What to do with products once they have reached their end of life? Can products be recycled, reassembled, or remanufactured? How can products be properly disposed of? These questions help create a new business model for the future, one of a "cradle to cradle" systems approach.

The applied sustainable development best practices described in this section include Design for Environment (DfE), a fundamental shift in the way products are designed using Life Cycle Analysis (LCA). This tool describes the use of low impact materials, less overall raw material, efficient production techniques, reduction of environmental impact, initial lifetime, and efficient life systems. One application of this tool is for the development of green and LEED buildings that are designed and constructed to higher performing standards and certifications. In some instances LEED buildings can be constructed for the same costs as conventional buildings and are 25-30 percent more efficient in the use of water and energy. However, the primary driver for design and engineering is the use of clean and green technologies. There is a major shift underway today in the use of green chemistry and disruptive clean technologies versus petrochemical based chemistry and technologies. One area of application is the use of green cleaning products for hospital and healthcare applications.

6. DESIGN FOR THE ENVIRONMENT

Introduction

Many companies today are at the "leading edge" of product development, both for new products, as well as for reformulated products. These leading edge companies are now using a "cradle to cradle" life cycle design known as Design for the Environment (DfE) process. While this process is most demanding in its nature and approach, it provides breakthrough results that are difficult for competitors to match or emulate. The office and institutional furniture industry in West Michigan provides a prime example for the use of the DfE and LCA. Companies such as Herman Miller with their Aeron chair and Steelcase with its Leap chair have established product and leadership positions in the marketplace.

Case studies in this section include Herman Miller, Amway Corporation, and Harbor Industries.

Description

The DfE Tool is essentially a Life Cycle Design Strategies Wheel[1] that can be used by businesses and companies, as it applies to many functional departments including product development, research and development, engineering, etc., when designing a product or service for today's marketplace. The DfE contains eight steps or phases including:

1. New concept development
2. Selection of raw materials
3. Optimization of product design
4. Optimization of production techniques
5. Efficient distribution system

6. Reduction of the environmental impact in the user stage
7. Optimization of initial lifetime
8. Optimization of end-of-life system

As can be seen, companies can compare the priorities of an existing product with those of a newly created product using the life cycle design strategies wheel.

The DfE Tool for Life Cycle Design

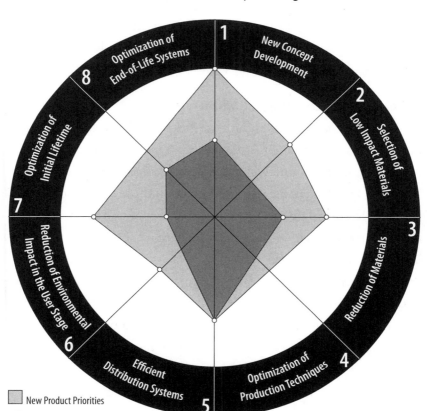

New Product Priorities

Existing Product Priorities

Source: Carolien van Hemel and Han Brezet for UNEP Ecodesign Manual (1997) adapted by Norman Christopher, 2012.

1. New Concept Development

This innovative and creative stage defines a new or reformulated product with breakthrough features and benefits. First of all, the product concept must be validated in the marketplace through feedback from potential customers as well as expert panels. Some of the product features or characteristics may include the following: The product being made of fewer raw materials and less total weight, thereby saving energy for manufacturing and overall costs. The product may also have a shared use thereby enhancing overall utilization. Additionally the product may have the ability to integrate more functions to reduce duplicity. Products may also be designed to have optimized functions to achieve breakthrough performance.

2. Selection of Low Impact Materials

In this stage material selection is critical. Nonhazardous materials are the most important for the selection process, including those made from green chemistry. Materials made from renewable resources are of keen interest to users versus those that are produced from depletable resources. Materials and processes made with lower embedded energy content are potentially more cost-effective as well. Today, the use of recycled or recyclable raw materials is becoming an art and science itself. Many recycled materials today, such as metals and plastics, are more cost-effective and also of consistent quality. What one company might consider as waste or a by-product might become an attractive raw material for use by another company, especially if the companies were in close proximity.

3. Reduction of Materials

There are a number of innovative strategies that can enhance product design and product attributes such as overall product weight reduction. Determining breakthrough high quality product design as a threshold and milestone at the outset is key, as it is more difficult and costly to add an additional feature or product dimension at a later date. Consideration should be given to shipping components and completing final assembly near the market or customer served in order to save on freight volume and transportation costs. Another significant opportunity exists in using recycled and biodegradable packaging materials.

4. Optimization of Production Techniques

One of the prime strategies is to optimize existing processes and production equipment for manufacturing. Green chemistry and water-based systems should be utilized where possible so that processes are more efficient and generate lower emissions. Instead of separate production or manufacturing techniques for components, manufacturing processes should be combined and integrated where possible. Targets should be set to reduce energy and water consumption, as well as to minimize waste generated. Shifting manufacturing processes to renewable sources should be considered and implemented, if possible, where cost effective. Switching to green cleaning chemicals and optimizing their use is also important. Throughout operations and manufacturing, state-of-the-art pollution prevention measures should be undertaken including air emission control procedures. Additional consideration should be given to the sharing of services and use of by-product waste stream resources from nearby manufacturing companies as well.

5. Efficient Distribution Systems

In this stage packaging options should be evaluated and optimized, such as with the use of reusable packaging materials and containers. Reduction in packaging waste should also be targeted. One key area is the elimination of PVC containing materials. Efficient transportation alternatives should also be considered and implemented, such as consolidating and combining less than truckload (LTL) quantities of product into full truckload (TL) quantities. Back hauling techniques also are important for creating additional efficiencies. Partnering with other suppliers, customers, and even competitors can potentially enhance shipment efficiencies significantly within the overall supply chain.

6. Reduction of Environmental Impact in the User Stage

Manufacturers and suppliers should ensure that products used by customers and consumers have a reduced environmental impact versus other competitive products in the marketplace. One consideration would be the selection of benign materials for product manufacture and use so that the product could be disposed of safely after use. Another might be in the requirement for lower energy consumption. An example would be Energy Star rated products that provide energy consumption ratings on their label. Another example would include the use of renewable energy to manufacture the product. Herman Miller has now achieved the use of 100 percent renewable energy for their furniture product manufacture. This target was part of their 2020 Perfect Vision goals. Additionally, the product should be designed so that if other energy consumables are required with the use of the product, then those energy sources could use clean energy and consume overall less energy as well.

7. Optimization of Initial Lifetime

In this phase products should be developed and optimized for their initial lifetime use. There are a number of important product features that have resulting benefits. One characteristic includes reliability and durability for use. In essence, durable and reliable products are developed with high quality and built for long-term use. Examples of products that are well designed are those that are modular in structure so that additional components can be easily modified and adapted for use. The product should also be easily maintained and repaired simply, such as with the use of common tools and procedures. Maintenance, repair, and warranty instructions should be clearly readable and understandable so that the product can be well maintained during use.

8. Optimization of End-of-Life Systems

A clear distinction when using the DfE tool is that products are designed for both initial lifetime and end-of-lifetime uses. Products developed for this final stage would include a reuse if at all possible. Products could be reclaimed or "taken back" by the manufacturer or supplier and then remanufactured or refurbished for additional reuse, either domestically or for developing third world countries, once end-of-life systems have been established and attained. The product parts and components can also be recycled either for scrap value or for use as other raw material sources. Moreover, since the product would only contain clean components and raw materials, and contain nontoxic or nonhazardous substances, there would not be the need for incineration or other costly disposal procedures.

The overall traditional product life cycle can also be modified into a sustainable product life cycle when using the DfE. The sustainable product life cycle stages would contain important "gates" or critical reviews where designed products would need to meet required new milestones before moving on to the next stage.

Application

The DfE process, life cycle analysis, and cradle to cradle protocol can be applied to any manufactured product. However, there are several industries and markets today where their processes and protocols have been used to design, develop, and commercialize new "green" and sustainable products that attract an increasing base of customers. These customers seek to purchase products that: have a reduced impact on the environment, demonstrate the company's commitment to environmental stewardship, and are eco-efficient.

Some of these sustainable and green product areas include:

- Chairs and office furnishings for a number of market segments such as higher education, healthcare, hospital, and professional services within the office furniture industry.
- Carpets and carpet tiles from the textile industry. In the late 1990s Ray Anderson of Interface, Inc., became one of the first companies to change the landscape of the carpet and textile industry by leasing carpet instead of selling it. Interface would manufacture, install, and maintain the carpet for its customers. They would then take back the carpet upon end-of-life, recycle it, and remanufacture the old carpet into new product (www.interface.com).
- Sustainable clothing and outerwear gear. Clothing Matters in Grand Rapids has been offering sustainable and eco-apparel since 1996 (www.clothingmatters.net). Their clothing products are manufactured with fibers such as bamboo, soy, hemp, organic cotton, as well as recycled materials to help reduce or prevent pollution, conserve material and natural resources, and help foster social responsibility and social justice.

Results and Benefits

By using the DfE, companies can enjoy enumerable benefits. The DfE will enable management to make more informed decisions regarding cost, risk, and performance issues.[2] Some of the potential benefits include:

- Reduced environmental health and safety risks and concerns
- Increased efficiencies in manufacturing
- Improved customer acceptance
- Improved employee morale and productivity
- Reduced material usage
- Minimized generation of waste

- Less liability and overall reduced risk regarding environmental regulations and compliance
- Expanded product, market, and business opportunities
- Reduced environmental impact
- Cleaner production processes

Companies today are also challenged to develop and provide high quality products, goods, and services at competitive prices in the global marketplace. The DfE process, when effectively implemented, will position the business favorably with customers as many customers are looking to purchase more environmentally friendly eco-efficient products.

The Environmental Protection Agency (EPA) has established the Design for the Environment logo that is recognized for safer chemistry, promotes green chemistry, and protects the health of families and the environment.[3]

Case Studies

The Herman Miller Aeron Chair was originally designed, developed, and introduced in the 1990s.[4]

It is one of the most successful products to have used the design for the environment process and the McDonough–Braungart Cradle-to-Cradle protocol. The use of these processes and protocols enabled the design of the chair to go well beyond regulatory compliance and helped "raise the bar" for overall product development within the furniture industry.

Some of the important features and benefits of the Aeron chair include:
- Up to 94 percent recyclable at the end of its useful life.
- Comprised of 66 percent recycled materials (44 percent post-consumer and 22 percent pre-consumer content).

- All die cast aluminum components are made from 100 percent recycled material.
- Aluminum components can be segregated and returned to the recycling stream as a technical nutrient.
- Steel components contain approximately 25 percent recycled content and are 100 percent recyclable as a technical nutrient.
- Most metal components have a powder-coat paint finish that emits negligible volatile organic compounds (VOCs).
- Plastic components are identified with an ASTM International (formerly known as American Society for Testing and Materials) recycling code whenever possible to aid in returning these materials to the recycling stream.
- The seat frame and back contain over 60 percent recycled content, made from approximately 50 recycled two-liter plastic beverage bottles per chair.
- Foam and textile materials are part of an open loop system and can be recycled into everything from automotive components to carpet padding at the end of their current life.
- Materials include corrugated cardboard and a polyethylene plastic bag. Each material is part of a closed loop recycling system, for repeated recycling capabilities.
- Whenever possible, shipments between Herman Miller and its suppliers include the use of pallets and other returnable packaging to minimize waste.
- On large North American orders, disposable packaging can be replaced with reusable shipping blankets.

Additionally, the Aeron chair:
- Is Greengard certified as a non-emitting product
- May contribute to LEED credits for building performance
- Has a 12 year 24/7 warranty
- Is manufactured in West Michigan at an ISO 14000 certified facility

Amway Corporation has also made a corporate commitment to life cycle assessment (LCA) to improve overall total product performance as well. LCA helps support Amway's goal of making the environment cleaner and more sustainable. One such example has been with their eSpring water purification system. Using a new GaBim product sustainability software system, Amway has been able to examine the total environmental impact of a product starting from design and ending with product disposal. Amway was able to redesign the eSpring product from its first generation "Arata" product model to a new "Calypso" product model.[5]

According to Mark Gammage, the senior Research and Design product leader, there were significant benefits of using the LCA process:

- Prioritization of environmental improvement areas in the design phase
- Better and more informed Research and Design decision making
- Ability to confirm and validate product environmental performance claims
- Development of more relevant product sustainability impact measurements and sustainability indicators
- Increased awareness about environmental sustainability throughout the company

The results of the product design using the LCA process has generated impressive outcomes including:

- Reduction of the product's plastic content by 51 percent
- Reduction of its global warming potential by 46 percent
- Reduction of its energy use by 46 percent

For this effort Amway was recognized by the Society of Plastic Engineers (SPE) in the spring of 2010 as the winner of its Environmental Stewardship Award. Amway has future plans to expand and complete LCAs on more of its product lines and has a goal to have every product complete an LCA by 2014.

Another West Michigan company that has also used the DfE process to great success is Harbor Industries. This family owned company, founded in 1946, has locations in Grand Haven and Charlevoix. They are one of the largest producers of custom point-of-purchase displays and fixtures.

The company has been using a DfE based Eco-Design Sustainability Wheel[6] that provides innovative tools and processes for life cycle product design including:

1. Innovation (e.g., design to mimmic nature)
2. Low impact materials (e.g., use thoroughly tested materials)
3. Optimized manufacturing (e.g., minimize waste, energy, number of materials used)
4. Efficient distribution (e.g., reduce packaging weight)
5. Low impact use (e.g., minimize emissions)
6. Optimized product lifetime (e.g., design for take back programs)
7. Optimized end-of-life (e.g., offer ease of disassembly provisions)

Current metrics are focused on environmental performance including electricity, natural gas and water consumption, and waste materials generated. Additional performance measurements are being developed for recycled and renewable content of materials; off-gassing waste stream reduction, and cleaner production processes.

Call to Action

- What design and engineering processes does the company have in place?
- What type of product development process does the company use?

- Does the product development process utilize sustainable development best practices?
- Does the company utilize Design for the Environment (DfE) and Life Cycle Analysis (LCA) in its engineering and product activities?

References

1. J. C. Brezet, e. Andal, 1994. Promise Handling Voor Milleugerichte Product Ontwikkeling (Promise Manual for Environmentally, Focused Product Development), SDU, Vitgewverij, The Hague, The Netherlands Hemel, C.G.V. and Keldmann, T., 1996 "Applying DFX Experiences in design for Environment, Design for x: Concurrent Engineering Imperatives, Chapman and Hall, Landon, pp.72-95.

2. Adapted: www.sidhal.com/green/EPA-OPPT-Design%20for%20the%20 Environment-About%20DfE.htm.

3. Design for the Environment, www.greenworkscleaners.com/about-us/ design-for-the-environment, accessed August 2011.

4. Herman Miller, Environmental Product Summary Aeron Chair, www.hermanmiller.com/content/dam/hermanmiller/documents/ environmental/eps/EPS_AER.pdf, accessed August 2011.

5. Source: Amway Corporate Blog, Life Cycle Assessments Prove Sustainability Claims, www.blogs.amway.com/onebyone/2010/03/11/ life-cycle-assessments-prove-sustainability-claims, accessed April 2012.

6. Source: Harbor Industries, 2011 Corporate Social Responsibility Report, http://www.harborind.com/documents/Harbor_CSR.pdf, accessed July 2012.

7. GREEN AND LEED DESIGN, BUILDING, AND CONSTRUCTION

Introduction

William McDonough and Michael Braungart, in a 1998 article for the *Harvard Business Review* entitled the *Next Industrial Revolution*, were quoted as saying: "Today even the most advanced building in the world is a kind of steamship, polluting, contaminating and depleting the surrounding environment and relying on scarce amounts of natural light and fresh air. People are essentially working in the dark, and they are often breathing unhealthy air. Imagine, instead a building as a kind of tree. It would purify air, accrue solar income, produce more energy than it consumes, create shade and habitat, enrich soil, and change with the season."[1] Green building today has become a way of life and represents a new discipline for designing, building, and sourcing new and renovated construction. Essentially green building takes into account all environmental impacts. The entire design is developed as a closed loop system and includes all products, components, and systems being used. The key question is whether these newer green buildings, with additional desirable features and benefits, can be constructed without any added costs?

In West Michigan, office furniture leaders Haworth, Herman Miller, Steelcase, and others began to design and construct buildings with more environmentally sensitive requirements dating back to the 1970s. Today Leadership in Environmental and Energy Design (LEED) construction has become the standard and overall policy for all new construction in West Michigan among many companies, colleges, and municipalities, such as Grand Valley State University and the City of Grand Rapids.

Background

LEED building design and construction guidelines were developed by the U.S. Green Building Council (USGBC) starting in 1994. LEED has now transformed the construction industry and become an internationally recognized voluntary green building certification that requires third-party certification.

Today the USGBC includes a membership of 18,000 companies and organizations, 78 local affiliates, and 140,000 LEED professional credential holders.[2] The USGBC is the major driving force for the construction industry and is projected to contribute nearly $550 billion to the U.S. gross domestic product (GDP) from 2009-2015. The USGBC has focused its efforts on educating the industry about building characteristics and performance. It has been estimated that buildings account for:

- 39 percent of carbon dioxide (CO_2) emissions
- 40 percent of energy consumption
- 13 percent of water consumption
- 15 percent of gross domestic product (GDP) per year

The Center for American Progress has stated that green building efficiency can meet 85 percent of the future U.S. demand for energy and that a national commitment to green building has the potential to create 2.5 million jobs. The USGBC has indicated that 900,000 new jobs are a possibility by 2020 if building energy efficiency is fully advanced.

Source: http://www.greenbuildingadvisor.com/blogs/dept/think-spot/qa-rick-fedrizzi-president-and-ceo-usgbc

The case studies in this chapter include Bazzani and Associates, Nichols Paper and Supply, and Meijer.

Description

LEED building design and construction can be utilized and implemented for any building life cycle, phase, or type. It represents a holistic life cycle approach that embraces sustainable development best practices in a number of key performance areas. LEED is a voluntary certification program that promotes a whole-building approach to sustainability by recognizing performance in key focused areas that are integrative, comprehensive, and inclusive of buildings for commercial, institutional, and residential use:

Sustainable Sites

Choosing a building's site and managing that site during construction are important considerations for a project's viability and overall sustainability. The Sustainable Sites category: discourages development on previously undeveloped land; minimizes a building's impact on ecosystems and waterways; encourages regionally appropriate landscaping; rewards smart transportation choices; controls stormwater runoff; and reduces erosion, light pollution, heat island effect, and construction-related pollution.

Water Efficiency

Buildings are major users of our nation's potable water supply. The goal of the Water Efficiency credit category is to encourage smarter and more efficient use of water, both inside and outside the building. Water reduction can typically be achieved through the use of more efficient appliances, fixtures and fittings inside, and water-wise landscaping outside of the building.

Energy & Atmosphere

According to the U.S. Department of Energy, buildings use 39 percent of the energy and 74 percent of the electricity produced each year in the United States. The Energy & Atmosphere category encourages a wide variety of energy strategies: commissioning; energy use monitoring; efficient building design and construction; use of efficient appliances, systems and lighting; the use of renewable and clean sources of energy, generated on-site or off-site; and other innovative strategies.

Materials & Resources

During both the construction and operations phases, buildings generate a substantial amount of waste and use a lot of materials and resources. This credit category encourages the selection of sustainably grown, harvested, produced, and transported products and materials. It also promotes the reduction of waste as well as reuse and recycling, and it takes into account the reduction of waste at a product's source. Purchasing locally sourced materials can also generate additional credits as well.

Indoor Environmental Quality

The U.S. Environmental Protection Agency estimates that Americans spend about 90 percent of their day indoors, where the air quality can be significantly worse than outside. The Indoor Environmental Quality credit category promotes strategies that can improve indoor air quality and circulation as well as providing access to natural daylight and views, and improving acoustics and noise levels.

Locations & Linkages

The LEED for Homes rating system recognizes that much of a home's impact on the environment comes from where it is located and how well it fits into the community. The Locations & Linkages credits encourage homes to be built away from environmentally sensitive places and instead located on infill, previously developed, and other preferable sites. It rewards homes that are constructed near existing infrastructure, community resources and transit, and it encourages access to open space for walking, physical activity, and time spent outdoors.

Awareness & Education

The LEED for Homes rating system acknowledges that a green home is only truly green if the people who live in it use its energy efficient features to maximum effect and performance. The Awareness & Education credits encourage architects, home builders, and real estate professionals to provide homeowners, tenants, and building managers with the education and tools they need to understand the features and benefits of what makes their home green and how to make the most of those advantages.

Innovation in Design

The Innovation in Design credit category generates bonus points for projects that use new and innovative technologies and strategies to improve a building's performance well beyond what is required by other LEED credits or in green building procedures that are not specifically addressed elsewhere in LEED. This credit category also rewards projects for including a LEED Accredited Professional on the team to ensure a holistic, systems integrated approach to the design and construction phase.

Regional Priority
USGBC's regional councils, chapters, and affiliates have identified the local environmental concerns that are most important for every region of the country. Six LEED credits address those local priorities that have been selected for each region. A project that earns a regional priority credit will earn one bonus point in addition to any points awarded for that credit. Up to four extra points can be earned in this manner.

Icons courtesy of U.S. Green Building Council, accessed April 2012.

The LEED building design and construction process is also a rating system that requires third-party verification. The USGBC has updated the LEED 2009 certification process for new construction and major renovation by establishing 100 base points, 6 possible points for Innovation in Design, and 4 regional priority points for the following certification levels:

- LEED Certified 40-49 points
- LEED Silver 50-59 points
- LEED Gold 60-79 points
- LEED Platinum 80 points and above

Application
The following are the established LEED rating system categories:
- New Construction and Major Renovations (LEED-**NC**): This rating system is for achieving high performance commercial and institutional building projects and practices.
- Existing Buildings (LEED-**EB**): This rating system was designed for owners of current buildings to improve their overall operations and maintenance performance.

SUSTAINABILITY DEMYSTIFIED!

- Commercial Interiors (LEED-**CI**): This rating system was established for tenants so that they could take advantage of sustainable development choices for the interior design of their occupancy area within the overall building infrastructure.
- Core and Shell (LEED-**CS**): This rating system was developed for new building owners, designers, and developers regarding implementation of sustainable development design features for the core and shell construction of the building structure.
- Retail: This rating system was established so that specific sustainable design features could be incorporated into retail spaces. Meijer, a West Michigan based retail giant, has recently opened a LEED approved retail store and anticipates opening more in the future.
- Healthcare: This rating system enables healthcare facilities to achieve high performance sustainable design features and benefits. The Metro Health complex in Grand Rapids is a good example.
- Homes: Residential homes can now be built to high performance LEED rating systems. Habitat for Humanity in 2009 built 23 LEED approved low income residential homes in the greater Grand Rapids area.
- Neighborhood Development (LEED-**ND**): This rating system enables the integration of sustainable design principles such as smart growth, sustainable urbanism, and green building for community and neighborhood development. The City of Grand Rapids has been evaluating the LEED-ND protocol for the Wealthy Street Neighborhood Corridor.

Although LEED is the premier building design and rating system protocol, there are alternatives to LEED Certification. These alternatives to LEED standards and certifications include:

- The Sustainability Tracking and Assessment Rating System (STARS) (http://stars.aashe.org): STARS is a transparent, self-reporting framework for colleges and universities to gauge their progress toward sustainability. STARS was developed by the Association of Advancement for Sustainability in Higher Education (AASHE) with broad participation from the higher education community. The STARS framework is intended to engage and recognize the full spectrum of colleges and universities in the United States and Canada. STARS encompasses long-term sustainability goals for already high-achieving institutions as well as entry points of recognition for institutions that are taking first steps toward sustainability. Facilities and building are one of the key areas addressed in this assessment. GVSU was one of the first colleges and universities to use this protocol.

- BREEAM (BRE) Environmental Assessment Method (www.breeam.org): BREEAM is a leading and widely used environmental assessment method for buildings. It sets the standard for best practice in sustainable building design and overall building environmental performance. BREEAM addresses wide-ranging environmental credentials of their buildings for both building planners and clients. It uses a straightforward scoring system that is transparent, easy to understand, and supported by evidence-based research; has a positive influence on the design, construction, and management of buildings; and sets and maintains a robust technical standard with rigorous quality assurance and certification.

- Green Globes Design (www.greenglobes.com) is both a guide for integrating green design principles and an assessment protocol as well. Using confidential questionnaires for each stage of a building project's delivery, the program generates a comprehensive online assessment including guidance reports. Using Green Globes helps to design a building that will be energy and resource efficient, will achieve operational savings, and be healthier to work or live in.

Green Globes is the newest addition to the BREEAM/Green Leaf portfolio of environmental assessment tools. The program's core premise is that environmental leadership and responsibility makes business sense.

- The Green Building Certification Institute (GBCI), established in January 2008, provides third-party project certification and professional credentials recognizing excellence in green building performance and practice. GBCI administers project certification for commercial and institutional buildings and tenant spaces under the U.S. Green Building Council's LEED Green Building Rating Systems addressing new construction and ongoing operations. GBCI also manages the professional credentialing programs based upon the LEED Green Associate and LEED Accredited Professional (AP) credentials.

- Living Building Challenge (www.ilbi.org): The purpose of the Living Building Challenge, a program of the International Living Building Institute (ILBI), is to define the most advanced measure of sustainability possible today in the built environment. This certification program covers all buildings and sizes and is an integrative tool for transformative design, allowing the envisioning of a future that is socially, culturally, ecologically, and economically balanced and sound. The West Michigan chapter of the USGBC is interested in creating a Living Building Challenge project in the Greater Grand Rapids area.

Results and Benefits

LEED buildings have demonstrated the following performance benefits over the years. These benefits have been substantiated through written project case studies, such as the research and studies from Greg Kats:

- Energy conservation estimated at 25-30 percent
- Water conservation estimated at 30-40 percent
- Wastewater savings through the use of rain gardens and irrigation ponds
- Reduced waste such as through the recycling of construction and demolition (C and D) debris. GVSU now recycles over 90 percent of C and D debris when building to LEED standards
- Improved indoor air quality through the use of CO_2 sensors and circulation of fresh air
- Greater employee comfort and productivity, such as with natural lighting use
- Reduced employee health costs, such as those from respiratory ailments, by using circulation of fresh air and air filtration measures
- Overall lower operational and maintenance costs due to reduced energy and water consumption
- Competitive first costs due to the implementation of integrative building design features, benefits, and overall synergies
- Increased value and overall return on investment for capital outlays and costs
- Marketing advantage for the company through the attraction of customers and community stakeholders, and other interested parties
- Overall reduced liabilities through improved risk management and decreased insurance costs for the building project

In 2003 Greg Kats, in his study the Costs and Financial Benefits of Green Buildings, determined the true cost of building green and overall financial benefits ($ per square foot). At that time the total 20 year net present value (NPV) for LEED Certified and LEED Silver buildings was reported as $48.87 per square foot and for LEED Gold and LEED Platinum buildings as $67.31 per square foot.[3] Recently, Greg Kats completed another survey of green schools built in 10 states during 2001-2006.

When evaluating a potential new building or construction project, there are a number of successful steps that can be undertaken when designing the building to green and LEED building performance standards. In his article Building the Green Way, Charles Lockwood identified ten practical design and construction rules.[4]

Ten Practical Design and Construction Rules

1	Focus on the big picture • Look for significant 40 percent potential savings and 40 percent better performance versus traditional buildings
2	Choose a sustainable site • Use infill lots and redevelopment sites where possible; e.g., brown field redevelopment • Provide access to public transportation
3	Do the math • Conduct a cost/benefit analysis for each project step, milestone, and activity before allocating funding • Include financial assistance, tax breaks and incentives wherever possible
4	Make the site plan work • Ensure proper layout of the building for maximizing natural lighting and capturing cross ventilation
5	Landscape for savings • Minimize heat island effects through natural landscaping strategies • Plant locally grown trees and shrubs for shade cover
6	Design for greater "green" • Use natural lighting and ventilation where possible • Glaze windows • Locate fixed systems near building core
7	Take advantage of technology • Utilize green and clean technologies • Evaluate distributed power generation sources

8	Save and manage water • Establish irrigation systems • Purchase waterless urinals and low flush toilets • Provide storm water management best practices
9	Use of alternative materials • Use green, sustainable, nontoxic certified building materials and components • Use 100 percent recycled carpet
10	Construct green • Coordinate wet and dry activities, such as painting and cleaning air vents • Recycle construction waste • Crush used concrete and asphalt • Paint with low VOC interior finishes • Purchase Energy Star equipment

Source: Courtesy of Building the Green Way, by Charles Lockwood, Harvard Business Review.

In the fall of 2010, the West Michigan Chapter of the USGBC completed its *Green Buildings of West Michigan* book. Forty-five LEED certified buildings in West Michigan were featured and profiled in a September 2010 report.[5]

Most recently Keith Winn, President of Catalyst Partners, received LEED-NC v 2.2 Platinum Certification for his office building on 502 Second Street NW in Grand Rapids (www.catalyst-partners.com).

Case Studies

Currently they are 156 LEED certified building projects in West Michigan. Worthy to note is that the City of Grand Rapids in 2011 ranked number 14 on the number of LEED certified buildings versus all other cities including major metropolitan areas such as Seattle, Portland, Chicago, and New York. Grand Rapids also ranked number two in LEED buildings per capita behind only Cambridge, Massachusetts, according to the West Michigan chapter of the USGBC.[6]

In West Michigan one of the more significant LEED building recognitions was received by Bazzani and Associates for the first double gold LEED certification in the United States for the East Hills Center (Of the Universe) building. LEED Gold certifications were awarded for both LEED-CS and LEED-CI. The 7,200 square foot building that received the LEED-CI award is home to Marie Catrib's restaurant, Cobblestone Home, and the 2,700 square foot building of the West Michigan Environmental Action Council (WMEAC).[7]

The double gold LEED certified project had several key features:

- All of the decisions for furniture for the WMEAC offices were environmentally sound
- A wide variety of sustainability fabrics and finishes were used including carpets
- The building uses 35 percent less energy and contains significant insulation
- A green roof was installed to reduce cooling costs and help extend the life of the roof membrane
- The south side of the building collects passive solar energy to help heat the building in winter
- The building contains energy efficient lighting and HVAC equipment
- A rain garden filters rainwater and helps minimize storm water runoff
- It is the first building in the city of Grand Rapids designed to be a zero water discharge installation

Nichols Paper and Supply Company also recently received a LEED-EB Gold certification for their company and warehouse in Muskegon, Michigan, in June 2010. Nichols was the 7th LEED for Existing Building certification in the State of Michigan; first in their industry in Michigan; and, to the best of their knowledge, the second distribution company of custodial and packaging supplies in the United States to achieve LEED-EB status and certification.[8]

Nichols is the largest independent distributor of cleaning, protection, and packaging supplies in the state of Michigan, has been in business for over seventy years, is headquartered in Muskegon (112,000 square foot building), and services over four thousand customers. Nichols also has branches in Wixom, Holland, Traverse City, and Grand Rapids.

The LEED for Existing Buildings Rating System helps building owners and operators measure operations, improvements, and maintenance on a consistent scale, with the goal of maximizing operational efficiency while minimizing environmental impacts. LEED-EB certification also addresses whole-building cleaning and maintenance issues, including chemical use, recycling programs, exterior maintenance programs, and systems upgrades.

According to Mike Olthoff, CEO of Nichols Paper: "This was a major undertaking for our organization and an important achievement. It demonstrates to our customers and potential customers that we are serious about green buildings and can help them achieve their goals when it comes to creating their own clean and healthy facilities. An organization can earn a significant number of LEED credits by implementing a Green Cleaning Program. We felt going through this process would add to our credibility. We are very proud of this important achievement and feel it demonstrates our leadership in helping Michigan create a new economy."

Renae Hesselink, LEED AP and Vice President of Sustainability, said it took them approximately two years to get through the process. "It is about culture change and implementing policies and procedures that support living in a green building." Hesselink also said, "It also doesn't end with achievement of certification; it is an on-going continuous improvement process, a journey because technology and innovation will continue to change products and processes."

In March of 2010 Meijer Inc. became the first retail supercenter in the nation to receive LEED remodel certification from the

USGBC. The location was in Norton Shores, Michigan, one of the oldest stores in the Meijer chain.[9] Many retailers have followed LEED guidelines for new construction projects, but no retailer had ever undertaken LEED guidelines for such a large reconstruction project. Some of the key features of the 50-year-old Muskegon retail store reconstruction and upgrade include:

- Floor plan reduction from 224,759 feet to 195,386 feet
- Store rebuilt on its original site, saving virgin land and property
- Use of 6 roof mounted wind turbines for energy savings
- Replacement of older refrigeration systems
- Addition of a gasoline station that sells 85 percent ethanol fuel (E85)
- Installation of a solar reflective roof that covers 100 percent of the roof and reduces the heat island effect of the building
- Planting of drought resistant plants
- 90 percent of the rainwater is captured and treated on the property before entering the municipal sewer system
- Diversion of over 95 percent of the demolition and reconstruction waste from the landfill
- Over two-thirds of the building materials came from local sources
- 28 percent of all building materials contained recycled content
- Reduction of 38 percent of water use through design efficiencies and installation of low-flow fixtures

Meijer remains committed to LEED design, building, and construction standards for its buildings and locations that help reduce its overall environmental footprint and improve upon its environmental stewardship.

Call to Action

- Is the company familiar with green and/or LEED design building and construction procedures? Does the company have a trained LEED AP on staff or access to one?
- Does the company anticipate any design, building, and construction capital projects in the near future? Can LEED-NC, EB, CS, or CI certification standards be applied to this capital project?
- What local design and engineering firms can help provide the company and organization knowledge and expertise in green and LEED design, building and construction?
- What are some of the available LEED case studies for similar capital projects that are in the local area and can be benchmarked?

References

1. The NEXT Industrial Revolution, http://www.theatlantic.com/magazine/archive/1998/10/the-next-industrialrevolution/4695/, accessed July 2011.
2. United States Green Building Council, www.USGBC.org, accessed August 2011.
3. The Costs and Financial Benefits of Green Buildings, http://www.calrecycle.ca.gov/GreenBuilding/Design/CostBenefit/Report.pdf, accessed August 2011.
4. Charles Lockwood, Building the Green Way, *Harvard Business Review,* http://summits.ncat.org/docs/HBR_building_the_green_way.pdf, June 2006.
5. Green Buildings of West Michigan, http://www.usgbcwm.org/green-buildings-book, accessed August 2011.
6. Renae Hesselink, LEEDAP, Chair West Michigan USGBC, www.usgbcwm.org.
7. East Hills Center (Of the Universe) receives first Double Gold LEED Certification in the universe, http://www.rapidgrowthmedia.com/devnews/easthillsgoldleed0928.aspx, accessed July 2011.
8. Nichols Achieves LEED EB – Gold Status, www.enichols.com/sustainability-2/our-journey, accessed August 2011.
9. Source: www.mlive.com/news/muskegon/index.ssf/2010/03/norton_shores_meijer_receives.html, accessed April 2012.

8. GREEN AND CLEAN TECHNOLOGIES

Introduction

Green and clean technologies have become an increasingly important platform for businesses in recent years as manufacturers and service providers try to reduce or shift away from "environmentally unfriendly" and petroleum based technologies. These new "green" and "clean" technologies have been developed and commercialized in order to conserve resources in our natural environment, to reduce our overall needs and demands for desirable resources, and to reduce or eliminate emissions and waste from their use. In addition to being environmentally friendly, many of these "green" and "clean" technologies are cost competitive in the market place. Today chemical companies with commercially available products based on these technology platforms include global icons such as Dupont, Dow Chemical, and Dow Corning. Other companies are further developing green chemistry initiatives as well. The American Chemical Society is also a strong proponent of green and sustainable chemistry.

Case studies in this chapter include LG Chem, Louis Padnos Iron and Metal, and Irwin Seating.

Description

Many of the "green and clean" technologies that have been commercially developed are based on renewable and environmentally friendly sources of energy and feedstocks. Today, these technologies provide new product concepts, entrepreneurial market approaches, and spark innovation and creativity. These technologies can also generate demonstrated efficiencies in operations and enable users to develop various breakthrough solutions. Many corporations and businesses now recognize that not only are green and clean technologies the right technologies to use, but their use also makes sound business sense with favorable bottom line performance, overall organizational benefits, and distinct competitive advantage. Many primary customers and their secondary customers are now requesting, and in some cases demanding, the use of these technologies in their supply chain and are seeking the value created. Through their use, these technologies can also improve the quality of life for end users, especially in emerging markets and third world countries.

One of the key characteristics of these new green and clean technologies is that they are highly disruptive with the opportunity to significantly change and transform many market segments and industries, accelerate economic growth, develop new markets, and create new jobs. In fact in March 2010 the Bureau of Labor Standards (BLS) acknowledged that they have begun to track green jobs in their database. The green jobs database includes new North American Industry Classification System (NAICS) and Standard Occupational Classifications (SOC) codes.[1] Green jobs are considered ones that help a company produce goods or services that benefit the environment, conserve natural resources, or assist in making production processes more environmentally friendly and use fewer natural resources.

The Fuji-Keizai group conducted a market study on the future for Clean-Tech: Current Status and World Wide Outlook.[2] They estimated that the current global-market for clean-tech goods and services was $284 billion in 2008 growing to over $1.3 trillion by 2017 for an annual growth rate of 17 percent.

Key Clean-Tech Segments and Areas

Segment	Clean-Tech Area
Agriculture	Bio-based materials, bio-remediation
Air and the Environment	Air-purification; air-filtration; energy efficient HVAC
Materials	Nano-technologies; thermoelectric materials; composite materials
Energy	Renewable energy generation, infrastructure, storage and efficiency
Recycling and Waste	Hazardous waste remediation; recycling technologies; waste treatment
Manufacturing	Advanced packaging; natural or green chemistry; sensors; precision manufacturing
Transportation	Smart logistics; hybrid vehicles; fuel efficiency
Water and Wastewater	Ultra-filtration systems; desalination; UV membrane; ion-exchange

Andrew McWilliams of BCC Research, the market forecasting company, in his recent study on the U.S. Market for Clean Technologies, estimated the U.S. market for clean technologies at $54.2 billion in 2007 and $57.8 billion in 2008 growing to $88.6 billion in 2013 with an estimated compounded annual growth rate (CAGR) of 8.9 percent.[3] Clean energy estimated at $30.6 billion is the largest anticipated market. Clean building is the second largest market with a projected $28.2 billion in 2013. Clean transportation is the next largest market with an estimated $16 billion in 2013.

Also, according to the 2009 Michigan Green Jobs Report,[4] the primary markets for green and clean technologies include:

- Clean transportation and fuel
- Energy efficiency
- Pollution prevention and environmental clean-up
- Agriculture and natural resource conservation
- Renewable energy production

However, it should be noted that the market for green building was not covered in the Michigan Green Jobs Report, nor were several other major application areas for clean technologies.

There are many examples of green and clean technologies that are being developed in the marketplace today. Some of these technologies and product applications include:

- Advanced Batteries (e.g., Lithium)
- Advanced Packaging
- Bio-based Materials and Biopolymers (e.g., Poly Lactic Acid (PLA) Polymers)
- Bio-fuels (e.g., biodiesel, ethanol)
- Biomimicry (e.g., the study of nature and its systems)
- Carbon Sequestration
- Demand Response and Sensor (e.g., Motion Detectors)
- Environmental Remediation
- Filtration Media, Devices, and Systems
- Green Building, Design, and Construction (e.g., LEED)
- Green and Natural Chemistry (e.g., Nontoxic Materials)
- Green Information Technology
- Green Transportation (e.g., Electric Motors, Plug-In Hybrids)
- Hydrogen
- Nanotechnology
- Renewable Energy (e.g., Biomass and Waste to Energy; Geothermal; Hydropower; Solar Power (e.g., Thermal, Photovoltaic; Wave/Tidal; Wind Power)
- Smart Logistics
- Solid State Lighting (e.g., Light Emitting Diode (LED), Compact Fluorescent Lightbulb (CFL))

Application

Many clean and green technologies have a significant impact on both existing as well as new markets. These technologies are highly innovative and potentially disruptive in the marketplace. Companies are redesigning existing products as well as developing new products for these markets using clean and green technology platforms in order to gain competitive market positioning and improved sustainable supply chain management.

Examples of market sectors impacted by green and clean technologies include:

- Air Quality
- Building and Construction
- Carbon Management
- Energy and Power Generation
- Energy Efficiency
- Energy Storage
- Fuel Recovery
- Manufacturing
- Packaging
- Pollution Prevention
- Transportation and Logistics
- Waste Management
- Water and Wastewater Management
- Water Purification

Results and Benefits

There are numerous benefits to the use of these technologies. Some of the major benefits include:

- Reduced energy consumption, such as with heating, cooling, and lighting
- Cost savings (e.g., raw material consumption, energy, and water use)

- Reduced or eliminated emissions such as with greenhouse gas, carbon dioxide, and particulate emissions
- Reduced waste
- Less treated wastewater
- Reduced overall environmental footprint and environmental impact
- Increased productivity from manufacturing processes
- Improved health and wellness of employees
- Improved quality of life in emerging and third world developing countries
- Accelerated growth of newly created jobs
- Access to tax credits and other incentives
- Reduced potential liabilities and risks

Case Studies

Advanced battery technologies for a number of applications such as for the emerging plug-in hybrid electric vehicle market consist of more than 20,000 jobs in Michigan, according to the Michigan Economic Development Corporation (MEDC) which has made more than $2 billion in investments in these technologies. Former Michigan Governor Jennifer Granholm viewed batteries as the "21st century equivalent of the development of the internal combustion engine in the early 20th century." Advanced battery production in Michigan is directly tied to the future growth of electric vehicles and the green automotive industry nationally and globally.[5]

The Boston Consulting Group (BCG) has predicted that the sales of electric vehicles including hybrids, plug-in hybrids, and pure electric vehicles will grow to 9-12 percent of the U.S. market by 2020, up from 3 percent in 2010. Michigan has been able to attract nearly 20 battery manufacturers through lucrative tax credits.

In West Michigan there are two advanced battery manufacturing plants, Johnson Controls–Saft and LG Chem. According to some estimates, advanced batteries could be a $100 billion market over the next 20 years. The BCG also expects battery costs to fall by approximately 65 percent by 2020 as well.[5]

LG Chem Ltd. is the largest chemical company in Korea and offers a broad platform of products worldwide through its diversified and integrated operations. The company also is focusing on advanced rechargeable battery technology for the future. LG Chem Ltd. has established plans for a $300 million advanced battery manufacturing plant for electric vehicles in Holland, Michigan, which will produce products using lithium ion battery technology. Eaton Corporation has partnered with LG Chemical and Compact Power Inc., the LG Chem subsidiary who will operate the battery plant and manufacture batteries for specific Eaton hybrid electric drive systems, for such customers as FedEx, UPS, Coca-Cola, PepsiCo, and Walmart. In addition, LG Chem will produce lithium ion batteries for both the Chevy Volt and Buick Envision plug-in hybrids[6] and Ford Motor Company will also purchase battery packs for their new Ford Focus. The LG Chem plant is expected to open in 2013 and employ 450 people.

These developments in advanced battery manufacturing, with four battery plants in the regional area, will assure West Michigan's place as a worldwide hub for lithium battery research and development.

The commercialization of renewable energy technologies is also making progress in West Michigan. In March 2010 Louis Padnos Iron and Metal announced the largest solar energy installation in the state of Michigan at its plastic and paper Recycling Center on 500 44th Street SW in Wyoming, Michigan. Developed in partnership with Louis Padnos Iron and Metal and Cascade Renewable Energy Solutions, a division of Cascade Engineering, the joint solar energy project cost $1.27 million and featured 636 solar panels that were arrayed and covered on the rooftop of the building. Consisting of 3 foot by 5 foot panels covering 15,000 square feet of the roof, the solar project will generate 150 kilowatts of energy which is sold to Consumers Energy Company. Consumers had launched a buyback program for energy generated by the solar facility so that the public utility could meet new guidelines of generating 10 percent of their overall electrical supply from alternative and renewable energy sources by 2015. State property and tax credits also played an important role in giving the overall solar energy project a payback period of approximately 8 years.

This showcase project highlighted several key mutual learning experiences including joint partnership innovation, environmental commitment, generation of data, and building of a mutual knowledge base. Overall the solar project was forward looking in that it signaled to the marketplace the potential long-term value of solar energy as a viable renewable energy solution for Michigan. Additional information about the real time solar energy data for the facility is also available.7

Irwin Seating began purchasing green energy through Consumers Energy in 2002 and recently earned Consumer's Green Generation customer of the year. Irwin Seating is the largest participant in the Green Generation program in West Michigan and third largest overall in the state. Today, Irwin Seating purchases about 20 percent green energy which totals nearly 700,000 kWh per year. Win Irwin, President, indicated that the green energy costs approximately $6,000 more annually. Today the company can purchase nearly twice as much green energy as it could back in 2002 at much lower costs, as the price of green energy has continued to decline over this period of time. Irwin Seating is a company that has been built on environmental stewardship best practices over the years. As a business leader, Irwin Seating is helping to build a market for green energy in Michigan and West Michigan that will enable Consumers Energy to sell more green power and allow for Irwin Seating and other industrial manufacturers to use more green energy in their operations over time.[8]

About 30 years ago, Irwin Seating was the first company in the industry to convert paint operations from conventional solvent based coatings to powder coating technology. Today, the company is also in its second year of a no waste campaign with all waste being recycled or incinerated.

Call to Action

- Does the company still primarily use petrochemical based products either directly in manufactured products within company operations or with outsourced materials, products, or components?
- What green and clean technologies can or does the company embrace in its operations?
- Does the company see the opportunity to reposition or reinvent itself using green and clean technologies? If so which clean technologies and with what applications?
- Can green and clean technologies be used in the supply chain to differentiate the production and supply of value-added products and services?

References

1. Overview of the BLS Green Jobs Initiative, www.bls.gov/green/#overview, accessed August 2011.
2. Clean-Tech: Current Status and Worldwide Outlook, www.fuji-keizai.com/e/report/cleantech_e.html, accessed August 2011.
3. BCC Research, http://www.bccresearch.com/report/clean-technologies-us-market-env011a.html, accessed July 2012.
4. Michigan Green Jobs Report, http://Michigan.gov/documents/nwlb/GJC_GreenReport_Print_277833_7.pdf, accessed August 2011.

5.   Special Report: Michigan goes big on batteries, thecenterformichigan.net/special-report-michigan-goes-big-on-batteries, accessed August 2011.
6.   Eaton Selects LG Chem Plant to Supply Battery Technology for Hybrid Power Systems, www.mlive.com/business/west-michigan/index.ssf/2010/07/eaton_selects_lg_chem_plant_to.html, accessed August 2011.
7.   Louis Padnos Iron and Metal, www.padnos.com, accessed June 2012.
8.   *Grand Rapids Business Journal,* August 20, 2012, page 15, accessed August 21, 2012.

PART THREE

MARKETING AND SALES

Marketing and sales usually are described in similar capacities, yet have distinctively different responsibilities. Marketing management always describes the "what" for sales (e.g., What industry? What market? What segments? What are the overall marketing targets for sales to achieve?). Many times marketing identifies and budgets the more profitable markets and segments to sell into as well. Sales management provides the "where" and the "how" (e.g., Where will the customer sales come from? How will the customer and market sales goals be achieved?). Marketing and sales work hand in hand. Both functions have campaigns, advertising, and promotional programs and activities. Market share is a critical goal for many companies. The higher the market share and overall brand recognition, the more apt the company is able to drive bottom line performance. Customer relations are built upon successful key account marketing and sales strategies.

Today, however, new customers have arrived in the retail and industrial marketplace and these customers are more discerning about the products they desire to purchase. Customers and consumers are more educated today and aware of specific criteria and that must be met before a purchasing decision can be made. In fact nearly 45 million U.S. consumers in the retail market, or roughly 20 percent prefer to purchase products that meet green or sustainability criteria. Additionally, many of these customers desire to seek out locally manufactured products over other national brands.

These customers are also willing to pay a higher price for these products. It has also been shown that purchasing locally manufactured products enables roughly an additional 25 percent of the purchasing dollars to remain in the local economy versus those dollars being spent on the purchase of a similar products from a non-locally owned business. Therefore, companies today have the opportunity to target new business opportunities in the New Economy, as well as the local and regional marketplace, and create new marketing and sales opportunities for their products and services.

In this section there is a discussion of the New Economy and the Lifestyle of Health and Sustainability Market (LOHAS). The retail LOHAS market has been tracked as a consumer market for several years and continues to grow as customers now select and purchase products with a life cycle approach based on pre- and post-consumption criteria. Additionally, the importance of sustainability standards and certifications are reviewed in light of the many false and misleading "green" label claims. The marketplace today is undergoing a "greenwashing" and shakeout that will enable the New Economy to have a stronger base moving forward.

9. NEW ECONOMY MARKET OPPORTUNITIES

Introduction

The "New Economy", as discussed, is composed of many new exciting product and service offerings, new market segments, entrepreneurial new start-up businesses and companies, and the beginnings of new industries for tomorrow. The roots of this "New Economy" in West Michigan can be traced back to the 2000 timeframe – over ten years ago!

Today, we can see the progress being made in this New Economy in West Michigan. Results include: a revitalized downtown business district in Grand Rapids; new and refurbished lodging, downtown accommodations and conference settings that meet the Michigan Green Venue certification standards; new and rebuilt commercial buildings that meet green and LEED building standards; Renaissance improvement zones; Brownfield Redevelopment sites that have improved the landscape; capital investments in life science research, a new medical school, and several new hospitals along Michigan Street and "Medical Mile;" and the cleaning and restoration of water resources such as the Grand River that flows through West Michigan and the city of Grand Rapids.

The case study in this chapter is Eden Foods.

What is this New Economy that we live in today?

Description

The world we live in today is much "different" than in the past. This New Economy has distinct and different characteristics than the "old" or traditional economy of the past.

What Kind of World do We Live In?

"Old" Economy	Characteristics	"New" Economy
Slow	Change	Fast
Long	Life Cycle	Short
Predictable	Development	Volatile
Financial, Asset, and Human	Capital	Natural, Financial, Social, and Shared
Linear	Processes	Continuous Improvement
Petrochemical	Products/Technologies	Clean and Green
Command and Control	Business Model	Empowerment and Collaboration
Big Eats Small	Competition	Fast Eats Slow
Mass	Marketing	Differentiation
Degrees and Training	Skill Sets	Multi-Skilled Learning
Cradle to Grave	Decision Making	Cradle to Cradle
Profit	Success	Value Creation

Source: Adapted, Mike Rafferty, CSI, Unilock, slide, adapted by Norman Christopher, 2012.

Marketplace change today is extremely fast and dynamic. Businesses are now required to constantly reinvent themselves, looking for any strategy they can to develop a new product or service that will differentiate the competition and positively influence the marketplace. Product life cycles are much shorter than in the past—sometimes no more than 1-2 years. All we have to do is look at a product like golf clubs, which in the past had few changes from season to season. Now with all the new composite materials that are being used, "hot" new putters and drivers may only last one season before a new breakthrough product enters the marketplace driven by disruptive technology.

As a result new product, market, and business development tends to be volatile and disruptive versus evolutionary and predictable, and now comprised of many challenging hurdles accompanied by milestone breakthroughs. In the past, traditional capital sources for the "new economy" included financial, human, and assets. Today, many other capital options are available and used for sustainable development such as knowledge, cultural, community, social, advocacy, natural and shared capital resources and assets. Development processes used in the past were linear and predictable. Once achieved, the results of these processes "leveled off" and became normalized. Manufacturing operations today have a new philosophy—one of continuous improvement! Companies and businesses today, regardless of their size, have found many project areas of "low hanging" fruit in their operations that conserve resources and increase overall eco-efficiency. Paybacks for these type of projects usually take only a few years. The successes should be celebrated and the savings reinvested to provide a track record of progress.

Today's business model is also not one of "command and control" business management practices, such as with large corporations in the past who were structured with strategic business units (SBUs). Many successful new business models and start-up business ventures today are being created through partnerships and alliances. Employees are being empowered to make a difference, rather than waiting for management to make a decision to change. It is the essence of a "bottom up" versus "top down" management style that is allowing companies to be more responsive, employees to be more productive, and management teams to obtain breakthrough results with applied sustainable development best practices.

The new economy competitive marketplace is also characterized by businesses and enterprises that are "fast" and fleet afoot besting competitors that are "slow" and entrenched. Yesterday it was about "bigger being better," which is not the case today. Marketing has also become much more sophisticated. Today markets are being segmented and fragmented with products being more tailored, "niche" in their application, and easily differentiated. Employees today are also more multi-skilled and well-rounded. Employees are highly trained and capable of filling in for other employees and managers, rather than just being considered as "specialists" in specific professional fields.

What drives this new economy are the decisions for change that the business owners and managers are being required to make. In the past, decisions were reached via a "cradle to grave" mentality. Many times the "status quo" was considered good enough. As long as products were manufactured within proper regulations, met compliance standards, were sold for their appropriate applications, attained warranty claims fit for their intended purpose, and customers paid for them within 30 days, that was considered a successful business.

However, no longer is a cradle to grave business model mentality good enough to ensure success, or in some cases allow businesses to survive and just "tread water." Today's marketplace is requiring a "cradle to cradle" business mission and visionary approach. Customers are asking and demanding to know answers to questions like: What is the product made of? What raw materials have been used? Where was the product made and by whom? Can the product be recycled? Can it be disassembled and reassembled? How can it be disposed of? The buyer or customer is thinking both pre- and post-consumption as well. The consumer today is now a more educated buyer than ever before that is looking at more than just the price of the product.

The Natural Marketing Institute has looked at the consumer's approach to the life cycle analysis of purchased products today.[1] As can be seen, the educated consumer and buyer today have many criteria that must be met before a purchasing decision can be made.

A Consumer's Approach to Life Cycle Analysis

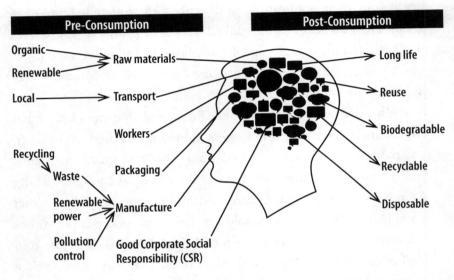

Source: The LOHAS Market and Consumer Trends: The Rise of the Ethical Consumption Reveolution, The National Marketing Institute (NMI), adapted by Norman Christopher, 2012.

Since the 18th century, there have been five waves of innovation. Today we are passing through the fifth wave—the age of digitization. Social media communications and outlets have been developing at an exponential pace. The growth of Facebook, LinkedIn, and Twitter participation has become the norm for business leaders as well as their family members. Software programs are being refined and revised for new rollouts. Just look at Microsoft Word and Adobe Acrobat Reader who are both in their seventh and eighth versions and beyond. Each new upgrade changes the rules of the game and sets a new bar of expectations.

But what about tomorrow? What lies ahead? What is the next wave of innovation?

The Natural Edge Project was established in 2004 as a collaborative partnership that engaged research, education, and policy formation regarding innovation in sustainable development.[2] They advocated that the sixth wave of innovation, including clean technologies and sustainable development, was already taking place and gaining a foothold.

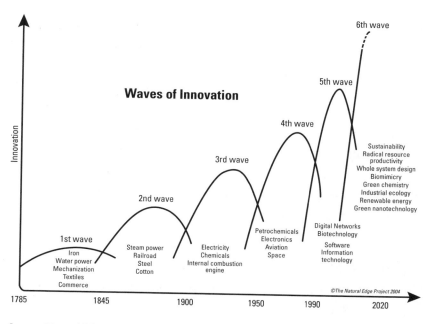

Source: Natural Edge Project, 2004.

The sixth wave of innovation will drive the new and green economy! It will contain many new systems, processes, techniques, technologies, and best practices. First and foremost will be the use of applied sustainable development best practices. One example will be the pursuit of radical resource productivity, generating savings of 15-20 percent annual savings or greater. Whole system "cradle to cradle" product design features will be employed, such as the Design for the Environment (DfE) protocol. Some breakthrough products will be developed by "mimicking nature," such as with biomimicry. One can think about studying the flight patterns of different birds and how that has enlightened us to build and grow the airplane and aerospace industry. Products and bio-materials based on green chemistry will be used, not those developed just from petroleum based chemicals and derivatives. Industrial ecology will be pursed whereby industrial open-ended processes will shift to closed loop systems that minimize waste and help achieve a balance with the natural environment. Renewable energy sources, from both grid and distributed systems, will provide power and energy for many industrial processes. Today, for example, Herman Miller has recently acknowledged that they have achieved their 100 percent renewable energy goal as part of their 2020 Perfect Vision. Another major manufacturing opportunity will emerge with green nanotechnology. "Nanotechnology is the design, characterization, production, and application of systems by controlling the shape and size at the nanometer scale. A nanometer (nm) is one billionth of a meter."[3]

Application

Today the marketplace for sustainable products and services in the United States is real, growing, and now tracked as a consumer market. It is known as the Lifestyles of Health and Sustainability (LOHAS) market.

In 2008 U.S. consumers spent approximately $300 billion on LOHAS related products and services.[4]

U.S. Consumer Spending on LOHAS Related Products and Services

Segment	Consumer Spending (Billions of Dollars)
Personal Health; e.g., natural and organic food, personal care, vitamin and natural supplements, etc.	$117.41
Green Building; e.g., Energy Star appliances, certified homes, etc.	100.35
Eco-Tourism; e.g., adventure travel in nature, botanical gardens and parks, etc.	42.14
Alternative Transportation; e.g., hybrid and electric vehicles, car sharing, etc.	20.7
Natural Lifestyles; e.g., natural apparel, natural home furnishings, etc.	10.3
Alternative Energy; e.g., renewable energy; i.e., solar photovoltaic.	1.0
Total	$291.9

The estimated $300 billion U.S. LOHAS market encompasses only consumer retail sales, not business-to-business (B2B) transactions. This market began being tracked in the year 2000. In 2005 the LOHAS market was estimated at $209 billion. Most recently the LOHAS market has been growing at a rate more than 15 percent annually in the U.S. The methodology for developing this data comes primarily from secondary sources according to the Natural Marketing Institute (NMI). Today, there are some estimates that the global consumer LOHAS market has reached $1 trillion.

Recently, the NMI has also conducted exhaustive studies to determine consumer buying behavior. In 2010 the LOHAS market and overall "Green Industry" reached a tipping point in terms of connecting values with consumer buying behavior.

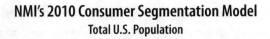

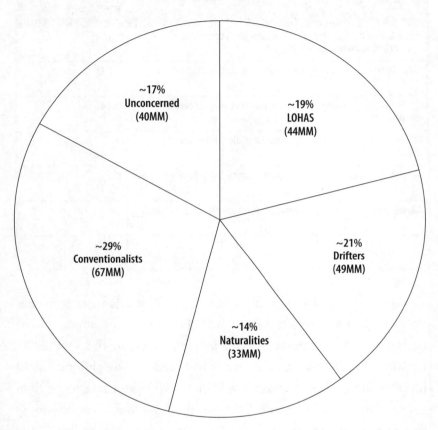

NMI's 2010 Consumer Segmentation Model
Total U.S. Population

~17%
Unconcerned
(40MM)

~19%
LOHAS
(44MM)

~21%
Drifters
(49MM)

~29%
Conventionalists
(67MM)

~14%
Naturalities
(33MM)

Source: The National Marketing Institute (NMI) 2010, adapted by Norman Christopher, 2012.

LOHAS purchasers in today's marketplace represent an estimated one out of every five consumers in the United States or approximately 44 million consumers that are dedicated to the purchase of "green" products, even at a higher price. They also support advocacy and embrace environmental stewardship. Naturalites, representing 14 percent of consumers, are focused on their health and purchase natural and organic foods and beverages. Drifters, or approximately

49 million consumers, are the second largest segment. They are considered to be price sensitive and are influenced by decisions other than the environment. Conventionalists, the largest consumer segment, do not have an overall green attitude, but recycling and conservation are important to them. Those that are unconcerned do not have an environmental and social buying behavior and are not easily influenced to purchase LOHAS goods and services.[5] The sustainable development mindset of businesses today "thinks globally" and "acts locally," but also builds regionally such as with the use of clean technologies within West Michigan.

Michael Shuman in his book *The Small-Mart Revolution: How Local Businesses Are Beating the Global Competition* discusses the importance of building local economies and that there are eight "de-globalizing" trends that are the major driving forces.[5] These trends include:

- Inefficiencies in global scale manufacture. One size doesn't fit all. Beverages are a good example, such as with the many local West Michigan micro-breweries.

- Global distribution also creates great inefficiencies. Sometimes distribution costs are greater than production costs. The importance of sustainable agriculture and local and regional food production in West Michigan is now being seen by many as a significant economic driver for key crops such as blueberries, strawberries, apples, and peaches.

- Rising energy prices will enable local production for local consumption to become more economical. West Michigan parts suppliers for automobiles and furniture are regaining an economic foothold.

- Personalized services such as healthcare and banking are usually offered in the same metro area. "Medical Mile" in Grand Rapids now has a number of first rate well-recognized medical facilities, hospitals, research facilities, including health profession, nursing, and medical school programs.

- Location and size does not limit a community in the skills and knowledge it can retain and develop. Grand Rapids is now home to the Michigan State University (MSU) Medical School and the Van Andel Research Institute, thereby building upon medical research capabilities. Grand Valley State University keeps over 80 percent of its graduates in West Michigan and has close working relationships with nearly 100 key employers.
- The decline of the U.S. dollar has given rise to the cost of imported goods and services. This marketplace dynamic has enabled import substitution and local production of renewable energy technologies, alternative vehicles, bio-fuels, and bio-materials.
- Some global industrial firms have been known to show less loyalty to their workforce and more willingness to outsource and relocate manufacturing plants to less expensive wage scale areas. Hard and durable goods suppliers are examples.

The importance of the local economy as a driving force is key to the recovery of regions like West Michigan. A civic economies "local works" study was commissioned by Local First in 2008. It showed when you spend $100 at a non-locally owned business, $43 stays in the local economy and $57 leaves it. However, if you spend $100 at a local business for the same or similar product, $73 stays in the local economy and only $27 leaves it. The difference represents an improvement of 30 cents on the dollar remaining in the local economy. The study also indicated that if there was a 10 percent shift in Kent County in consumer spending to locally owned businesses, $140 million in new local economic activity would result. It would also create 1,600 new local jobs and provide $50 million in new local wages.[7]

One of the key market opportunities that were noted in *The Small-Mart Revolution* that helps build the local economy is localizing your household. Some of the most important areas include eating out locally, using local healthcare, buying fresh local food, and localizing household energy use and car services. The most significant area is overall home improvement by purchasing from local hardware and retail stores.

Results and Benefits

There are a number of important benefits to resupplying products and services for the New Economy and local customers. These benefits include:

1. A 30 percent improvement to the local economy when you purchase a product from a locally owned business versus purchasing the same product from a non-locally owned business.
2. LOHAS consumers now represent approximately 20 percent of all U.S. retail consumers and many of them are willing to purchase green and sustainable products at a higher price.
3. Naturalites who prefer green and sustainable products and Conventionalists that practice environmental stewardship, such as recycling and conservation, represent over40 percent of consumers that can be influenced to purchase LOHAS products.
4. Eight out of 10 consumers are interested in some type of green products offered in the LOHAS market.
5. A 10 percent shift in Kent County consumer spending to locally owned businesses would generate an estimated $140 million in new local economic activity, create 1,600 new local jobs, and provide $50 million in new local wages.
6. Some of the more important sustainable development trends and challenges of the New Economy include: access and availability of clean water; energy and fuel efficiency and optimization; nutrition; disease prevention; and waste minimization.

Companies that address these dynamic change forces today will have competitive advantage in the marketplace tomorrow.

Case Study

One of the fastest growing segments of the LOHAS market is natural and organic food. According to the Organic Trade Association's 2011 Organic Industry Survey, sales of organic food and beverages reached $26.7 billion with organic fruits and vegetables having the largest growth rate.[7]

Eden Foods located in Clinton, Michigan, is a family owned company that was started in 1968 and has pioneered the development of natural and organic food since that time. Today the company offers more than 250 natural and organic food products.[8]

Company goals include:

- Providing the highest quality food with accurate life supporting information
- Establishing a healthy, respectful, challenging, outstanding, and productive environment for employees
- Cultivating sound relationships and partnerships
- Developing an adaptive and flexible management style to social, environmental, and economic change forces
- Having strong positive impact on farming and food processing practices

It should be noted that organic food no longer has to be natural. Today many chemicals are still allowed by the USDA in their natural organic program. Eden Foods has pioneered their own organic authenticity.

All Eden Foods products meet or exceed United States Drug Administration (USDA) requirements for using the organic seal. Eden Foods does not use the organic seal because it does not represent

Eden standards. Their products avoid genetic modification, are irradiation free, exhibit superior food safety, and use organic pest control management practices.

Eden Foods also is concerned about the environment. Their practices include:

- Local First purchasing
- Custom can biphenyl free linings for organic beans
- 100 percent recycled paperboard for organic pasta boxes
- Recycled pallet wrap
- Post-consumer recycled materials and biodegradable packaging
- Reduce, reuse, recycle practices
- Ecologically designed truck fleet practices

Some of Eden Foods organic food products include: chili, tomatoes, grape juice, beans, pasta, and whole grains. Eden Foods is one of the few remaining independent organic companies of any size. Company emphasis is on organic sustainability, local sourcing, sustainable and organic farming, transparency, and social justice issues. Estimated annual sales are $50 million.

Some of the highlights of Eden Foods include:

- In 1972 Eden opened its first warehouse and began to build working relationships with artisan Japanese traditional food makers.
- Eden is the oldest natural and organic food company in North America and the largest independent manufacturer of dry grocery organic foods.
- Over 95 percent of Eden foods are sold in natural food stores, co-ops, and supermarkets versus traditional distribution channels.
- A 70,000 sq. ft. warehouse was built and certified to LEED gold standards in 2008

- In 2009 Eden Foods was recognized as the best food company in the world and the third best overall company as selected by the Better World Shopping Guide.

Call to Action

- How does the company define and view the current marketplace economy it competes in?
- Is the future marketplace economy considered new, green, and sustainable?
- Does the company offer consumer products for the LOHAS marketplace? If not, can the company learn anything about the LOHAS consumer marketplace trends and behaviors for its base of customers?
- How can the company capitalize on the new economy? What strategies should be undertaken and employed?

References

1. The LOHAS Market and Consumer Trends: The Rise of the Ethical Consumption Revolution, Natural Marketing Institution (NMI), May 15, 2007.
2. The Natural Edge Project International Keynote Speaker Tours, www.naturaledgeproject.net/keynote.aspx, accessed August 2011.
3. California Department of Toxic Substances Control, www.dtsc.ca.gov, accessed July 2011.
4. http://www.mediapost.com/publications/article/126836/report/-lohas-market-nears-300billion.html.
5. http://www.renewableenergymarkets.com/docs/presentations/2010/Thurs_Customer%20Trends%20and%20Profiles_Gwynne%20Rogers.pdf.
6. The Small-Mart Revolution, www.scribd.com/doc/14707250/The-SmallMart-Revolution-How-Local-Businesses-are-Beating-the-Global-Competition, accessed August 2011.
7. Why Local First, http://www.localfirst.com/why_local_first, accessed August 2011.
8. Eden Foods, www.edenfoods.com, accessed July 2012.

10. SUSTAINABILITY STANDARDS AND CERTIFICATIONS

Introduction

Over the last few years there have been great influxes in the number of new products that are trying to become mainstays in the emerging new, green and clean economy. Many of these products have pushed the envelope regarding their claims, attributes, and overall product labeling. Some of these products are reformulations of previous existing products, while others are brand new entries into the marketplace and trying to capture market presence and market share.

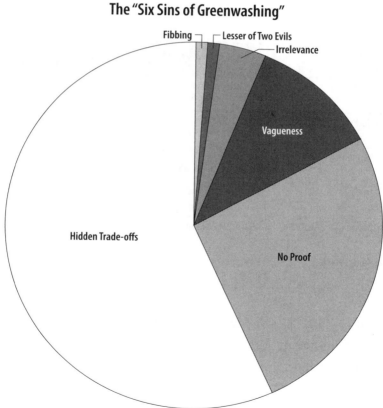

The "Six Sins of Greenwashing"

Source: The "Six Sins of Greenwashing," www.terrachoice.com/files/6_sins.pdf, August 2011.

In either case, some of these products may have falsified claims. For example what does a "green" product really designate and mean? Consumers are demanding to know. As a result today we are undergoing a major shakeout period of "green washing" which, over the longer-term, will help stabilize and grow the new economy and overall marketplace. Only those products that have been substantiated and certified to authentic sustainability and green standards and claims will gain market share, brand recognition, and overall product leadership.

What can be learned by looking at the "lens of green washing?"

In 2007 Terra Choice, the environmental marketing firm, conducted a study that showed 99 percent of 1,018 consumer products were guilty of green washing.[1]

Sin	Description/Example
Sin of Hidden Trade-Off (57%)	Narrow recycle content vs. broader energy, water use; energy efficiency products that contain hazardous materials
Sin of No-Proof (26%)	"Green" cleaning products, shampoos claiming to be organic
Sin of Vagueness (11%)	"Nontoxic" products; "eco" products, 100% natural products that contain formaldehyde
Sin of Irrelevance (4%)	"CFC – Free" products even though the CFCs were banned 20 years ago
Sin of Lesser Two Evils (1%)	Organic tobacco, environmentally friendly pesticides
Sin of Fibbing (1%)	Misrepresentation of certification; falsified claims

Three "sins" account for over 90 percent of false "green" and sustainability claims. The number one false claim is the sin of hidden trade-off which accounts for over 50 percent of false claims. These claims, such as acknowledging a very narrow or specific recycle content, may misrepresent that the product, on the other hand, may require a greater energy or water use to manufacture.

The case study in this chapter is Zeeland Farm Service.

Description

Today the customer is driving the marketplace and demanding products contain substantiated claims that can be easily differentiated versus the competition. Why? One very important reason is that customers now read labels very carefully. Consumers and customers will look at products from both a pre- and post-consumption perspective. Cost may not be the sole determining factor in terms of purchasing decisions. Health and nutrition concerns also have buyers and customers demanding more available product information than ever before.

From a pre-consumption standpoint, questions will be raised as to what sustainable raw materials were used to make the product. Were fewer raw materials used in the process? Were renewable energy sources used to manufacture the product? Does the product contain recycled raw material content?

Once consumed, customers also raise a number of questions regarding post-consumption. Can the product be recycled? Can it be disassembled with ease? Is there a location where the product can be dropped off for disposal after use, rather than being landfilled? Compact Fluorescent Light bulbs (CFLs) are a good example. In response to consumer complaints about disposal, Home Depot and other locations now accept CFLs after use since they do contain some hazardous material components. Other questions include: Can the product be remanufactured for additional use until final end of life? Are there parts that can be salvaged?

Remember, however, that all labels are not created equal.[3] Some labels contain a seal of approval, while others may have unreliable claims.

All Labels Are Not Created Equal
ISO Defines Different Types of Labels

Type I	Seal of approval	• For meeting a multi-attribute set of predetermined requirements • Based on life cycle date • Requires 3rd party validation • Used for comparison
Type II	Verifiable Single Attribute Claims (self-declared or 3rd party certified)	• Recycled content • Energy consumption
Type III	Display comprehensive and detailed product information	• Environmental declaration • Requires 3rd party validation

Source: Bob Willard slide, Sustainability Practice Group, adapted by Norman Christopher 2012.

Type I labels (such as certified cradle to cradle) represent a seal of approval for meeting multi-attribute requirements.

Type II labels (such as Energy Star) represent a verifiable single attribute claim.

Type III labels display comprehensive detailed product information and require third-party validation.

Green and Sustainability Standards and Certifications can contain a number of qualifications and prerequisites. Some can be voluntary in nature, such as the well-known International

Organization for Standards (ISO). Many companies are familiar with the globally recognized ISO 9001 standard that helps businesses document and improve upon waste reduction, operational efficiencies, and product quality. Many companies today are pursuing ISO 14000 standards. ISO 14000 represents a family of standards dealing primarily with environmental management systems. The most recognized standard is ISO 14001. (www.iso.org)

Other voluntary standards include those of the American National Standard Institute (ANSI) standards. These voluntary standards are also consensus based and have broad based public review and comment. An appeal process is also included. Some of the ANSI standards are specific to biofuels, healthcare, homeland security, chemicals, nanotechnology, and nuclear energy, etc. (www.ansi.org)

Standards and certifications can also be consensus based. Examples of consensus based standards and certifications include the Leadership in Environmental and Energy Design (LEED) green building rating system. As discussed, the LEED rating system and certification process is a points based third-party verification program that deals with design, construction, building, and operations of high performance green building structures. The greater Grand Rapids area has over 160 LEED certified building projects. Some of these buildings are also LEED "firsts" in the U.S. including the David Hunting YMCA, the Grand Rapids Art Museum (GRAM), and Keystone Community Church.

Other examples of consensus based sustainability standards and certifications include Forest Stewardship Certified (FSC) and Sustainable Forest Initiative (SFI) standards that pertain to the global sustainable responsible management of forest and wood based products. (www.fsc.org; www.sfiprogram.org)

Other standards are proprietary in nature such as the GREENGUARD standard. The GREENGUARD Environmental Institute was established in 2001 and today oversees the third-party certification of low emission product standards for healthy homes and schools. (www.greenguard.com) The Cradle to Cradle product design and certification program was established by Bill McDonough and Michael Braungart. This proprietary product design protocol measures the positive effect upon the environmental, health, and social impacts such as through the use of green chemistry. (www.mcdonough.com)

Other sustainability certifications and standards are single purpose in nature, such as Green Seal. Green Seal was formed in 1989 and provides transparent and credible science based environmental certification standards. An AGS C-1 Pilot Standard is also available. Technical assistance is also provided to the government sector in green purchasing and operations. (www.greenseal.org)

Based in West Michigan, The Business and Institutional Furniture Manufacturers Association (BIFMA) has recently established a breakthrough open and consensus based method to evaluate the sustainable characteristics, attributes, and benefits of furniture products. Sustainable "Triple Bottom Line" product attributes relating to energy; natural resource impact, human and ecosystem health, and corporate social responsibility are evaluated in an overall rating system. The BIFMA e-3 Furniture Sustainability Standard was jointly developed by BIFMA International, the National Science Foundation, NSF International, and ANSI. (www.bifma.org; www.nsf.org) The Furniture Sustainability Standard can be used by companies to evaluate and rate their products and then certify them to Level performance.

Application

Kiplinger's Personal Finance magazine in July 2010 published an article titled "How Green is Your Label?"[4] Quoted from the article: "Shopping for eco-friendly products has become confusing as green seals of approval proliferate. Now the Federal Trade Commission has weighed in and begun cracking down on "greenwashing"— advertising that may be deceptive or confusing to consumers. The guide below lists some of the common labels and will help in understanding what they mean. Some signify real achievement, while others merely indicate that a product has good intentions."[3] Their comments highlight the important differences that may exist in sustainable product standards and certifications themselves.

Energy Star

- **Certified By:** The Environmental Protection Agency and the Department of Energy
- **Products:** Appliances, building supplies, and consumer electronics
- **Comments:** An Energy Star product is certified to be energy-efficient without sacrificing performance, and savings can be significant. For example, replacing a clothes washer made before 2000 with a new Energy Star appliance can save $130 a year. You'll find the seal on products from companies such as GE, Panasonic, Philips, Samsung, and Whirlpool. The Energy Star label has become well recognized in the marketplace by consumers.

Green Seal

- **Certified By:** Green Seal is a nonprofit environmental certification organization
- **Products:** Paint, cleaning and paper products, for hotels and other services
- **Comments:** Products and services are evaluated for compliance with Green Seal's standards for safety, among others. You'll see the seal, for example, on Staples products and at Great Wolf Lodge water park resorts. The seals come in three levels:

bronze, silver, and gold. Bronze means progress toward meeting standards; silver shows that some standards have been met; and gold means all standards have been achieved.

UL Environment

- **Certified By:** UL Environment, a division of Underwriters Laboratories
- **Products:** Consumer electronics, lighting, appliances
- **Comments:** UL Environment tests products that tout eco-friendly features – ones that are compostable, say, or contain recycled materials. Those that pass, including some products from LG Electronics and Owens Corning, earn the label. Products are reevaluated twice a year, and UL posts its findings on its website, www.ulenvironment.com.

Design for the Environment

- **Certified By:** The Environmental Protection Agency
- **Products:** Detergent, window cleaners, degreasers, car washing products
- **Comments:** Products that win this seal are made with chemicals that are the safest for humans and the environment as determined by the EPA. Standards are strict; only 15 percent of those that apply receive the seal on their first try. Products with the seal include Bissell cleaning supplies, Palmolive dishwashing liquids, and Scrubbing Bubbles cleanser.

USDA Organic

- **Certified By:** U.S. Department of Agriculture's National Organic Program
- **Products:** Raw, fresh, and processed food
- **Comments:** Foods bearing this seal have been grown with no conventional pesticides and without many kinds of fertilizers.

In the case of livestock, animals may not be given antibiotics or growth hormones and must eat organically grown feed. The label can read either "100 percent organic" or "organic," which means it is 95 percent organic.

Cradle to Cradle

- **Certified By:** McDonough–Braungart Design Chemistry, consultants
- **Products:** Include cosmetics, personal-care products, diapers, and shipping supplies
- **Comments:** This certification measures products' all-around sustainability, from manufacturing to recycling and reuse. The four-tier program rates products from basic to platinum. Basic indicates a company's intent to abide by the standards; platinum signifies achievement of the standards. Look for the label on Aveda products, diapers, and Method cleaning products.

GREENGUARD Environmental Institute

- **Certified By:** The GREENGUARD Environmental Institute
- **Products:** Furniture, flooring, paint, doors, and windows
- **Comments:** Products with GREENGUARD seal have been evaluated for chemical emissions that affect indoor air quality and human health. Each product is tested for more than 10,000 possible chemicals and retested four times a year. You can find the seal on some 3M products, Benjamin Moore paint, Liquid Nails adhesives, and Rubbermaid Home products.

Other well-known green labels include:[5]

- The universal recycling symbol indicates that the product is recyclable.

- The Leaping Bunny label indicates that the product is manufactured by a company that follows the corporate standard of companies for animals.
- The certified biodegradable label indicates the product breaks down into carbon dioxide, nontoxic minerals, and water.
- The Smart Choice label is a Pepsi program. "Products must contain at least 10 percent of the daily value of a targeted nutrient such as a protein or vitamin and meet limits for fat, saturated fat, trans fat, cholesterol, sodium, and added sugar." Over 250 juice and snack products use this label.
- The Fair Trade certified label from Trans Fair USA ensures that the product has been manufactured sustainably to Fair Trade standards including price, labor conditions, trade, transparency, community development, and with environmental stewardship. This label is growing in importance as some companies and their products have been shown to be manufactured using substandard wage and living conditions. Today many consumers use Fair Trade as the basis to select their favorite coffees and teas.
- The label civility free is not substantiated by the government, but implies that no animal testing was performed on the product or its ingredients.
- The Rain Forest Certified label supports sustainable agriculture, social responsibility, and integrated pest management practices.

Today companies and businesses need to readdress their product standards and certifications in light of the opportunity to meet "green" and sustainability customer requirements. Consumers and customers today are driving the marketplace, manufacturers, and service providers toward authentic "green" certification standards.

The American Consumer Council, when discussing the Sins of Greenwashing, has identified key "green" product certification and standards questions to be addressed. These include:

- Is the green certification program sponsored by a credible nonprofit?
- Does it have written criteria and standards that govern the application and certification process?
- Does it have a verification and validation process?
- Once your company is certified, are there accountability steps and a process of continued improvement?
- Does the green product standard have credibility in the marketplace?

Results and Benefits

Companies that pursue eco-label product standards and certifications will be able to build upon a number of strategic advantages and opportunities. These benefits can come from a number of areas such as:

- Obtaining sales with LOHAS consumers and customers that are looking first to purchase eco-label certified products and are willing to pay more for these products. LOHAS customers represent approximately 20 percent of the overall consumer marketplace. Additionally other LOHAS classes of customers, such as the Conventionalists and Naturalites, should also be considered for targeting. LOHAS Conventionalists and Naturalites make up another 40 percent of consumers.
- Building upon the company's reputation
- Enhancing the brand image of the product
- Capturing eco-efficiencies within manufacturing and overall business operations

- Gaining market presence and market share in the green, clean, and new economy
- Increasing levels of productivity among employees because of the pride associated with the eco-label and what it stands for
- Helping to diffuse potential customer complaints because of higher product standards associated with the eco-label
- Having sustainability become an overall core business strategy and a driving force for the company's strategic plan

Case Study

Zeeland Farm Service (ZFS) is a 60-year-old family service business located in Zeeland, Michigan, consisting of four companies owned by a single family:[6]

- Zeeland Farm Services, Inc. comprised of grain, ingredients, and specialty seed divisions.
- Zeeland Freight Services, Inc.
- Zeeland Farm Soya, Inc. which contains a soybean processing plant and soy biodiesel production.
- Zeeland Food Services, Inc. which contains a soybean oil refinery and Zoye specialty soybean oils.

Zoye soybean oil is a unique specialty oil that has been created, developed, and grown via a disciplined process that involves:

- Planting low saturated and low lineolic seeds via the ZFSelect seed brand
- Growing the seed in contracted fields monitored via GPS process
- Harvesting the soybeans under identity preserved methods and controlled conditions ensuring Zoye oil is pure and always meets the highest quality standards all-natural 100 percent pure soybean oil

- Manufacturing with renewable energy, with the soybeans being processed into food grade oils via extraction processing

The resulting Zoye pure and natural soybean oil has many features and benefits including:
- Made from the highest quality, non-GMO, and identity preserved soybeans
- 100 percent pure soybean oil
- 0 grams of trans fat
- 0 grams of cholesterol
- No hydrogenation
- Only 1 gram of saturated fat per serving which is half the saturated fat per serving of regular soybean oil

It should be noted that food products that contain genetically modified organisms (GMOs) are coming under scrutiny in the marketplace. GMO containing products usually experience faster growth cycles as well as improved resistance to growing conditions. Most of the ZFS soy based products are non-GMO as well.

Zoye oils were created to capture the growing market for healthier options for eating and cooking with vegetable oils. Zoye oils come in a variety of product forms such as liquid fry shortening, frying and cooking oils, salad and cooking oils, and buttery flavor pan and grill oils.

Today, Michigan grown and processed Zoye oils are available at all Meijer store locations and participating Spartan stores. In addition, college and university food service locations, such as Grand Valley State University and their Campus Dining, now use Zoye oils in their food service preparation. Zeeland Farm Service has developed products and targeted applications for customers in the commercial, institutional, and retail markets.

Some of the sustainability highlights about ZFS include:

- Adhering to strong values including premium healthy products for customers and the community
- Operating on renewable energy capturing methane gas from a local landfill
- Supporting farmland preservation and conservation

Call to Action

- What are the primary product and/or business standards and certifications that the company pursues?
- Does the company emphasize or require that their business products or raw materials meet sustainability and/or green product standards and certifications? If not, which products might easily be adopted to meet sustainability product standards and certifications?
- What raw materials or products that are purchased meet sustainability and green standards and certifications?
- Is there any opportunity for the company and its supply chain partners, including customers and suppliers, to establish sustainability and/or green standards and certification for its overall products and services?

References

1. The "Six Sins of Greenwashing," www.terrachoice.com/files/6_sins.pdf, August 2011.
2. Greenwashing, www.squidoo.com/envirogreenwashing, accessed June 2011.
3. Bob Willard slide, Sustainability Practice Group, adapted by Norman Christopher 2012.
4. How Green is Your Label?, *Kiplinger's Personal Finance* magazine, www.kiplinger.com/magazine/archives/how-green-is-your-label.html?si=1, accessed July 2011.
5. Green Labels – Know What You Are Buying, www.greenecoservices.com/green-labels-know-what-you-are-buying/, accessed August 2011.
6. Zeeland Farm Services Inc., www.zfsinc.com, accessed August 2011.

PART FOUR

OPERATIONS AND MANUFACTURING

Production facilities are the heart and soul of any manufacturing business. Many times businesses and organizations have viewed plant manufacturing facilities as primarily cost centers. A great deal of effort was spent making sure there was a readily available supply of raw materials, that process and plant equipment was properly maintained, and that local and environmental regulations were met. The mentality centered on a "cradle to grave" approach to manufacturing. Capital budgets were targeted for new plants and equipment, but many times this equipment was designed and used for the steady state and linear manufacture of products. Production planning could usually be scheduled with minimal concerns through daily shifts, as well as specific manufacturing runs on certain product lines. However, there were many inefficiencies and waste created with these types of operations.

What's changed today for all companies and organizations is a "cradle to cradle" systems approach to operations and manufacturing. The fundamental shift is based on a life cycle approach to manufacturing and production. Facilities and operations that were once viewed as cost centers are now being managed through new processes and manufacturing systems and strategies. Many new approaches are being pursued including where raw materials come from. Do they contain ingredients of concern? What type of labor was used to produce them? Waste generation has also become an important area to address and in many instances can create a new business opportunity. Can we produce products that use fewer raw materials and also generate less waste? Another important issue deals with the concern for the health and safety of plant workers as well as overall environmental regulations. How can companies and businesses ensure the optimum safety of plant operations for their workers as well as the community in which they are manufactured? Because of the extremely competitive marketplace for most companies and organizations, many enterprises are embedding continuous improvement processes for their operations to create additional cost savings. Also new clean technologies, such as the use of green chemistry, now drive many facilities and plant operations.

There are a number of applied sustainable development best practices described in this section. First, there is a discussion of environmental impact as companies seek to become better environmental stewards in the operations including how to reduce their overall environmental footprint. Another important practice is waste generation as companies have moved from recycling strategies to overall reduction and minimization of waste. Some companies in the office furniture industry have also now set new goals and targets around "zero waste" for their plant operations. Operations and manufacturing are now pursuing environmental management systems including ISO 14000 certification as both suppliers and customers now demand specific sustainability purchasing certifications and standards for their products and services. Additionally, companies through the pursuit of eco-efficiencies including the use of less energy, electricity, and water are also now able to demonstrate reduced climate impact as well for their manufacturing operations. Sustainable manufacturing approaches are encouraged since many times they represent a "win-win" situation for both business and customer. They are a "win" for business in that they can create eco-efficiencies and cost savings. They are also a "win" for customers as they demand and desire to purchase environmentally friendly products at competitive prices.

11. ENVIRONMENTAL IMPACT

Introduction

Environmental impact has now become an area of significant attention and concern to consumers and customers and is on the radar screen of all companies and businesses. However environmental impact cannot be viewed as an important issue for only internal company and business operations. It has now become an integral part and focus of the entire supply chain from incoming raw materials to finished products and services. Environmental impact can be defined as the impact or effect of any activity or substance on the environment such as land, water, and other components.[1]

Case studies in this chapter come from the furniture industry such as Herman Miller, Steelcase, and Haworth. These companies and others seek continuous improvement in environmental sustainability in their overall business operations and supply chain management.

Description

All business activities contribute to environmental impact and must be viewed from a holistic system perspective and "cradle to cradle" approach. An essence of this approach requires a life cycle process. Forbo Flooring Systems, a division of Swiss based Forbo Group, offers a guide on how to look at the process elements of a product's life cycle along with the overall environmental impact of each element.[2]

Process Life Cycle Analysis

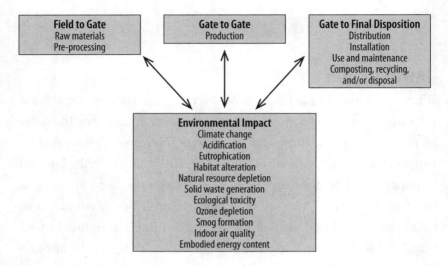

Source: Looking at Product Life-Cycle Assessments, Building Magazine, August 2008, accessed June 2011, adapted by Norman Christopher, 2012.

A process life cycle analysis and approach will enable the company to breakdown the environmental impact into three major component areas. These areas include:

- Field to gate area (includes raw materials and pre-processing input)
- Gate to gate area (includes production, manufacturing, processing, and packaging)
- Gate to final destination (involves distribution of the product, installation, warranty and use, maintenance and service, remanufacturing and reassembly, and final disposal)

All three areas can contribute to and adversely affect environmental impact. Each area raises important questions that need to be addressed by the business in order to minimize the overall environmental impact from company operations.

Do the raw materials, manufacture, and distribution of products:

- Improve or reduce indoor air quality?
- Contribute to or reduce smog formation?
- Contribute to reduced ozone depletion?
- Contribute to or reduce human toxicity concerned issues?
- Contribute to or adversely affect ecological toxicity to land, water, and air quality?
- Increase or help reduce the amount of solid waste generation?
- Contribute to natural resource depletion or help minimize the amount of natural resources used as raw materials?
- Increase eutrophication or the amount of algae blooms?
- Increase acidification such as through atmospheric, soil, and water pollution thereby increasing human exposure to toxic substances?
- Increase the amount of green house gas emissions potentially contributing to global climate change?

Once the company understands the life cycle process for evaluating environmental impact, a business environmental footprint or environmental impact assessment and analysis can be undertaken.[3]

Business Environmental Footprint

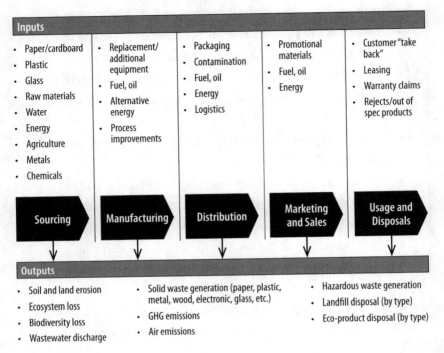

Source: Deloitte Development LLC, adapted by Norman Christopher, 2012.

As the flowchart shows, the best way to implement this analysis is through a value chain or supply chain approach by carefully determining inputs and outputs along each step in the supply chain including:

- Sourcing
- Manufacturing
- Distribution
- Marketing and sales
- Usage and disposal

A critical path analysis for each stage needs to be undertaken including both inputs and outputs in each of the above steps.

First, it is important to determine the expectations and objectives from the environmental risk assessment as well as what information will be collected to:[4]

- Identify hazards and environmental concerns by type as well as potential areas of concern and harm
- Understand the effects that these risks might cause and what the potential areas of harm might cause
- Evaluate the risks of these potential hazards and harms and the likelihood that they will actually occur
- Use key performance indicators to track and monitor environmental impact data and overall environmental stewardship measurements
- Record the results of the assessment, implement precautions, and develop contingency plans
- Monitor, review, and report progress regarding the assessment at regular intervals with departments and management

Information. Support. Compliance. (http://www.businesslink.gov.uk/bdotg/action/home), accessed August 2011.

Let us take a look at one of these supply chain stages, manufacturing, in more depth.

Primary input areas to address include:

- Amount and quality of water consumption
- Amount and type of chemicals used, such as hazardous, or toxic materials
- Amount and type of cardboard, plastic, glass, and metals used as raw materials for processing as well as packaging, including their recycle content
- Amount and type of energy consumption such as petroleum based or from alternative sources

- Amount of electrical consumption
- Amount of steam consumption
- Amount of fuel oil used for machinery and equipment

Primary output areas to address during processing and manufacturing include:

- The amount and quality of water and wastewater being stored and generated
- Type and integrity of storage and disposal containers including toxic and spent materials containers being safely separated
- Air emissions such as through the required EPA Toxic Release Inventory (TRI) as well as smoke, dust, particulate, and GHG emissions
- Drainage, storage, and disposal of liquid wastes, such as into the sewer
- Solid waste generated by type and amount as well as overall disposal techniques

Application

By applying a life cycle and critical path analysis to a company's value and supply chain, it allows the development of an overall environmental impact analysis and assessment for the business.

A more in-depth look at the product life cycle assessment can help determine the overall environmental impact and footprint of a product.

Kraft Foods provides an interesting example as they grow many of their raw materials. Cocoa is fertilized, grown, and harvested from seed. Many operations are used during processing including fermentation, drying, roasting, and grinding. The final product developed is chocolate.

Product Life Cycle Assessment and Environmental Impact

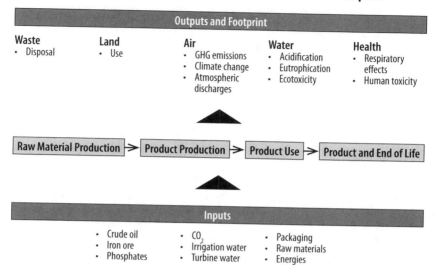

Source: Jon Dettling, Quantis International: Example of a Corporate Environmental Footprint for a Leading Food Products Company, LCA XI Conference 9/11/11, adapted by Norman Christopher, 2012.

Kraft Foods has hundreds of inputs and raw materials including; energy, crops, water, packaging, and minerals, that become part of their product life cycle assessment and overall environmental impact. Many processing steps are also undertaken in the development of their final products. Using a product life cycle assessment, Kraft Foods determines their outputs which they have broken down into major areas including: waste, land, air, water, and health. From the data generated, the overall environmental footprint and environmental impact can be determined.[5]

The data revealed that:

- 90 percent of the carbon footprint is generated outside of its locations, with nearly 60 percent coming from farm commodities
- 12 percent of the carbon footprint is from transportation and distribution

- 80 percent of the land impact is from agriculture
- 70 percent of the water footprint is from growing raw materials

Using this information and the better understanding of its overall environmental footprint and impact, Kraft Foods, the world's second largest food producer, has established specific goals to be accomplished between 2010 and 2015 including:[6]

- Increase sustainable sourcing of agricultural commodities by 25 percent
- Reduce energy use by 15 percent in manufacturing plants
- Reduce energy-related CO_2 emissions in manufacturing plants by 15 percent
- Reduce water consumption in manufacturing plants by 15 percent
- Minimize waste generated in manufacturing plants by 15 percent
- Eliminate 50,000 tons of packaging materials
- Reduce 50 million miles from its transportation network

Source: www.2sustain.com/2012/01/kraft-foods-environmental-survey-reveals-impact-of-supply-chains.

Results and Benefits

For those companies that complete an in-depth environmental assessment in conjunction with environmental impact analysis, there are many potential benefits that can be captured and realized. These benefits can be qualified, quantified, measured, and reported, such as:

- Decrease in energy and water consumption
- Reduction in solid and liquid waste generation and overall discharges
- Minimization in the generation of GHG emissions

- Reduction in overall air pollution including toxic air and particulate emissions
- Reduction in the exposure of toxic and hazardous materials to humans
- Improvement in the recycling of electronic, metal, plastic, paper, cardboard, and other materials
- Reduction in the amount of fuels consumed
- A shift to green procurement and local raw material purchases
- A reduction in overall environmental risk thereby preventing the occurrence of an environmental incident or potential disaster with subsequent legal fees and potential fines
- Creation of recyclable products
- Minimization in the use of packaging materials
- Improvement in the management of supply chain partners and working relationships
- Education and training of supply chain partners and employees to help reduce their overall environmental impact by department area
- Creation of an efficient local distribution and logistics network

These benefits can be easily quantified by selecting the right performance measurements and metrics thereby creating both eco-efficiencies and savings as well as minimizing overall environmental risk to the company.

Case Study

The furniture industry in West Michigan is leading the way in reducing their environmental footprint and driving sustainable development best practices.[7] There are many best practices that have been embraced and adopted by leading furniture companies.

Steelcase has issued their 2010 Corporate Sustainability Report. In 2006, as the world's largest office furniture manufacturer, they set the goal to reduce their environmental footprint by 25 percent by 2010. They reported the following results since 2001:

- Decreased GHG emissions by 59 percent
- Reduced volatile organic compounds (VOCs) by 94 percent
- Decreased water usage by 71 percent
- Reduced waste material that otherwise would have gone to the landfill by 63 percent
- Additionally, Steelcase has replaced the bond edging on 12 product lines with a PVC free polyolefin material and trained greater than 400 employees in LEED version 3 in the last year

Haworth recently acknowledged they have achieved zero landfill waste from their U.S. manufacturing operations in 2009, compared to the 4.6 million pounds in 2008. Haworth has stated the goal of reaching zero landfill waste globally by 2011.

Herman Miller has also reached a goal of obtaining all of its electricity globally which amounts to 8 million kilowatt hours (kWh) annually from renewable energy sources.

Additionally, Herman Miller has also established a futuristic 2020 vision for their company that requires "Perfect Vision." Herman Miller has set major goals in reducing their environmental footprint and impact including targets of zero landfill, zero hazardous waste generation, zero VOC air emissions, zero process water use, 100 percent green electrical energy use, all company buildings constructed to a minimum LEED Silver certification, and 100 percent sales from DfE approved products. As of May 2011 they also reported their progress in these areas since introducing the initiative in 1994:[8]

Herman Miller 2020 Perfect Vision

During the 1994-2011 timeframe, Herman Miller also grew their total business approximately 60 percent.

As can be seen below there are many applied sustainable development best practices that have been implemented with great success.

Herman Miller has laid out a set of very aggressive sustainability Goals and targets to be achieved by the 2020. These goals include:

- Zero landfill disposal
- Zero hazardous waste generation
- Zero VOC air emissions
- Zero process water use
- 100 percent green electirical energy use
- All building construction meeting a LEED silver certification rating
- 100 percent of sales coming from DfE approved products

Source: www.hermanmiller.com/about-us/our-values-in-action/environmental-advocacy/our-vison-in-action-and-policy.html.

Herman Miller used 1993 as a baseline year for these aggressive sustainability goals and targets. How successful have they been and what has been their overall progress to date using the 1993 baseline year information? The company recently issued A Better World Report for 2011 that highlighted their overall progress and improvements.

- 90 percent progress against their landfill disposal goal
- 95 percent progress against their hazardous waste goal
- 81 percent progress against their VOC air emission goal
- 75 percent progress against their process water use goal
- 100 percent progress against their green electrical energy use goal
- 88 percent overall reduction in their operational footprint

- 14 LEED rated building projects have been constructed in the U.S. and U.K.
- 54 percent of sales now come from DfE approved products

Source: www.hermanmiller.com/about-us/our-values-in-action/a-better-world-report.html.

Call To Action

- What are the major issues of concern to the company in the areas of environmental impact?
- Does the company have good baseline data in the areas of environmental impact such as air emissions, greenhouse gas emissions, landfill waste, wastewater runoff, process water returns, hazardous waste disposal, etc?
- Has the company set target goals in the overall areas of environmental impact?
- Does the company monitor environmental impact areas for its manufacturing operations and facilities on a regular basis?
- Have aggressive measures been established to ensure improvement in the key areas of environmental impact?

References

1. Wastes – Education Material, www.epa.gov/waste/education, accessed August 2011.
2. Looking at Product Life-Cycle Assessments, *Building* magazine, August 2008, www.buildings.com/tabid/3334/ArticleID/6355/Default.aspx, accessed June 2011.
3. Deloitte Development LLC, www.deloitte.com, accessed August 2011.
4. Information. Support. Compliance., http://www.businesslink.gov.uk/bdotg/action/detail?itemId=1097094950&type=RESOURCES, accessed August 2011.
5. Kraft Foods, http://2sustain.com/2012/01/kraft-foods-environmental-survey-reveals-impact-of-supply-chains.html, accessed August 2011.

6. Kraft Foods, http://2sustain.com/2012/01/kraft-foods-environmental-survey-reveals-impact-of-supply-chains.html, accessed August 2011.
7. Mark Sanchez, www.mlive.com/business/west-michigan/index.ssf/2010/05/steelcase_herman_miller_reach.html, accessed July 2011.
8. Environmental Advocacy – Our Vision and Policy, www.hermanmiller.com/about-us/our-values-in-action/environmental-advocacy/our-vision-and-policy.html, accessed August 2011.

12. WASTE MINIMIZATION

Introduction

For many years companies and businesses followed the Three Rs associated with waste—reduce, reuse, and recycle—when applying process life cycle analysis and techniques to the inputs and outputs of waste. Many businesses now ask themselves: Why do we generate so much waste in the first place and how can we minimize it?

Waste minimization, as defined by the EPA, refers to "the use of source reduction and/or environmentally sound recycling methods prior to energy recovery, treatment of, or disposal of wastes."[1] This includes source reduction and environmentally sound recycling of wastes regulated under the Resource Conservation and Recovery Act (RCRA), particularly hazardous waste materials. In the past, waste minimization focused primarily on reducing the generation and subsequent release into the environment of the most persistent, bioaccumulative, and toxic chemicals in hazardous waste.

Today the concepts of waste minimization have grown to include many other materials beside toxic waste such as metals, plastics, paper, cardboard, and other industrial wastes. Also, today many companies and businesses are trying to reduce and minimize their electronic waste, construction demolition debris waste, and packaging waste, etc.

The case studies in this chapter include Cascade Engineering, Nichols Paper, and Spectrum Health.

Description

The concept of waste reduction or waste minimization has also been embedded into the overall best practice of waste management which is described as "the collection, transport, processing, recycling, or disposal, managing, and monitoring of waste materials.[2] Most businesses and organizations are familiar with the "Three Rs" of recycling our waste, reducing our trash, and reusing whatever waste materials we can.[3] The Three Rs have been the primary process and methodology used to minimize waste. In the past it was almost second nature to send waste to the landfill and not even think twice about it. Landfill costs in West Michigan have always been less expensive than other areas. The Kent County Michigan landfill charges $34.50 per ton for general refuse or the tipping fee that a landfill charges to dump waste or refuse. However, in Michigan the cost to landfill waste is quite inexpensive compared to other states. A current bill in the Michigan legislature to raise the "tipping fee" from 7¢ to 12¢ per cubic yard was passed in September 2011.

Due to the importance of environmental stewardship and the importance of resource recovery, the cost of raw material and waste minimization has become a key business strategy and focus.

- First of all, companies should try and reduce their consumption of raw materials including conservation of energy and water for processing, heating, and cooling. One way to accomplish this would be to measure material intensity for their products on a per unit basis.
- Secondly, companies should try and reuse as many products, materials, and components as possible. This can be accomplished by using durable goods, reusable products, and refillable products. These types of goods, products, and containers will help cut down on the "throw away" and "pitch it" mentality of the past.
- Thirdly, companies can recycle materials for their own use, for use by others as raw materials, or for salvage value. Local companies such as Louis Padnos Iron and Steel offer extensive recycling services of industrial waste materials and components, as well as resource recovery best practices.

- Using efficient equipment such as Energy Star products is also a good way to conserve energy.

Daniel Esty and Andrew Winston, in their book *Green to Gold*, explored the opportunity of how smart companies use environmental strategies to innovate, create value, and build competitive advantage.[4]

Expanding our Rs

Traditional Practices			New Priorities	
Reduce	**Reuse**	**Recycle**	**Redesign**	**Reimagine**
• Conservation • Energy Star products	• Durable goods • Reusable products • Refillable products	• Plastics • Paper • Metals • Food • E-waste	• DfE and LCA processes • Recycled raw materials	• Industrial symbiosis; e.g., waste as a raw material

Source: *Green to Gold Business Playbook*, Daniel C. Esty and P.J. Simmons (Wiley, 2011) adapted by Norman Christopher, 2012.

Many companies today are going well beyond the "Three Rs" with additional creativity and innovation by redesigning their products and processes such as with DfE and LCA and using recycled raw materials obtained either from in-house or purchased sources. Using products and components that have high recycled content as raw materials is also becoming more and more of a strategic business strategy that promotes environmental stewardship and generates eco-efficiencies. Many companies today are sharing or selling their by-products and waste streams, a process known as "industrial symbiosis."

An example of this strategy is Cascade Engineering and their use of recycled plastic in the manufacture of injected molded waste containers for industrial and commercial use. Cascade Engineering has established a very effective supply chain for recycled plastic materials in the local community including customer pick up of the recycled plastic products and materials that can be accepted in various shapes and forms. In many instances recycled raw materials can be reprocessed and can work just as effectively as virgin source raw materials and provide cost savings and other efficiencies. Additionally, if virgin raw materials are sourced from distant locations, availability may also become an issue including total cost of delivery and freight.

Application

As discussed, the development of waste minimization and waste management business strategies has extended the Three Rs process beyond the minimization of waste to "zero waste," something that a number of local companies such as Cascade Engineering, Herman Miller, and others are pursuing.

"Waste" isn't thought of as waste anymore. Using recycled waste materials can lead to a number of eco-efficiencies including cost savings, reduced environmental impact, and overall improved environmental stewardship. To support this effort, the University of South Florida, Division of Environmental Health and Safety, developed a practical Waste Minimization Guide.[5]

Solid waste minimization techniques and processes can be applied to a wide variety of products, materials, and components such as:

- Metals including aluminum, steel, and copper
- Glass
- Plastics such as low density and high density polyethylene (LDPE, HDPE)
- Paper
- Cardboard
- Electronics
- Biomass including woody, agricultural, and food sources, etc.
- Construction and demolition debris, etc.

Additionally, liquid waste minimization techniques can also be applied in a number of areas such as:

- Industrial waste
- Wastewater
- Process water
- Acids
- Alkalies
- Solvents
- Other chemicals

Valley City Environmental Services in Grand Rapids offers a broad range of hazardous and industrial waste transport services.

Listed below are some of the waste minimization process techniques companies can use in their business operations.

- First of all, determine quantities of waste output that are generated by type or waste class that is currently being landfilled and at what total cost.
- What are the key higher volume waste streams that can be targeted for reduction?
- Is the staff, department and management team of your business trained and educated on the importance and principles of recycling, waste minimization, and "zero waste" techniques and processes?
- Establish a cross-functional waste minimization team composed of employees, department heads, management, and support staff to establish guidelines, generate new minimization strategies, and conduct walk-throughs of company operations, and identify business and project opportunities.
- Determine and define inventory control procedures of incoming raw materials, work in progress, and finished goods to reduce overall waste.

- Use, reuse, recycle, and reduce material components and packaging to optimize business operations and reduce waste.
- Shift to green and local purchasing of products, equipment, materials, components, and services that are less harmful or nontoxic as well as those that reduce overall waste outputs.
- Change over to green cleaning chemicals for maintenance and away from harsher acids and alkalies that are more toxic and can effect wastewater discharges.
- Establish the right performance metrics to be used to track and monitor data, as well as to report progress on an ongoing basis.

Results and Benefits

There are enumerable benefits to waste minimization techniques that can generate substantial eco-efficiencies and cost savings in business operations. These benefits include:

- Avoided landfill and disposal costs
- Lower processing, manufacturing, and operational costs
- Reduction in overall environmental impact of business operations
- Use of less expensive recycled and reused raw materials
- Increased health and safety of employees due to less exposure to toxic and hazardous materials
- Reduced potential environmental liabilities and overall environmental risk and exposure
- Improved brand and public image
- Lower energy and water consumption due to installation and use of more efficient equipment such as for energy, water, and air use

Case Studies

Cascade Engineering has an established process for implementing their waste reduction program.[6] Their process includes:

- Analyzing landfill waste materials
- Targeting high volume high impact waste streams
- Educating their staff on waste reduction guiding principles and strategies
- Establishing performance metrics to track progress and improvement

In 2002 Cascade Engineering began to address their landfill cost which had grown to $268,000.

To accomplish this task, Cascade Engineering formed Waste Reduction and Zero Waste Teams. The teams worked to proactively address how the company was impacting the environment and to put in place a systemic process to reduce its negative impact on the environment. Cascade's environmental management system evolved from the understanding of the importance of reducing waste to landfill as well as turning waste into a profitable commodity.

Cascade Engineering's Waste Reduction Team is a cross-functional team that includes members from relevant disciplines and departments. The process begins with a thorough analysis of the waste being generated and leads to an understanding of how reducing, reusing, and recycling impacts the company's environmental footprint, provides cost savings, and generates revenue. Employee feedback, visual methods, and vendor partnering allow the Zero Waste Team to implement a sustainable system that provides continuous feedback and improvements to the organizations's recycling programs and overall environmental management system.

In 2009 landfill costs had been reduced to $8,000 and Cascade Engineering had realized a number of significant benefits including:

- A reduction in their overall environmental footprint and environmental impact
- Reduced landfill costs
- Employee pride through the company-wide effort
- Positive recognition by the community
- Increased earnings as waste became a commodity and raw material

As a result of the success of this project team, waste to landfill reduction has become a foundational platform of their environmental management system.

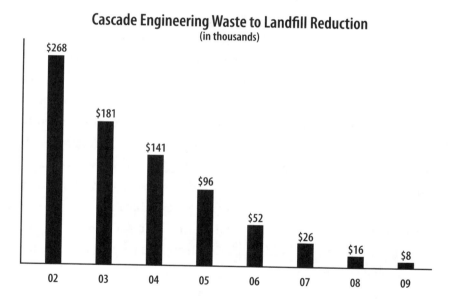

Cascade Engineering Waste to Landfill Reduction
(in thousands)

Source: Cascade Engineering, Corporate Newsletter 2010, adapted by Norman Christopher, 2012.

Nichols Paper in Muskegon has also had a successful recycling program.[7] In July 2009 Nichols reported that since 2007 their recycling program had:

- Recycled over 100,000 pounds of material

- Reduced waste pick-ups from 5 days per week to one pick-up every 2-3 weeks on a will-call basis
- Reduced tipping fees to 10 percent of what they were in 2006, a 90 percent savings

The Nichols' recycling program was undertaken with Louis Padnos Iron Metal Company of Holland, Michigan. It has been such a success that Nichols is currently working toward attaining the highest rating certification from the Michigan Recycling Coalition. In addition, Nichols has implemented recycling programs at its branch locations to maximize its overall recycling efforts. As part of the program, Nichols associates are being educated about what kind of materials can be recycled and closing the loop on the importance of purchasing products made from recycled and reused materials.

Labeled containers are placed in convenient locations throughout its facilities. The containers clearly communicate which bins contain metals, plastics, and paper. In addition, each associate is encouraged to bring in items that can be recycled if they are not currently recycling at home (items such as batteries and grocery T-sacks). Each associate's desk is equipped with a recycling bin for white and mixed paper as well. The company also conducts a quarterly "dumpster dive" to identify opportunities for more recycling and reminders of what items can be recycled rather than thrown away.

The company also holds periodic electronic recycling events for its associates, customers, and neighbors. A February 2009 week-long E-Recycling event collected 4,500 pounds of e-waste. Other events have included Recycling Stretch Film programs that helped customers in the recycling of plastic films which are difficult for organizations to dispose of in low quantities.

Nichols Commitment to Sustainability

"Nichols is committed to sustainability. As a leader in our industry, our goal is to engage our associates, suppliers, and customers to develop sustainable business practices that meet the needs of today without compromising future generations and their ability to meet their own needs.

We believe this is our corporate responsibility and we commit to the following:

- Promote environmental stewardship
- We will continue to assist our customers in maintaining clean and healthy facilities while meeting sustainability standards
- Provide support to our community through donated time and funding where we can make a difference"

Source: Nichols Paper Recycling Program, newsletter.

Today many West Michigan companies engaged in sustainable development best practices are continuing to improve their recycling, reduce and minimize their waste streams, and set a goal of zero waste impact for their business operations.

Spectrum Health has also been a leader in waste minimization efforts and overall waste management best practices. In 2009 Spectrum Health implemented a single stream recycling program at Butterworth Hospital, Blodgett Hospital, and United Hospital. This initiative allowed non-confidential, non-contaminated, and recyclable materials to all be placed in the same container. Recyclables include: plastics, metals, glass, newspaper, magazines, cardboard, paper, shrink wrap, styrofoam packaging, blue sterile wrap, etc. All sorting is done off-site by a vendor. In addition, Spectrum Health has also established best practices in regulated medical waste reduction, food waste composting, and pharmaceutical waste management. As one can see, waste minimization efforts encompass broad categories covering industrial, food, medical, and pharmaceutical waste categories. To date, Spectrum Health has achieved impressive results:[8]

- Achieved a recycling rate of 20 percent with 560,000 pounds per year being diverted from the landfills
- Experienced $13,000 in savings per year at Blodgett and Butterworth Hospitals
- 25,000 pounds of batteries in 2009 were recycled
- Implemented a reusable sharps program and in 2009 diverted 55 tons of sharps containers from landfills, saving $22,000 in waste disposal fees
- Established reprocessing and remanufacturing procedures for single use devices (SUDS) and in 2009 reduced medical waste by 5,951 pounds, saving $394,350 in SUS inventory and supply costs
- Implemented food waste composting at Blodgett Hospital with projected savings of $9,000 annually by reducing their waste stream by 8 percent and diverting 65 tons of food waste from the landfill
- Instituted pharmaceutical waste management best practices to ensure that pharmaceuticals are properly disposed of and do not adversely impact the environment by entering surface, ground, and drinking waters

Other sustainable development best practices embraced by Spectrum Health include: green cleaning, alternative transportation, LEED building and construction, energy efficiency, and water conservation. They have made a management commitment to improve the health of the communities they serve, to make a connection between the environment and human health, and to overall sustainability.

Call To Action

- Does the company track its waste to landfill costs?
- Does the company track its waste stream categories (e.g., paper, plastic, metal, glass, cardboard, e-waste, etc.) by amount generated?
- Does the company track the amount of materials it recycles by-product type or waste stream category?
- Has company set specific goals to divert waste from the landfills, reduce the amount of overall landfill waste, and/or set specific goals to increase the amount of recycled products used as raw materials?

References

1. Wastes – Hazardous Waste Minimization, www.epa.gov/waste/hazard/wastemin/tools.htm, accessed August 2011.
2. Waste Management, http://en.wikipedia.org/wiki/Waste_management, accessed July 2011.
3. eHow Essentials, http://www.ehow.com/topic_166_green-recycling.html, accessed July 2011.
4. Daniel C. Esty and Andrew S. Winston, *Green to Gold* (Yale University Press, 2006), page 197.
5. Waste Minimization Guide, http://usfweb2.usf.edu/eh&s/hazwaste/wminimizationguide.pdf, August 2011.
6. Waste Reduction Team, www.cascadeng.com/pdf/quest/Quest_WasteReduction.pdf, accessed August 2011.
7. Nichols Recycling Program, www.enichols.com/downloads/nichols_truestory_0609.pdf, accessed August 2011.
8. Spectrum Health, www.spectrumhealth.org/body_tabs.cfm?id=1897, accessed April 2012.

13. ENVIRONMENTAL MANAGEMENT SYSTEMS

Introduction

Virtually all businesses and organizations are in a cause and effect relationship with the environment. Sometimes environmental causes are known as environmental aspects, which can be both direct and indirect.[1] Environmental aspects are the components and activities of an organization, along with its products and services that interact with the environment, such as the use of raw materials, energy consumption, consumption of natural resources, air emissions from buildings and operations, motor vehicle operations, cleaning and custodial maintenance, ground maintenance, use of hazardous materials, and office products, etc. These examples represent environmental aspects that a company can influence and have direct control over.

However, all of these business activities also have a resulting environmental effect or impact. These impacts can be described as any positive or negative change to the environment which is either partially or wholly the result of the company's activities, processes, manufacturing, operations, products, and services. Examples of environmental impacts include air pollution, green house gas emissions, waste generation, soil and water contamination, and reduction in natural resources, etc.

To address these concerns, many businesses and companies have developed and implemented an Environmental Management System (EMS) to improve upon or reduce their overall environmental impact. An EMS can help consolidate the work force, plans, policies, and procedures of an organization that are used to manage environmental issues. Many businesses also develop and establish environmental policies for their organization that focus on environmental compliance, pollution prevention, environmental training and education, and overall improvement for reducing environmental impact issues. The U.S. EPA has developed Environmental Management Systems procedures including an Implementation Guide for Small and Medium-Sized operations.[2]

The case studies in this chapter are Cascade Engineering and Herman Miller.

Description

Most companies that have developed Total Quality Improvement (TQI) protocols for their business operations are also ISO certified. The level of ISO certification that many companies are pursuing today is the ISO 14001 certification level. An ISO 14001 checklist has been developed to help companies and organizations pursue this certification level that is built upon a thorough and complete Environmental Management System.[3]

What must an ISO-Registered Environmental Management System (EMS) contain?

All ISO-registered EMS has the following 17 procedural and provisional areas:

- A statement of environmental policy
- Procedures to identify and consider environmental aspects
- Procedures to identify and gain access to legal and other requirements
- Environmental objectives and targets
- Environmental management programs for achieving the objectives and targets
- Defined structure and responsibility
- Procedures for internal (and possibly external) communication
- Description of and directions to all EMS documentation

- Procedures for document control
- Procedures of criteria for operational control
- Procedures for emergency preparedness and response
- Documented procedures for monitoring and measuring
- Procedures for corrective and preventative actions
- Procedures for identifying, maintaining, and disposing of environmental records
- Programs and procedures for periodic EMS audits
- Provision for regular management reviews of the EMS
- Provision for ensuring employee training awareness and competence

An ISO-registered Environmental Management System must meet these 17 different requirements. The EMS is put in place with preventive proactive strategies to ensure overall environmental compliance, stewardship, and responsibility.

The EMS should also contain environmental objectives and goals with corresponding targets and measurable performance outcomes. Some of the more important environmental objectives include: regulation, compliance, waste stream reduction, reduction in energy consumption, recycling, green purchasing, and pollution prevention.

An example of an environmental objective might be to improve overall environmental performance. A corresponding target could be to reduce the number of compliance audit noncompliance violations by 50 percent or more on an annual audit to audit basis.

Application

Environmental Management Systems follow a plan-do-check-act process that many companies are familiar with.[4] The primary outcome for this EMS process is one of continuous improvement.

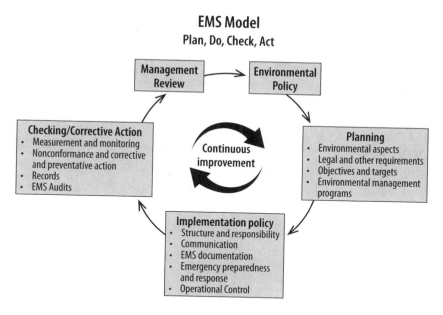

EMS Model
Plan, Do, Check, Act

Source: The Environmental Protection Agency (EPA) 2010, adapted by Norman Christopher, 2012.

For an EMS that is based on ISO 14001, the primary major requirement is the development of an environmental policy and statement. Once that is in place, the first phase of "planning" can begin. Key activities include identifying the company or business environmental causes or aspects. The company then reviews its regulatory compliance in all areas of its operations. At this time it is important to set preliminary environmental goals and objectives, as well as specific targets and metrics. Environmental management programs including training should be established as well.

In the second phase of "do" or implementation, clear roles and responsibilities should be defined for department heads and employees. Training programs and communications should be developed for departments and employees as well. EMS document control and operation control systems should be set in place. An emergency preparedness and response system will be needed in case of catastrophes or disasters. Environmental accounting and green procurement best practices can also be implemented and demonstrated in this phase.

In the "checking" and corrective action phase, there are a number of specific action steps that need to be undertaken. One key item is the need for periodic auditing and monitoring of environmental performance. Identifying root causes of environmental issues is critical as well as conducting EMS audits. Each EMS nonperformance area should have corresponding corrective action steps. Appropriate records should be maintained for review and compliance.

All of the auditing, monitoring, and reporting of EMS for the company should be forwarded to and reviewed by the management team. For the company or organization to have an effective EMS in place, there first must be commitment from top management. Secondly, the EMS must be owned by everyone including management, departments, and employees. And thirdly, the EMS must be consistent with other management systems or processes that are in place. Since the EMS is a continuous improvement process, management can continually "Act" upon the EMS plan through performance targets, milestones, and measurements to ensure that progress and corrective action steps have been undertaken in noncompliance areas.

Results and Benefits

There are many benefits to the "Triple Bottom Line" when an effective EMS has been developed and embraced by a business or organization from both the top-down and bottom-up.[5]

EMS Benefits
Environmental
- Improved environmental performance
- Enhanced compliance with environmental procedures

- Reduced pollution
- Conserved resources

Economic
- Reduced or mitigated risks
- Attraction of new and retention of existing customers
- Increased efficiencies within operations
- Reduced costs and savings

Social
- Increased employee morale
- Enhanced recruitment of new employees
- Improved image with public, regulators, lenders, inventors, and others
- Achieved or improved employee awareness of environmental issues and responsibilities
- Qualification for recognition and incentive programs

Source: EPA, Environmental Management System, adapted by Norman Christopher, 2012.

Some of these key benefits include a direct positive impact to the bottom line by increasing efficiencies and reducing overall operating costs. Environmental performance can be improved by reducing environmental causes and effects and preventing sources of environmental issues and liabilities. Employees will have direct involvement in and engagement with environment programs and feel responsible and empowered for their contributions. The company or organization will have an enhanced image with internal shareholders and external community stakeholders and may also be recognized for its efforts.

Overall, by implementing an EMS, a company can further integrate environmental programs into the mission and vision of the organization, as well as reduce and mitigate potential environmental risks at the same time.

Case Studies

Cascade Engineering was encouraged to develop an EMS by their customers who were beginning to demand third-party certification to the global ISO 14001 standard. A formal EMS was then developed and created to manage the company's environmental causes and effects. Environmental responsibility was fully integrated into all aspects of the company's operations and facilities. Environmental audits were undertaken, training programs were developed, and progress and results were monitored and reported. By fully embedding and embracing the guiding principles of environmental stewardship, Cascade Engineering has been able to improve all aspects of its operations and achieve positive environmental, economic, and social impact.

The results from 2005-2009 are significant and include: [6]

- Reducing landfill waste to $8,000
- Reducing GHG emissions to approximately 33,000 metric tons of CO_2 equivalents
- Creating a neighborhood recycling center for the company and its residential neighbors
- Increasing the use of post-consumer and industrial recycled material to 9.5 million pounds
- Encouraging employees to help and serve others on community environmental responsibility issues

Herman Miller, a well-known leader in the furniture industry, has also established a proven management model and process that can be followed by other companies regarding overall environmental management.

Herman Miller Environmental Quality Action Team (EQAT)

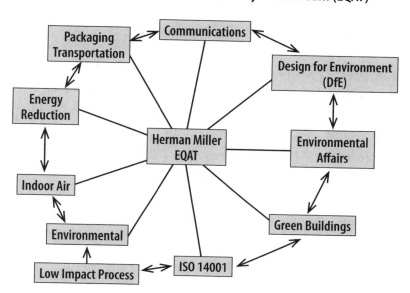

Source: Herman Miller, adapted by Norman Christopher, 2012.

The company created the EQAT that represented a cross functional steering committee comprised of employees. It was first started in 1969 to set the environmental compass for Herman Miller, establish priorities, and monitor and report results. In 1991 the EQAT team created the company's first environmental policy.[7]

This environmental policy that was created helped establish a road map at Herman Miller for a sustainable development journey of best practices and ongoing continuous improvement by:

- Going beyond compliance and raising the bar within the company
- Pursuing pollution prevention and eliminating waste of any kind
- Implementing new clean technologies to use resources more efficiently

- Designing products, buildings, and services for the environment
- Promoting environmental awareness and knowledge

In 2004 Herman Miller established their 2020 Perfect Vision program that highlights specific, challenging and stretch environmental goals for the company in the areas of Volatile Organic Content (VOC) air emissions, hazardous waste, solid waste, process water, energy use, LEED buildings, and DfE products.

To satisfy the 2020 Perfect Vision goals, Herman Miller has a documented EMS that satisfies the requirements of ISO 14001 and is fully integrated into the company's management system. Progress and updates can be accessed through the company website.

Call to Action

- Does the company have an effective Environmental Health and Safety Management system (EHS) in place?
- Has the company centralized its environmental compliance and regulatory procedures in an overall Environmental Management System (EMS)?
- Has the company been certified in any of the ISO certification protocols such as ISO 9000, 9001, or 14001 standards?
- What ISO certification or other environmental standard requirements are being driven by the company's key customers and major suppliers?

References

1. Environmental Aspects: The Basics, www.environment.infocrux.com/Environmental-Aspects.html, accessed August 2011.
2. Environmental Management Systems: An Implemented Guide for Small and Medium-sized Organizations, http://www.epa.gov/owm/iso14001/ems2001final.pdf, accessed August 2011.

3. ISO 14001 Checklist, http://www.ecaas.com/system/forms/frm_checklist_14001.pdf, accessed August 2011.
4. Environmental Management Systems: An Implemented Guide for Small and Medium-sized Organizations; page 19, http://www.epa.gov/owm/iso14001/ems2001final.pdf, accessed August 2011.
5. Environmental Management Systems, http://epa.gov/ems/, accessed July 2011.
6. Environmental Management System, www.cascadeng.com/pdf/quest/Quest_EMS.pdf, accessed August 2011.
7. Environmental Advocacy; How We Do It, www.hermanmiller.com/about-us/our-values-in-action/environmental-advocacy/how-we-do-it.html, accessed July 2011.

14. CLIMATE IMPACT AND MITIGATION

Introduction

Many greenhouse gases (GHG) such as water vapor, carbon dioxide (CO_2), methane (CH_4), nitrous oxide (N_2O), and ozone occur naturally. Others, such as hydroflurocarbons (HFCs), peflurocarbons (PFs), and sulphur hexafluoride (SF_6) result exclusively from human sources and industrial processes.

Levels of GHG can be increased from many human activities such as: [1]

- Burning solid waste wood, agricultural products, and fossil fuels
- Using fertilizers
- Decomposing organic waste such as land fuels and with livestock farming
- Eliminating trees through deforestation that use CO_2 and give off oxygen

In 2008 the U.S. Energy Information, which is part of the Department of Energy, estimated that the U.S. GHG emissions were 7,052.6 million $MTCO_2E$ which was down slightly from 2007. As evidenced in the pie chart, there are many sources of heat trapping and GHG emissions in the U.S. Energy related CO_2 emissions such as burning petroleum and coal fuel sources which account for over 80 percent of all U.S. gas emissions. [2]

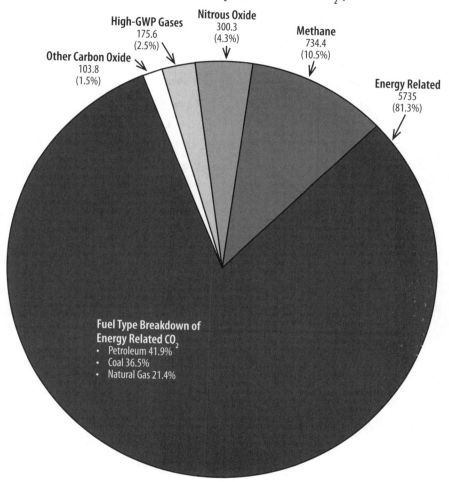

Sources of U.S. Heat Trapping Emissions
2008 Sources of U.S. Greenhouse Gas Emissions
(Million metric tons of CO_2E equivalent or MMT CO_2E)

High-GWP Gases
175.6
(2.5%)

Nitrous Oxide
300.3
(4.3%)

Methane
734.4
(10.5%)

Other Carbon Oxide
103.8
(1.5%)

Energy Related
5735
(81.3%)

Fuel Type Breakdown of
Energy Related CO_2
- Petroleum 41.9%
- Coal 36.5%
- Natural Gas 21.4%

Source: EIA Estimates, published in Emissions of Greenhouse Gases in the United States (Dec. 2009), adapted by Norman Christopher, 2012.

GHGs allow sunlight to enter the atmosphere naturally and freely. When sunlight hits the earth's surface, some sunlight is reradiated back into the atmosphere as heat. GHGs absorb the infrared radiation and trap the heat in the atmosphere. However,

GHGs vary in the capacity and capability to trap, absorb, and hold heat in the atmosphere. This process and phenomenon is known as Greenhouse Effect. Why?

- HFCs and PFCs are not naturally occurring and are the most heat absorbing GHGs
- N_2O is naturally occurring but absorbs approximately 70 times more heat per molecule than CO_2
- CH_4 is naturally occurring but absorbs approximately 21 times more heat per molecule than CO_2
- For each unit of energy produced, natural gas emits about half what petroleum fuels emit and about three-quarters of the CO_2 produced by coal

The natural GHG effect is a normal process and provides a covering of gases that help ensure that the earth is warm, so both humans and wildlife can survive comfortably. The enhanced GHG effect is not considered normal and is caused by humans and animals generating an excessive amount of these gases that trap and absorb additional heat, thereby creating a warmer climate than usual for humans and wildlife to live in.[3] Companies today are pursuing both climate mitigation, as well as climate adoption strategies.

Description

There are several climate change mitigation and adaptation approaches that companies and businesses can follow or implement.

- First of all, companies could take a "do nothing" approach or adopt a "wait and see" attitude. Businesses could acknowledge that they need more information to make a decision since climate change and GHGs are not being regulated at this point. Another perspective might be to discount the climate change discussion due to conflicting data regarding the science.

- Another, scenario that could happen is that GHGs and CO_2 might become regulated by the government and EPA at some point in the future. A mandate, such as a carbon tax, could be put in place and further regulated. If carbon management became regulated, business operations could be subject to a highly reactive situation where compliance is required within a short amount of time. Businesses might not make the best decision for their operations given these set of circumstances.
- On the other hand, businesses could commit to current climate mitigation and adaption best practices being advocated by trade associations and implemented by their members on best effort basis. In Michigan, Governor Granholm established the Michigan Climate Action Counsel which developed a Michigan Climate Action Plan and established goals of reducing 80 percent of GHG emissions by 2050 and 20 percent of GHG emissions by 2020, using 2006 as a baseline year.

The City of Grand Rapids, along with thirty other cities in Michigan, have endorsed the U.S. Mayor's Climate Change Protection Agreement. The City has also endorsed the Michigan Municipal League's Green Communities Challenge. In addition, the City has also embraced the "CLEAN" Cities for Climate Protection (CCP) protocol. Grand Valley State University and other colleges and universities have endorsed the American College and University President's Climate Commitment program (ACUPCC). GVSU has completed a GHG inventory, developed a Climate Action Plan, and set a climate neutrality date for the future.

Many companies and businesses today are also establishing a baseline for their carbon footprint as part of their overall environmental impact for their business operations.

Carbon Footprint of Typical Person

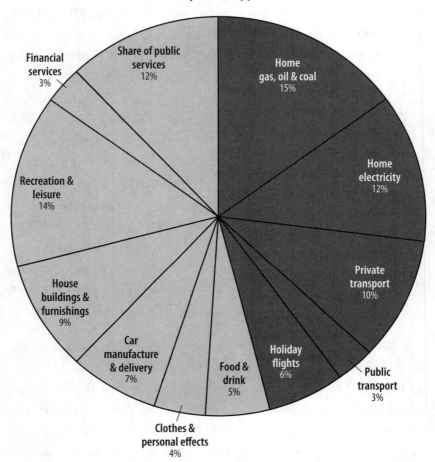

Source: What is a Carbon Footprint?, accessed August 2011, adapted by Norman Christopher, 2012.

Carbon footprints can be determined for individuals by looking at many sources of GHG emissions for our various activities.[4] Climate change impact relates to the amount of greenhouse gases produced in our day-to-day lives through burning fossil fuels for electricity, heating, and transportation, etc. As can be seen in the pie chart, there are approximately twelve different sources of a carbon footprint for an average person.

Primary footprints are measure of the direct emissions of CO_2 from burning of fossil fuels energy consumption and transportation fuels that we have direct control over.

Secondary footprints are those generated by the whole life cycle of products and services we consume and use.

For businesses, there are many climate action protocols and market tools that can be used to develop an inventory of GHG and CO_2 emissions.

There are voluntary standards and programs that businesses can look at for their overall operations.[5] Many of the climate action protocols are still under development.

Voluntary Standards and Programs
• ISO 14064-2 — Climate Action Reserve • GHG Protocol for Project Accounting (WBCSD/WRI) — Gold Standard (International) • Carbon Neutral Protocol — Green E-Climate Program • California Climate Action Registry (CCAR)

Source: Stockholm Environment Institute, A Review of Offset Programs: Trading Systems, Funds, Protocols, Standards, and Retailers, adopted by Norman Christopher, 2012.

There are also a number of market tools that can be used to gain access to best practices such as:

- Office Carbon Footprint
- Clean Air Cool Planet Climate Protection Software
- International Council for Local Environmental Initiatives (ICLEI) Local Government GHG Protocol

Individual and family carbon footprints can be determined from personal carbon calculators such as from EcoHatchery.[6] These personal carbon calculators can act as educational tools as well.

Application

There are a number of important steps in generating a GHG and CO_2 baseline inventory and then developing and implementing an overall Climate Action Plan.

Once an appropriate software program has been selected and chosen, a preliminary GHG inventory can be developed and established as a baseline. All of these inclusive software programs usually have the following scopes for assessment:

- Scope 1: on-site source generation such as steam
- Scope 2: purchased source generation such as electricity, natural gas, fuel oil, etc.
- Scope 3: travel source generation such as for products purchased and sold, employee travel, etc.

It is recommended that businesses focus on Scope 1 and 2 emissions first in establishing their GHG baseline inventory. Once a baseline GHG inventory has been established by the company, an overall Climate Action Plan can be considered.

Important steps to developing a Climate Action Plan include:

- Establishing an inclusive climate action team
- Developing and refining the GHG and CO_2 inventory
- Evaluating and implementing doable and achievable climate mitigation projects
- Setting CO_2 emission reduction targets
- Monitoring performance and reporting progress

Business operations and administration need to take the lead by setting visible examples of their commitment to becoming better environmental stewards, reducing environmental impact, and adhering to climate mitigation strategies. Companies, as well as cities and communities, can become climate leaders by raising the bar and mutually sharing and establishing best practices together regarding the development of climate action plans and generating carbon mitigation and adaptation strategies.

The following are some steps that can be taken in developing a Climate Action Plan:

- Obtain commitment and support from management, operations, employees, etc.
- Become a signatory to a defined protocol Climate Action Reserve, Green E-Climate program
- Commit to a sustainable culture by creating awareness, establishing understanding, and learning applications for sustainability best practices
- Establish an inclusive climate action team with representatives from administration, various functions and departments, employees, etc.
- Determine barriers, obstacles, and overall issues such as funding sources, time commitment, reporting, etc.
- Determine which protocol and software to use for GHG inventory such as market and web-based tools
- Establish baseline CO_2 emissions including scope 1 (direct), scope 2 (indirect), and scope 3 (emissions), such as travel, should be developed after scope 1 and 2 baseline emissions have been determined
- Refine baseline CO_2 emissions inventory including gaps, incomplete, and missing data
- Develop a body of knowledge around climate change and carbon management from internal and external sources including applied best practices
- Invite other stakeholders to the team as needed such as representatives from finance and IT departments
- Generate an inclusive list of potential carbon mitigation strategies through team discussions

- Evaluate potential climate adaptation strategies by looking at the overall heat island effect, tree and canopy cover, natural landscaping
- Evaluate and prioritize carbon mitigation projects by reviewing total costs and savings, and individual project returns
- Continue to refine CO_2 emissions data and model the future CO_2 inventory by finalizing the "status quo" baseline ensuring use of reliable data, and establishing reasonable valid projections
- Set target CO_2 emissions reduction goals for the short-, medium-, and long-term time frames, and focus on the next 3-5 year target milestones
- Finalize the overall climate action plan including goals, strategies, and action plans, ensure valid assumptions, and focus on scope 1 and 2 emissions reduction
- Monitor performance and report progress through metrics studies such as reduction in $MTCO_2E$, energy consumption, etc.

When developing a Climate Action Plan, it is most important to establish a list of prioritized and opportunistic carbon mitigation strategies.

Establishing Carbon Mitigation Strategies
There are a number of potential strategies that a business and organization can implement to reduce their overall environmental and carbon impact. These strategies include:
- Establishing climate change policies and procedures through carbon and energy management, environmental policies, and environmental management systems, etc.
- Reducing costs and reinvesting project savings through a green fund, revolving loans, Energy Service Company (ESCO) contracts, reinvestment incentives and options, etc.

- Pursuing environmentally preferred purchasing (EPP) and local purchasing options including the use of renewable energy credits (RECs)
- Developing "green" office procedures and guidelines
- Developing "green" information technology procedures and guidelines
- Determining climate change metrics, establish climate change reporting procedures, and incorporate into overall sustainability reporting
- Using "cradle to cradle" and life cycle analysis (LCA) processes within overall sustainable supply chain operations
- Redirecting air travel through video conferencing
- Conserving overall resources (e.g., energy, water, etc.) by incentivizing employees and departments
- Shifting accounting procedures to total cost accounting, activity based accounting procedures, etc.
- Considering flexible work schedules and 4-day workweeks
- Providing alternative transportation options for employees including urban transit

There are also a number of areas that business operations and manufacturing can specifically address for climate mitigation. These opportunities can create immediate short-term efficiencies and savings and long-term value, as well as reduce environmental impact and GHG emissions. These major areas include energy efficiency, waste minimization, and water conservation application areas.

Operations

Area	Opportunity
Alternative fuels	Bio-diesel; ethanol
Energy efficiency	Energy Star equipment; networked metering; restrictions on window units and space heaters; combined heat and power (CHP); radical energy conservation projects
Lighting	LED systems; motion sensors; day lighting
Onsite power generation	Renewable energy; e.g., biomass, geothermal, wind, solar, etc.
Building and construction	"Green" and LEED standards; insulation and weatherization; window and roof replacements, etc.
Alternative vehicles	Electric; hybrid; fleet downsizing
Urban transit	Bus; van; carpool; bike
Waste minimization	Zero waste; composting; recycling; waste minimization, etc.
Renewable energy purchases	Purchasing cooperatives; consortiums; RECs; renewable energy use
Water	Storm water runoff procedures; rain gardens; conservation techniques; low flush toilets; efficiency faucets and shower heads
Landscape	Natural landscaping; pesticide free grounds; green space
Computers	LED monitors; server virtualization; power management software; Energy Star equipment, etc.
HVAC	Variable frequency drives; natural ventilation

Additionally, administration can shift to green and local purchasing, develop sustainable supply chain management, and establish green office procedures for everyday operations. By establishing Climate Action Plan progress and milestone reports that are accessible to internal shareholders and external stakeholders, businesses can monitor progress and report improvements and results openly and transparently on a regular basis.

Results and Benefits

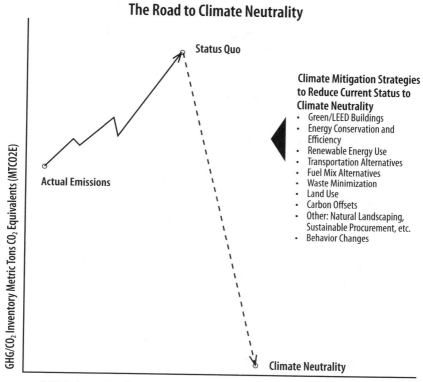

The Road to Climate Neutrality

Source: Norman Christopher, 2012.

Companies can address climate change, reduce their GHG and CO_2 emissions, and become better environmental stewards while creating eco-efficiencies and cost savings at the same time. Some of the primary areas of focus and cost savings include:

- Energy efficiency projects that include smart and networked metering as well as the use of Energy Star equipment, motion sensors, and upgraded lighting systems
- Building and construction guidelines including "green" and LEED building and construction standards, weatherization, and insulation

- Waste minimization and waste management systems such as recycling, composting, and zero waste initiatives
- Water conservation projects including establishing irrigation and retention ponds and storm water run-off procedures
- Natural landscaping
- Green and local purchasing guidelines and procedures
- "Cradle to cradle" sustainable supply chain management guidelines and procedures
- Renewable energy use from a portfolio of green and clean technologies where appropriate and cost effective
- Transportation alternatives including urban transit, biofuels, and alternative energy vehicles
- Purchase of carbon offsets, renewable energy credits, etc.

The real benefits from addressing climate change and implementing climate mitigation and reduction strategies come from the cost savings that can be generated from operations including the overall planning framework that climate mitigation helps to establish. Another benefit comes from continuous improvement efforts and changing behavior and habits, such as through energy efficiency awareness and conservation efforts.

Instead of having a number of isolated "one off" projects such as energy efficiency, waste minimization and water conservation, overall climate mitigation provides an integrated planning framework for all of these programs, initiatives and activities for tactical and strategic management planning. Nearly every environmental strategy has an accompanying environmental action metric that includes a GHG and CO_2 conversion factor.

Businesses can also recognize that there are a number of issues to be faced with climate action planning that can impede progress. Some of these key issues involve overall resistance to change, incentives to conserve, not setting clear quantifiable goals, lack of universally accepted carbon inventory systems, and overall accuracy of the GHG and CO_2 data that is being tracked and reported. These barriers represent the resistance level for behavior change.

Therefore organizations need to ensure that there is management commitment and leadership in place. Businesses should try and establish an inclusive rigorous disciplined protocol and process as well as an overall budget. Many times the budget can be justified through cost savings and cost reductions. The key is to take small steps, create company awareness and report success among management and employees as well as community stakeholders and advisors. Additionally, climate action planning best practices can usually be benchmarked against other organizations that have implemented these best practices. Many times climate action planning is done in partnership with others to mutually learn about best practices. The Grand Rapids Chamber of Commerce currently has established a Greater Grand Rapids Partnership for a Sustainable Community program that businesses can join and receive an easy to use carbon calculator with suggestions on environmental efficiencies.[7]

One company that has experienced significant cost savings as well as environmental benefits from pursuing climate mitigation strategies is Valley City Linen, the largest family owned linen company in Michigan. In addition to its facilities in Grand Rapids, the company also has operations in northern Michigan and Metro Detroit.

The company recently invested $700,000 of capital in new machinery and equipment that will help reduce its carbon footprint and also save approximately 8 million gallons of water. The new water-efficient commercial washers can process 4,000 pounds of laundry per hour using one-third of a gallon of water per pound of laundry compared to three to four gallons per pound of laundry with conventional equipment. The company can process 18.2 million pounds of laundry per year.

With its new equipment, each year Valley City Linen expects to:
- Save 8 million gallons of water

- Save $275,000 in fuel, electricity, and detergent costs
- Continually reduce its carbon footprint with the addition of heat reclamation systems, advanced wastewater systems, and finishing equipment
- Improve laundry quality and overall linen service[8]

Case Studies

The City of Grand Rapids, with the assistance of civil engineering firm Fishbeck, Thompson, Carr & Huber, Inc. (FTC&H), completed an Energy Efficiency and Conservation Strategy in 2009. In this project, a preliminary greenhouse gas inventory was established for both the City of Grand Rapids owned assets and properties, and the general community within Grand Rapids.[9]

City of Grand Rapids GHG Emissions

Department	Total Indirect CO_2E Emissions (metric tons)	Total Direct CO_2E Emissions (metric tons)	Total CO_2E Emissions (metric tons)	Percent of Total Emissions
Water	27,689.76	2,774.97	30,464.74	32
Environmental Services (wastewater)	22,603.10	2,685.60	25,288.69	27
Traffic Safety – Lighting and Signals	13,827.61	0.00	13,827.61	15
Facility Management, including Streets, Traffic Safety (buildings), Police	7,296.04	863.90	8,159.94	9
Vehicle Fleet	0.00	7,001.49	7,001.49	7
Parking	3,726.26	0.47	3,726.73	4
Library	2,197.12	722.51	2,919.63	3
Fire Department	754.95	909.80	1,664.75	2

Department	Total Indirect CO_2E Emissions (metric tons)	Total Direct CO_2E Emissions (metric tons)	Total CO_2E Emissions (metric tons)	Percent of Total Emissions
Parks and Cemeteries	999.68	433.82	1,433.50	2
DASH Buses	0.00	145.76	145.76	0
Miscellaneous	51.40	59.19	110.59	0
Gross CO_2E Emissions	79,145.93	15,597.50	94,743.43	NA
Renewable Energy Adjustment*	16,683.01	540.24	17,223.25	NA
Net CO_2E Emissions	62,462.93	15,057.26	77,520.18	NA

* Includes credits for both renewable electrical energy purchases and biogenic emissions from biofuels in fleet services.

Source: Kent County Department of Public Works.

Community of Grand Rapids GHG Inventory Summary (Metric Tons)

	CO_2	N_2O	CH_4	CO_2E	%
Residential	454,716	1.09	58.78	456,289	22.6
Commercial	379,245	0.72	35.74	380,217	18.9
Industrial	5,683	0.02	0.15	5,693	0.3
Transportation	1,128,275	54.52	47.04	1,146,164	56.9
Waste	-	-	1,299.31	27,285	1.4
Total	1,967,919	56.35	1,441.01	2,015,648	

Source: Kent County Department of Public Works, http://www.accessKent.com/yourgovernment/publicworks.wte.htm, Covanta Kent http://covantaholding.com/site/locations/covantakent.html Michigan Air Emissions Reporting System.

Direct CO_2 emissions are the primary carbon footprints and secondary CO_2 emissions are the secondary carbon footprints.

The City of Grand Rapids organizational boundary includes 265 properties such as city owned and leased buildings, water and wastewater infrastructure, parks, cemeteries, parking facilities, lighting, transit, maintenance, police and fire departments. The community of Grand Rapids inventory includes residential, commercial, schools and universities, hospitals, industrial, transportation, roadways, and rail traffic, etc.

The city has already achieved 20 percent use of renewable energy and has set a goal of 100 percent use of renewable energy by 2020. The city of Grand Rapids was the 156th city in the U.S. to sign the U.S. Mayors Climate Protection Agreement and has received national recognition for its climate mitigation and adaption strategies. More can be found on the website, http://www.sustainablegr.com.

"Progressive AE is the first architecture/engineering firm in North America to earn CarbonNeutral company status and make the tangible commitment to reduce carbon emissions and help slow climate change."[10]

"To earn this certification, the Grand Rapids firm measured its corporate carbon footprint using an independent third-party, quantifying all six Kyoto greenhouse gases and measured in units of carbon dioxide equivalent, or CO_2E. The finding was that Progressive AE produces 626 metric tons of CO_2E — most of it from the operations of buildings. Those emissions were reduced to net zero through a combination of internal reductions (e.g., improving operational efficiencies) and external reductions in the form of high quality carbon offsets."

"Progressive AE is proud to again be on the cutting edge of new business strategies and technologies," Bradley Thomas, P.E., Progressive AE's president and CEO, said in a news release. "Now that we have gone through this process ourselves, we can better use our team of architects, engineers, and consulting experts to perform this innovative service for our clients. If we can help our clients manage their carbon, we help them manage their costs."

"West Michigan businesses have consistently been on the forefront of the sustainability movement with initiatives that have put us on the map, proving that being responsible for your carbon emissions is good for the environment and for business," Grand Rapids Mayor George Heartwell said in a news release. "By being the first architecture and engineering firm in North America to be awarded CarbonNeutral status, Progressive AE has not only set the bar for other businesses across the country but also provides a low carbon alternative for clients looking for an architectural solution."

Internal reductions instituted by Progressive include:

- Installing new building HVAC controls and monitoring
- Recommissioning lighting, HVAC systems, domestic hot water systems, and all associated controls
- Creating a list of recommended efficiency improvements with associated Return on Investment (ROI) estimates
- Discontinuing mechanical snowmelt systems, except for special circumstances
- Upgrading lighting replacement fixtures, lamps, and ballasts
- Increasing materials recycled to include plastics, metals, glass, and other operational incidentals
- Replacing old two-stroke boat motors for the water resources department with low emission four-stroke motors
- Selling and not replacing an inefficient cargo van

Carbon offsets were accomplished in accordance with The CarbonNeutral Company's CarbonNeutral Protocol, an industry leading standard which guarantees all The CarbonNeutral Company programs "deliver robust, high quality, credible emissions reductions." The CarbonNeutral Protocol is reviewed by an Independent Advisory Group of academics, scientists, and businesses and covers the entire chain — from measurement to communication, including, for example, clear parameters for carbon footprints and CarbonNeutral certifications. The projects chosen for investment align with Progressive AE's corporate vision and applicable industries.

They are:

- Conservation-based forest management project in the Big River/Salmon Creek Forests in Northern California verified and certified to the Climate Action Reserve
- Wind power generated from three new wind turbines in the Dhule district of Maharashtra, India, verified and certified to the Voluntary Carbon Standard
- Small-scale hydropower in Guizhou Province China verified and certified to the Voluntary Carbon Standard

Progressive AE worked with The CarbonNeutral Company (www.carbonneutral.com), a carbon offset and carbon management business, working with more than 300 major businesses and thousands of small- to medium-sized companies.

Over the last 10 years, The CarbonNeutral Company has purchased carbon credits from more than 200 projects spread over six continents. They have two regional operating headquarters in New York and London, as well as offices in Grand Rapids, and Singapore, and a network of affiliates in Japan, Canada, France, and UAE.

"Progressive AE becoming CarbonNeutral is an important step not only for their business, but for the architectural, design, and engineering industry as a whole. By committing to reduce emissions to net zero, Progressive AE has set the benchmark. Progressive AE clearly recognizes that the built environment represents a critical bridge to a low carbon future and the firm is now demonstrating leadership to their clients by taking responsibility for the emissions associated with their businesses," Neil Braun, The CarbonNeutral Company CEO, said in the news release.

Progressive AE has a history of being "first" in many initiatives including being the first outstate firm to earn the American Institute of Architects (AIA) Michigan chapter award for Firm of the Year; the first firm to win the AIA Grand Valley chapter's award for Firm Achievement; and being the highest ranked architecture/ engineering firm on the *Grand Rapids Business Journal's* first list of LEED (Leadership in Energy and Environmental Design) accredited professionals.

Call to Action

- Has the company ever conducted a carbon inventory for its overall business operations?
- Does the company know how many metric tons of carbon dioxide equivalents it generates annually (e.g., $MTCO_2E$)?
- In what ways can the company reduce or mitigate the amount of $MTCO_2E$ it generates annually such as through energy conservation strategies to reduce the consumption of fuel oil, natural gas, steam, and electricity?
- Has the company considered climate adaptation strategies to reduce the overall heat island effect for its facilities and buildings as well as with operations including an anticipated 2-3 degree rise in average temperatures in the future?

References

1. The Encyclopedia of Environment, www.environmentabout.com/category/green-house-gases, accessed August 2011.

2. Total U.S. Greenhouse Gas Emissions Down 2.2 Percent in 2008, But Let's Not Celebrate Yet, www.treehugger.com/clean-technology/total-us-greenhouse-gas-emissions-down-22-in-2008-but-lets-not-celebrate-yet.html, accessed August 2011.

3. Energy and the Environment Explained: Greenhouse Gases, www.eia.gov/energyexplained/index.cfm?page=environment_about_ghg, accessed August 2011.
4. What is a Carbon Footprint?, www.carbonfootprint.com, accessed August 2011.
5. Voluntary Standards and Programs, http://sei-us.org/Publications_PDF/SEI-ReviewOffsetPrograms1.1-08.pdf.
6. Calculate Carbon Footprint, http://www.Ecohatchery.com/Calculator, accessed August 2011.
7. Community Sustainability, www.grandrapids.org/sustainability, accessed July 2011.
8. Valley City Linen, www.mlive.com/business/west-michigan/index.ssf/2010/11/after_75_years_automation_keep.html, accessed June 2012.
9. Energy Efficiency and Conservation Strategy 2009; pages 43, 57, http://mygrcity.us/departments/enterpriseservices/serviceareas/es/public/Documents/2009%20Energy%20Efficiency%20and%20Conservation%20Strategy.pdf, accessed August 2011.
10. Progressive AE first Architecture/Engineering Firm in North America to earn CarbonNeutral Status, www.carbonneutral.com/about-us/media-centre/press-releases/progressive-ae-is-1st-architectureengineering-firm-in-north-america-to-earn-carbonneutral-status/, accessed August 2011.

15. SUSTAINABLE MANUFACTURING

Introduction

Today's manufacturing processes have been transformed from a "cradle to grave" process orientation to a "cradle to cradle" holistic systems approach. This overall systems approach is known as sustainable manufacturing. The Department of Commerce International Trade Administration defines sustainable manufacturing as "the creation of manufactured products that use processes that minimize negative environmental impacts; conserve energy and natural reserves; are safe for employees, communities, and consumers and are economically sound."[1]

Sustainable Manufacturing Consulting defines sustainable manufacturing as "a business practice of the industrial sector, which expands all the company's processes and decisions into the social and natural environments it operates in and affects, with the explicit objective of reducing or eliminating any negative impact while pursuing the desired level of technological and economic performance."[2]

In the past many business executives and managers viewed sustainable manufacturing as just extra added costs to become better environmental stewards and more environmentally sustainable and responsible. Today, however, there is the increasing realization that sustainable manufacturing has gained more acceptance from eco-conscious customers in the marketplace. Moreover, Sustainable Manufacturing has become a "win-win." It is a win for businesses as they create eco-efficiencies and savings. It is also a win for customers who desire to purchase eco-efficient and more environmentally friendly products at competitive prices.

The case study in this chapter is The Business and Institutional Furniture Manufacturer's Association (BIFMA) voluntary e-3 Furniture Assessment Standard developed in conjunction with the American National Standards Institute (ANSI).

Description

Sustainable manufacturing should be viewed through the lens of closed loop systems rather than open-ended production processes. These traditional open-ended processes took raw materials extracted from the earth in the belief that there was an infinite supply of these resources. Eventually, products that were manufactured reached their "end of life" and were disposed of, many times to a landfill without much additional thought. Today, the sustainable manufacturing closed loop system begins and ends with an impact on the both environment and overall ecosystem. Many sustainable manufacturing processes use green and clean technologies that minimize the generation of waste, as well as reduce air pollution and the amount of greenhouse gas emissions and carbon dioxide produced.

Sustainable Manufacturing

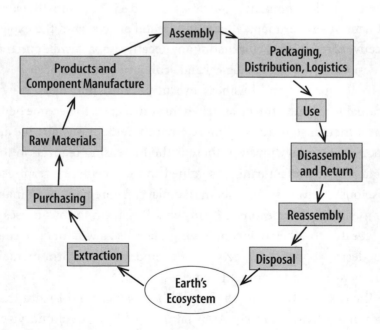

Source: What is Sustainable Manufacturing?, (http://www.ifm.eng.cam.ac.uk/sustainability/seminar/documents/050216lo.pdf), adapted by Norman Christopher, 2012.

As can be seen, the critical aspects of sustainable manufacturing deal with the production of products, components, assemblies, and systems in an overall closed loop system using a cradle to cradle life cycle process.[3]

Julian Allwood, of the Institute for Manufacturing at the University of Cambridge determined early on that there were a number of steps that could be followed in pursuit of sustainable manufacturing best practices. These steps include:

- Using less energy, water, and materials thereby improving overall resource use and productivity
- Substituting nontoxic input materials for toxic materials and renewable resources for nonrenewable resources
- Reducing unwanted waste outputs by shifting to cleaner production processes and industrial symbiosis, thereby minimizing waste generation and creating waste streams that can be used by others as new materials
- Converting outputs to inputs through recycling of materials for reuse
- Changing workload and organizational structures to improve supply chain performance and overall productivity

By looking at sustainable manufacturing as a closed loop system, the entire supply chain of the business can be transformed using clean technologies in conjunction with eco-innovation. In essence, sustainable manufacturing is a continuous improvement journey not necessarily a destination end point or steady state.

Today, sustainable manufacturing best practices are viewed as more than just "GREEN and LEAN" manufacturing initiatives. There is a focus on TBL economic, environmental, and social impacts and outcomes. Robert Pojasek in his article "When is Sustainable Manufacturing Sustainable?" advocates the use of protocol such as ISO 9001:2008 as the foundation to drive the process. This process can then easily integrate other sustainability TBL programs such as

Environmental Management Systems in ISO 14001, Risk management in ISO 31000, and Social responsibility in ISO 2600. Thus, integrated management systems pave the way for businesses to operate more efficiently and effectively in their day-to-day operations.

Application

Sustainable manufacturing should become part of the core business operations and then embedded and connected to the company's strategic plan and overall mission and vision. Employees, department heads, and top management need to be involved and engaged from the outset in the advocacy and the development of sustainable manufacturing best practices. Another great source of input and direction comes from the company's supply chain partners including raw material suppliers, customers, and other stakeholders who can help develop and implement the required closed loop sustainable manufacturing and production systems.[4]

The Closed Loop Production System

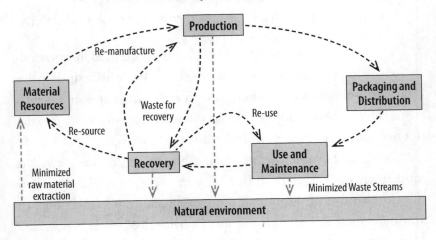

Source: Sustainable Manufacturing and Eco-Innovation: Framework, Practices, and Management-Synthesis Report, page 12, OECD 2009, adapted by Norman Christopher, 2012.

Sustainable manufacturing is based on inputs and outputs that address resource consumption, waste generation, efficiency, and recovery. Much can be learned from looking at industrial symbiosis as a process change opportunity. Marian R. Chertow in the Journal of Industrial Ecology defined Industrial Symbiosis as "engaging traditionally separate industries in a collective approach to competitive advantage involving physical exchange of materials, energy, and water and by-products. The keys to industrial symbiosis are collaboration and synergistic possibilities offered by geographic proximity."[5] The waste of one process might become a raw material for another process. Therefore, getting to know your neighbor and their business operations might be of mutual benefit. Recovery of materials and waste provide many opportunities for re-sourcing, re-use, and re-manufacturing.

The Evolution of Sustainable Manufacturing Concepts and Practices

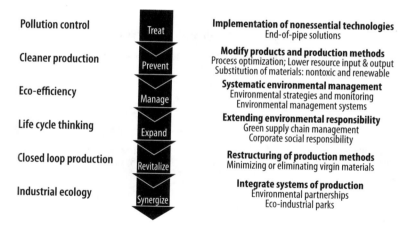

Pollution control	Treat	**Implementation of nonessential technologies** End-of-pipe solutions
Cleaner production	Prevent	**Modify products and production methods** Process optimization; Lower resource input & output Substitution of materials: nontoxic and renewable
Eco-efficiency	Manage	**Systematic environmental management** Environmental strategies and monitoring Environmental management systems
Life cycle thinking	Expand	**Extending environmental responsibility** Green supply chain management Corporate social responsibility
Closed loop production	Revitalize	**Restructuring of production methods** Minimizing or eliminating virgin materials
Industrial ecology	Synergize	**Integrate systems of production** Environmental partnerships Eco-industrial parks

Source: Sustainable manufacturing and Eco-Innovation: Framework, Practices, and Management-Synthesis Report, page 12, OECD 2009, adapted by Norman Christopher, 2012.

As sustainable manufacturing has evolved, so has the evolution of sustainable production and manufacturing concepts and best practices. There are many strategies and approaches that companies can take regarding the implementation of these best practices across the company's operations and overall supply chain.

Pollution control addresses all emissions and their treatment, as well as end of life solutions. Cleaner production prevents waste and optimizes resource consumption, input and outputs, and material use. Eco-efficiencies can be achieved through cost saving programs, environmental management systems, and audits. Life cycle analysis can be used to establish sustainable supply chain management and corporate social responsibility targets and leverage shared knowledge and resources. Closed loop production methodology helps to minimize use of virgin raw materials and overall generation of waste. Concern for industrial ecology encourages partnerships and leadership for environmental stewardship. Today, sustainable manufacturing and eco-innovation has become well integrated into company business plans and overall operations of many businesses.[4]

Conceptual Relationships Between Sustainable Manufacturing and Eco-Innovation

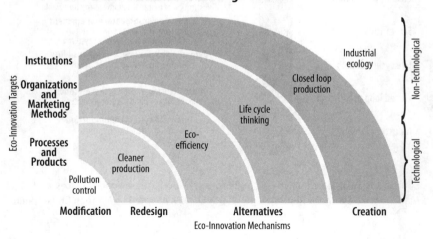

Source: Sustainable Manufacturing and Eco-Innovation: Framework, Practices, and Management-Synthesis Report, page 15, OECD 2009, adapted by Norman Christopher, 2012.

To achieve successful sustainable manufacturing also requires successful eco-innovation across a broad range of areas, systems, and processes. As sustainable manufacturing knowledge and experience is gained, and eco-innovation targets and milestones are set, both technological and non-technological resources can be applied. Greater TBL benefits can be achieved as more process modifications, product redesign, alternative business models and new organizational structures and procedures are created and used. However, these greater benefits go hand in hand with more complexities and integration challenges in sustainable manufacturing and overall operations.

Sustainable manufacturing performance measurements and metrics should be carefully developed, easily tracked, and monitored regularly to ensure progress against milestones. The following are examples of sustainable manufacturing indicators and metrics that can be developed and used.[6]

Sustainable Manufacturing Indicators

Category	Sub-Category	Metric Examples
Energy	Type Used	KWH used for electricity; MMBTU of natural gas for heating and cooling; lbs. of steam, etc.
Materials	Raw Materials	Tons of raw materials by type for manufacture; amount of packaging materials, etc.
	Auxiliary Materials	Amount of lubrication oils, compressed air, process water used, etc.
	Waste Materials	Amount of waste generated by type and sent to the landfill. Waste oils and chemicals generated; amount of toxic waste generated and disposed of, etc.
Emissions	Air Emissions	Amount GHG emissions generated by type; amount toxic air emissions released by type; e.g., TRI inventory; amount of heavy materials and particulates generated, etc.
	Water Emissions	Quality and amount of wastewater and groundwater released; e.g., sewer or into the environment, etc.

Category	Sub-Category	Metric Examples
Production	Time	Cycle times, through put times, etc.
	Production Quantity	Number of defective parts or components manufactured; e.g., per person, per hour, etc.
	Production Quality	Number of defective parts or components produced; e.g., per person, per hour, etc.
Logistics	Conveyance Mode	Vehicle type, freight rates and capacity, amount fuel used and overall mileage, etc.
Cost	Unit Costs	Raw materials used per unit output, energy cost and embedded energy intensity per unit output, etc.
	Investment Costs	Capital equipment costs, capital building and facility costs, etc.
Social	Staff and Employees	Number of man-hours of work, number of training hours per employee, number of sick and work absence days, etc.
	Customers	Number of warranty claims, number of customer order rejections by type, etc.

Selection of the exact sustainable manufacturing performance measurements and metrics is dependent on the specificity of the business goals and milestones. Many times these types of measurements are benchmarked against similar metrics of other companies to determine both company and industry competitive performance.

Sustainable manufacturing indicators can be specific singular measurements or composite indices and cover a number of areas including material flow analysis, life cycle analysis, eco-efficiency, as well as general environmental and social accounting.

Results and Benefits

There are a number of benefits that can be achieved by implementing sustainable manufacturing practices that will have a positive overall effect on reducing the environmental impact of manufacturing and facility operations.[3]

Sustainable Manufacturing Practices

Environmental Impact Issues	Use less energy, water, materials	Substitute for nontoxic input and renewable resources	Reduce unwanted waste outputs	Recovery and reuse	Change workload, organization and process structures
Greenhouse Gas Reduction	X	X		X	X
Air Quality Improvement	X	X	X		
Deforestation Reduction	X			X	
Biodiversity Improvement	X	X	X	X	
Toxic Chemical Reduction	X	X	X		
Nonrenewable Material Reduction	X			X	X
Hazardous Waste Reduction	X	X	X		
Waste Volume Decrease	X			X	X
Water Use Improvement	X		X	X	X
Agriculture	X	X			

Source:[3] What is Sustainable Manufacturing?, (http://www.ifm.eng.cam.ac.uk/sustainability/seminar/documents/050216lo.pdf).

Some of the key environmental benefits include reduction of greenhouse gas emissions, improvement in air quality, reduction of toxic chemical use, reduction in overall waste generation, and improvement in energy and water use. There will be economic benefits such as increased sales, eco-efficiencies, cost savings including cost avoidance and mitigation of risks and liabilities. Social benefits can be seen through increased productivity from employees and improved morale. Company reputation may also be enhanced through local community stakeholders. Many times business operations can set the tone of empowerment, innovation, and entrepreneurship for the company to help build the organizational culture and enhance the overall image of the company.

TBL sustainability benefits can be quantified and qualified through the proper selection of performance metrics and measurements for both inputs and outputs. Additionally, customized surveys can focus on specific eco-innovation areas. Moreover, most professional and trade associations now offer industry wide benchmarking data that can be used for comparative and competitive purposes. This data can help company management make better decisions as well as help improve overall manufacturing and operations. The Business and Institutional Furniture Manufacturer's Association (BIFMA) is a good example.

Case Study

Over the last few years the Furniture Industry and the leadership of BIFMA developed an industry wide voluntary sustainability standard and rating system for furniture products in conjunction with the American National Standards Institute (ANSI).

The ANSI/BIFMA e-3 Furniture Sustainability Standard is voluntary in scope.[7] The purpose for the development of this standard is several fold including the:

- Establishment of sustainable development performance across the furniture industry and its market segments
- Determination of an open assessment standard that minimizes the confusion over eco-labels
- Facilitation of a cost competitive environment for conformance and verification

The purpose of the standard is to:
- Provide measurable product-based conformance definitions for the advancement of sustainable furniture
- Minimize the proliferation of eco-labeling and green washing
- Become more cost competitive, made available to all market segments, realize authenticity through verification

The scope of the standard includes all business and institutional furniture products such as moveable walls, system furniture, desking systems, case goods, tables, seating, as well as other accessories, etc. Additionally, the standard is also pertinent and applicable to materials and components produced by suppliers in the value chain for furniture manufacturers. The BIFMA e-3 Furniture Sustainability Standard does require a third-party verification of a score that is broken down into four primary areas including: materials, energy and atmosphere, human and eco-system health, and social responsibility. Through third-party verification, furniture products can be Level certified.

There are a total of 90 points available in the rating system. The overall standards also apply to the company's organization and facilities, as well as the product(s) manufactured.

BIFMA Sustainability Rating System

	Organization	Facility	Product	Total
Materials	5	4	17	26
Energy Atmosphere	4	17	4	25
Human and Ecosystem Health	0	15	14	29
Social Responsibility	8	2	0	10
Totals	17	38	35	90

Once the total amounts have been determined, there are several conformance and certification levels that can be achieved.

Total Points	Conformance Level	Level Certification
32-44	Silver	Level 1
45-62	Gold	Level 2
63-90	Platinum	Level 3

Conformance levels must be first or second-party verified. Level certifications must be third-party only certified.

Currently there are 1,534 total products in nine furniture product categories that have been Level certified including 965 Level 1 products, 414 Level 2 products, and 155 Level 3 products.[8]

Call to Action

- What type of quality control processes does the company practice in its business operations today; e.g., "Kaizan," "Just in Time," Six Sigma Total Quality Management (TQM)?

- Does the company practice Green and LEAN manufacturing protocols and processes?
- What are the areas of largest concern in the company's manufacturing facilities and operations? Have the concerns been quantified and addressed?
- Does the company follow a closed loop production system?
- Has the company developed and established a set of performance metrics for sustainable manufacturing?

References

1. How does Commerce define Sustainable Manufacturing?, http://trade.gov/competitiveness/sustainablemanufacturing/how_doc_defines_SM.asp, accessed August 2011.

2. Sustainable Manufacturing Consulting, http://sustainablemanufacturing.biz, accessed August 2011.

3. What is Sustainable Manufacturing?, http://www.ifm.eng.cam.ac.uk/sustainability/seminar/documents/050216lo.pdf, accessed August 2011, adapted by Norman Christopher 2012.

4. Sustainable Manufacturing and Eco-Innovation: Framework, practices, and management Synthesis Report, page 12 & 15, OECD 2009, www.oecd.org/dataoecd/15/58/43423689.pdf.

5. Uncovering Industrial Symbiosis, Marian R. Chertow, page 12, http://www.rshanthini.com/tmp/CP551/M07R01JofIEUncoveringIndustrialSymbiosis.pdf, accessed July 2011.

6. B. Johnson, K. Lyons, S. Leong, "Framework and Indicators for a Sustainable Manufacturing Methodology," 2010 Winter Simulation Conference.

7. The BIFMA Sustainability Standard, http://bifma.org/public/e3docs/level_overview.pdf, accessed August 2011.

8. http://www.levelcertified.org/products, accessed March 2012.

16. ECO-EFFICIENCY

Introduction

Back in 2000 the World Business Council for Sustainable Development discussed "eco-efficiency as a management philosophy that encourages business to search for environmental improvement that yields parallel economic benefits. Eco-efficiency is achieved by the delivery of competitively priced goods and services that satisfy human needs and bring quality of life, while progressively reducing ecological impacts and resource intensity throughout the life cycle to a level at least in line with the earth's estimated carrying capacity. In short it is concerned with creating more value with less impact."[1]

Currently eco-efficiencies provide some of the best ways for companies to reduce costs and improve profitability, while reducing their overall environmental impact.

Over the last few years the Right Place Inc., through their Manufacturer's Council, has focused on green, lean, and eco-efficiency best practices through the Michigan Manufacturing Technology Center (MMTC) activities. A monthly work group consisting of many of the small- to medium-size businesses share best practices including visits to company plants and operations facilities. (www.mmtc.org)

The case studies in this chapter include Nichols Paper and Supply, Rapid-Line Manufacturing, and Spectrum Health.

Description

To successfully implement eco-efficiencies businesses must:
- Develop environmental assessments of their organization
- Identify gaps and issues
- Focus on "low hanging, high impact, eco-efficiency projects"

- Generate environmental reports and documentation
- Consider establishing an environmental management system

It should be noted that eco-efficiencies focus primarily on economic and environmental impacts and not social aspects and impacts, although environmental issues are beginning to command great socio-environmental attention due to human health issues relating to toxic chemical exposure.

The World Business Council on Sustainable Development (WBCSD) first coined the term eco-efficiency in 1992 and has identified seven primary elements of eco-efficiency that businesses should pursue.[2]

1. Reduce material intensity, such as with the reduction of water consumption and overall materials used
2. Reduce energy intensity and embedded energy used for processing and manufacturing
3. Reduce dispersion of toxic substances by shifting to the use of green and clean chemicals and technologies
4. Enhance recyclability by utilizing waste streams and minimizing waste sent to landfills
5. Increase the use of renewable energy technologies such as wind, solar, geothermal, and biomass for both grid connected and distributed power generation systems
6. Extend product desirability and function in use
7. Increase service intensity of products, thereby developing a recognized body of knowledge in the technology and its application

The WBCSD advocates that achieving successful eco-efficiencies be based upon three primary broad objectives.[3] The first objective deals with reducing overall resource consumption. Thus the initiative would include a number of important activities such as:

- Minimizing the use of energy, water, land, and materials
- Improving upon product durability
- Increasing recycling and reducing waste and minimizing generation
- Closing material open loop systems

The second objective addresses the reduction of environmental impact on nature. Some of the important activities would include:

- Minimizing and reducing air emissions and GHG; water discharges; waste disposal; and toxic waste generation
- Using renewable resources such as for power and energy consumption when cost effective and appropriate

The third objective focuses on increasing customer product and service value. Activities include:

- Improving product functionality, flexibility, durability, and modularity
- Providing for additional services such as technical support, maintenance, exchange, warranty, and upgrading
- Ensuring authentic product responsibility and ownership

The WBSCD goes on to say that eco-efficiency is not a panacea, cure-all, or end-all in itself. There are many things that eco-efficiency is not:

- A solution to all the problems and concerns of sustainability
- A certifiable standard
- A rigid framework
- A take-it-or-leave-it strategy

Eco-efficiency should be seen as an on-going continuous improvement process that enables companies and organizations to pursue a continuing spectrum of available opportunities to reduce their cost while making a supportive environmental contribution.

In order to accomplish these key objectives many companies have established an overall Environmental Management System (EMS) based on ISO 14000 standards as the most effective management approach.

There are a number of areas to find, develop, and implement eco-efficiency opportunities in the overall supply chain company business operations. Products may be tweaked or redesigned to meet new and existing customer needs and wants with more stringent environmental features and benefits. Processes can be reengineered to improve overall company operations, productivity, and environmental impact. Markets can be rethought and restrategized through industry segmentation and market fragmentation. Also value can be created through the sale of waste streams and by-products. All of these areas represent opportunities for efficiency and conservation in the use of air, water, energy, and waste. To assist organizations, WBSCD has developed an innovative business model to address eco-efficiency opportunities.[4]

Where to find eco-efficient opportunities?

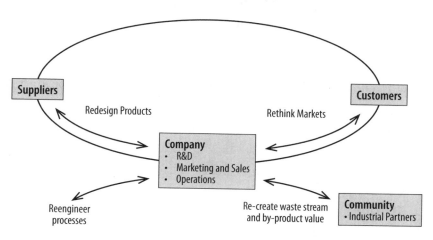

Source: Eco-efficiency, (www.wbcsd.org/web/publications/ecoefficiency_creating_more_value.pdf), adapted by Norman Christopher, 2012.

Application

There are a number of areas where eco-efficiency opportunities can be found. In order to identify and prioritize these opportunities, business owners are required to use a life cycle analysis (LCA) approach to their overall operations. This analysis can involve management, employees, shareholders, and stakeholders to gain in-depth insight and understanding and more fully comprehend risks, liabilities, and opportunities.

1. Reengineer

Companies can reengineer their processes and business operations to reduce resource consumption. Additionally pollution reduction technologies and carbon mitigation approaches can also be undertaken. These process changes can also take place with suppliers such as delivery of raw materials and with customers including distribution and logistics.

2. Redesign

Businesses can redesign their product for increased customer sales and overall improved customer satisfaction with the use of design for the environment (DfE) and life cycle analysis (LCA) processes —both of which are excellent protocols to use. By redesigning products to a higher ecological design, products can have additional functionality and improved durability. Many times these products are less expensive to manufacture as well as being easier to use by customers. Some of these attributes can also deal with ease of disassembly, improved serviceability, and reduced overall environmental impact upon disposal.

3. Rethink

Companies now have the opportunity to rethink their markets by finding new ways to meet customer needs and wants. It is also possible to further segment or fragment markets using this approach. Examples include the myriad of opportunities now with the various types of sporting goods such as running shoes, fishing gear, skis, and other sports equipment. Customer demand remains high as everyone wants to have the most technologically advanced product at a competitive price. Many times these products also have improved service and warranties, including future upgrade options.

4. Re-create

Businesses can also re-create product waste streams into by-product waste streams of value that can be used as raw materials. Companies can work with other local businesses in their industrial park or community on these waste stream opportunities. Industrial symbiosis has now become a common strategy for many companies that can provide these attractive results. In trying to achieve their goals, companies many times find that their waste is a cash generator that can be used by another local business as a raw material. Waste process heat, waste metals, waste wood products, and waste plastic materials are all good examples of cash generating waste streams. Companies such as Herman Miller have also set the bar at a very high level by establishing zero waste goals in the future.

Gil Friend in his book *The Truth about Green Business*, states "you don't have to choose between making money and making sense." Friend identified some additional ways to become eco-efficient."[5]

- Looking at defect rates to ensure product defects are kept to a minimum
- Ensuring that over production is under control by reviewing work in progress and finished goods inventories
- Keeping excess transportation costs at a minimum, especially less than truckload (LTL) shipments
- Keeping delays in production and delivery at a minimum, especially with special orders

- Having excess inventories of raw materials and finished goods in a "just in time" controlled process
- Keeping overprocessing under control such as reworking batches
- Performing unnecessary actions in excess production processes, such as with sampling orders and requests

Results and Benefits

There are a number of well-established benefits to eco-efficiency that include both cost savings and reduced environmental impact. Some of the key benefits have been validated through case study examples from Bob Willard, author of the book *The Sustainability Advantage*.[6] These benefits that can be realized on the "bottom line" include:

- Reducing material intensity and material requirements for products
- Minimizing energy intensity of products and overall energy consumption
- Minimizing overall water consumption
- Reducing dispersion of toxic chemicals by shifting to green chemistry
- Reducing the carbon footprint and overall environmental impact of the business
- Undertaking recycling, waste minimization, and "zero waste" initiatives
- Maximizing the use of cost effective renewable energy and clean technologies
- Increasing the service intensity of products through leasing, take back, and upgrade strategies
- Extending product durability and warranty claims

Case Studies

West Michigan companies and organizations have been able to pursue eco-efficient strategies and achieve dramatic results. Nichols Paper and Supply conducted a warehouse lighting case study in 2008.[7]

In the study, which was part of the company's transition to sustainability and LEED certification of their existing facilities, it was determined their existing warehouse lighting was in need of updating. At the time their warehouse lighting included 205 Metal Halide High Bay lamps. Each lamp contained 68 milligrams of hazardous mercury and lasted, on average, 20,000 hours. The existing bulbs, which were very bright, had a downside issue. Whenever a bulb broke each required proper disposal and could not be sent to landfills due to possible contamination issues.

After studying the positives and negatives of their existing lighting, Nichols decided to replace the existing lighting with 1134 T-8 florescent tube lamps which each contained only 3.5 milligrams of mercury per bulb and would last an average 30,000 hours. While the new bulbs did not provide lighting as bright as the bulbs they were replacing, by installing more bulbs the facility only experienced a 1 percent reduction in overall illumination. In addition, the new bulbs can be disposed of in landfills.

As a result, Nichols has experienced a 72 percent reduction in mercury; a 30 percent savings on electricity bills; and a payback of less than 2 years with tax incentives.

Nichols Paper Lighting Comparison

	Type of Light	Hours of Use (per bulb)	Milligrams of Mercury (per bulb)
Old	Metal Halide High Bay Lamp	20,000	68
New	T-8 Florescent Tube Lamp	30,000	3.5

Source: Nichols Paper case study August 2009, adapted Norman Christopher, 2012.

Rapid-Line Manufacturing Inc., a full-service metal fabrication and tooling shop based in Grand Rapids, Michigan, worked with Steelcase and the Green Suppliers Network to help conserve natural gas, as energy costs had skyrocketed to $12,000 per month. The Green Supply Network was established by the U.S. Department of Commerce and the U.S. Environmental Protection Agency (EPA) to assist small businesses in staying competitive and reducing their environmental impact. Established in 1926, Rapid-Line, which prides itself in being one of America's most capable metal fabrication shops, has approximately 66,000 square feet of manufacturing space divided among three locations with employment of around 100 workers. To lower costs and increase efficiency, Rapid-Line installed additional insulation and industrial grade fans to redirect excess heat. Variable speed ceiling fans were installed to heat and cool the plant more efficiently. The results have been a reduction in annual natural gas consumption by 4,400 MCF with annual savings of $46,000.[8]

At the time, Rapid-Line President Mark Lindquist compared the company's efforts in reducing its natural gas consumption as "taking small bites out of an elephant." Further explaining it wasn't a matter of one single improvement but through a series of small steps that added up to significant savings. He also credits the value in using resources such as the Green Suppliers Network training and assistance. Mr. Lindquist fest these resources were worthwhile and provided fresh insights into how costs can be reduced in conjunction with sustainability best practices.

Rapid-Line Natural Gas Savings Improvements:

- Installed insulation and industrial-grade fans to capture and redirect excess heat from the paint line ovens out into the plant during cold weather days, thereby increasing the efficiency of the oven heating units while providing enough heat to eliminate the need for furnace heating.

- Installed two, 20-foot diameter, variable speed ceiling fans along with baffles on the outer plant walls to heat and cool the plant more efficiently.
- Installed additional insulation around the paint line wash tanks as well as a computerized washer controller to keep the water system at a constant temperature and three new sets of air knives in the dry oven to help dry parts more efficiently while using less energy.
- Monitored the external temperature of curing ovens in order to locate and fix thermal leaks.

Additionally, Rapid-Line Manufacturing has been certified in establishing an Environmental Management System (EMS) that is in conformance with International Environmental System Standard ISO 14000: 2004.

Sources: Rapid-Line corporate website and Green Suppliers Network case study.

Spectrum Health has also invested in new LED technology for their parking decks. Fifteen hundred LED light fixtures will provide light to over 1.25 million square feet and 3,500 parking spaces. Tom Theoret, Director of Facilities, acknowledged that Spectrum spent about $700,000 for the light fixtures and about $100,000 for installation while saving $170,000 per year on costs. The LED light fixtures offer a better glow, consume less energy, and require less maintenance.[9]

Call to Action

- Has the company identified "low hanging" high impact eco-efficiency opportunities that can provide significant incremental performance improvements to the bottom line?
- What are the strategies the company and business can undertake to reduce material intensity; water consumption; energy use; waste generation; air pollution, etc.?

- Does the company practice a life cycle analysis in its business and operations?
- Has the business looked at secondary eco-efficiency opportunities such as defect rates, production delays, excess inventories, production reworking sampling procedures, etc.?

References

1. Eco-efficiency: Creating More Value With Less Impact, http://www.wbcsd.org/web/publications/eco_efficiency_creating_more_value.pdf, accessed July 2011.
2. Eco-efficiency, http://www.iisd.org/business/tools/bt_eco_eff.asp, accessed August 2011.
3. Eco-efficiency: Creating More Value With Less Impact, http://www.wbcsd.org/web/publications/eco_efficiency_creating_more_value.pdf, page 17, accessed August 2011.
4. Eco-efficiency: Creating More Value With Less Impact, http://www.wbcsd.org/web/publications/eco_efficiency_creating_more_value.pdf, page 18, accessed August 2011.
5. Gil Friend, *The Truth About Green Business*, (Que, 2009).
6. Bob Willard: WBSCD: Eco-efficiency learning module 5.
7. Warehouse Lighting Case Study, http://www.enichols.com/images/stories/pdfdownloads/Case%20Study%20-%20Nichols%20Lighting.pdf, accessed August 2011.
8. Success Story – Rapid-Line Inc., www.greensuppliers.gov/results/rapid-line.html, accessed August 2011.
9. LED Lights save Spectrum $170,000, The Grand Rapids Press, www.mlive.com/business/west-michigan/index.ssf/2012/08/how_many_led_light_bulbs_does.html, accessed August 2012.

17. GREEN CLEANING

Introduction

The cleaning industry today is comprised of vast amounts of surface preparation chemicals, floor strippers, cleaning chemicals, waxes, and many more products. The manufacturers and distributors of these products have seen a significant environmental and economic impact with the consumption of water, use of electricity, dispersion of toxic chemicals released into the environment, and disposal into the landfill associated with these traditional cleaning products.

The well-established basic chemicals used for traditional cleaning applications can increase risks to the environment, to those who use them, and to the employees of the companies that produce them. A recent survey of 32 facilities found approximately 250 janitorial products in use. Some interesting statistics indicated that 7 percent of the cleaning chemicals should not have been used at all, as they have been shown to cause cancer. Additionally, 56 percent of the cleaning chemicals in use required extreme care as the ingredients have been shown to cause blindness; severe skin damage; can be absorbed through the skin; can be inhaled and can cause damage to the liver, kidneys, blood, and nervous system.[1]

Furthermore, there are a number of paper janitorial supply products that are disposable such as toilet tissue, towels, and napkins. These products are also consumed in large quantities and require significant amounts of water to be produced. Many of these products wind up just being disposed of in landfills after use.

As one can see, traditional janitorial cleaning chemicals and service products have a significant environmental impact. Many of the basic cleaning chemicals were developed from petroleum and inorganic based chemistry. Numerous petroleum based products were harsh to the environment and contained volatile organic compounds (VOC) that were potentially hazardous to human health. Direct contact to some of these products can lead to asthma. burns, eye damage, organ damage, and even cancer. Other acid and alkali based chemicals can also cause respiratory and skin damage if not used properly and handled with appropriate safety equipment.

The case studies in this chapter include Nichols Paper and Supply Company, Metro Health, and Wyoming Public Schools.

Description

Currently there has been a significant shift from these traditional chemicals to green chemistry. What is green chemistry? Are new green cleaning products certified? Are new equipment and application techniques required? These are some of the many questions that deal with the use of green cleaning chemicals, equipment, and paper supply products.

Green chemistry is defined by the EPA as: "The design of chemical products and processes that reduce or eliminate the use or generation of hazardous substances. Green chemistry applies across the life cycle of a chemical product including its design, manufacture, and use." It is also known as sustainable chemistry.[2]

There are 12 principles of green chemistry that have been highlighted by both the EPA and the American Chemical Society Green Chemistry Institute.[3]

Twelve Principles of Green Chemistry

	Principle	Definition
1	Prevention	It is better to prevent waste than to treat or clean waste after it has been created.
2	Atom Economy	Synthetic methods should be designed to maximize the incorporation of all materials used in the process into the final product.
3	Less Hazardous Chemical Syntheses	Wherever practical, synthetic methods should be designed to use and generate substances that possess little or no toxicity to human health and the environment.
4	Designing Safer Chemicals	Chemical products should be designed to effect their desired function while minimizing their toxicity.
5	Safer Solvents and Auxiliaries	The use of auxiliary substances (e.g., solvents, separation agents, etc.) should be made unnecessary wherever possible and innocuous when used.
6	Design for Energy Efficiency	Energy requirements of chemical processes should be recognized for their environmental and economic impacts and should be minimized. If possible, synthetic methods should be conducted at ambient temperature and pressure.
7	Use of Renewable Feedstocks	A raw material or feedstock should be renewable rather than depleting whenever technically and economically practicable.
8	Reduce Derivatives	Unnecessary derivatization (use of blocking groups, protection/de-protection, temporary modification of physical/chemical processes) should be minimized or avoided if possible, because such steps require additional reagents and can generate waste.
9	Catalysis	Catalytic reagents (as selective as possible) are superior to stoichiometric reagents.
10	Design for Degradation	Chemical products should be designed so that at the end of their function they break down into innocuous degradation products and do not persist in the environment.
11	Real-Time Analysis for Pollution Prevention	Analytical methodologies need to be further developed to allow for real-time, in-process monitoring and control prior to the formation of hazardous substances.
12	Inherently Safer Chemistry for Accident Prevention	Substances and the form of a substance used in a chemical process should be chosen to minimize the potential for chemical accidents, including releases, explosions and fires.

Source: http://www.epa.gov/greenchemistry/pubs/principles.html adapted by Norman Christopher, 2012.

Cleaning products produced with green chemistry can also be eco-friendly and made from plant materials, plant minerals, and natural ingredients. Natural plant-based cleaning chemicals are also biodegradable.

Currently there are a vast array of green cleaning products and green janitorial supplies available in the marketplace. They include:

- Paper goods including towels, tissues, and napkins
- Trash bags and liners
- Accessories such as brooms, dust pans, buckets, brushes, sprayers, dispensers, and mops, etc.
- Equipment including sweepers, vacuums, dryers, and carts
- Cleaning chemicals and disinfectants for many surfaces including porcelain, glass, plastic, wood, metal, tile, carpet, and other hard surfaces

Applications

Green cleaning chemicals are composed of plant-based organic and natural materials and do not contain harmful chemical and synthetic ingredients. They are considered good for the environment and good for health.[4] The primary question has always been will these green cleaning chemicals perform as well as traditional ones, and do they cost more?

Green cleaning products can be used on a number of hard surfaces including concrete, wood, glass, tile, and metal, etc. Additionally, there are a number of other different applications for green cleaning chemicals including auto and truck detailing; HVAC cleaning and maintenance; carpet cleaning; degreasing; car, truck, and fleet operations, etc.

Companies, when purchasing green chemicals, can now find certified products in the marketplace that are not harmful to those that use them, to the environment, and suitable for recommended surfaces and applications. Many times the purchased green chemical is also more effective than the standard detergent-based product.

The marketplace today now has many institutional green cleaning products that have been certified for use and application. However, product labeling is a major concern. Many times manufacturers represent their products as being "nontoxic" or "biodegradable." However, these claims can be misleading, incomplete, or even inaccurate. The only real way to ensure that these products are "safe for use" is to look at label ingredients, as well as review the Material Safety Data Sheets (MSDS).

Currently, several organizations have taken leadership positions in the certification of green cleaning chemicals. These organizations include Green Seal, a U.S. nonprofit corporation, and EcoLogo, a Canadian certification program that was developed and is Canada's equivalent of the U.S. EPA.

In 2005 Green Seal issued their GS-37 protocol, an environmental standard for general purpose, bathroom, glass, and carpet cleaners and has already certified hundreds of products in these categories. EcoLogo issued a set of CCD-146 standards in 2005 for "hard surface cleaners" that include: bathroom cleaners, boat and bilge cleaners, cooking appliance cleaners, degreasers, dish cleaners, industrial cleaners, vehicle cleaners, window and glass cleaners, etc. EcoLogo has also certified hundreds of products in their environmental standard product categories.

Today many of the green cleaners now contain hydrogen peroxide, citric acid, and thyme oil versus disinfectants and sanitizers that in the past contained ortho-phenylphenol, bleach, quaternary ammonium compounds, pine oil, and other asthmagens that were health and safely concerns.

There are a number of green cleaning practices that companies and organizations should consider when using green cleaning chemicals to optimize overall efficiency and use.

- Keeping excess dirt out by using entranceway floor mats.
- Training on proper cleaning and disposal procedures with employees and custodians that can help reduce injury, illness, and pollution.
- Reading and following labels and instructions especially with dilution as concentrated products can prove to be a health risk.
- Switching from ready to use products to those in concentrate form. Many times disinfectants are diluted one ounce of concentrate with 64 ounces of water resulting in 6 to 14 fold cost savings.
- Using precise metering dilution equipment rather than hand mixing chemical products that minimizes health risk exposure while ensuring accurate chemical mixing and measurement.
- Reducing the number of types, brands, and vendors of cleaning products. Lower cost chemicals and frequent product switching does not equate to lower system costs. Many times green chemicals can now be used universally across many surfaces and applications to optimize cost and use, especially for LEED and green building use.[5]
- Using microfiber mops and clothes. Microfiber products have negative electrical charge that attract and hold dirt more effectively and have been shown to reduce water use by nearly 95 percent. They also exhibit less human energy to use and, in the case of mops, are more ergonomically designed.
- Purchasing green cleaning chemicals through longer-term contracts. Today many schools consolidate product and service requirements through longer-term janitorial supply contracts.

Additionally, companies and organizations can now purchase other green products besides green cleaning chemicals including:

- Recycled paper products for office use

- Recycled disposable products such as tissue, napkin, paper towel, and toilet paper
- Less toxic pest control products
- Green building products such as paint, furniture, carpet, and insulation that meet green certification standards for off-gassing and recycled content
- Compostable tableware for office use

Results and Benefits

Why should my company switch to the use of green cleaning chemicals? [6]

- Building owners that adopt overall green building practices can certify their buildings under USGBC LEED rating system. These building owners are environmental stewards who will support the development and use of green cleaning products in their buildings. Companies that develop, market, and sell green cleaning chemicals that have demonstrated benefits will have distinct competitive advantages in the market place.
- Businesses and companies that switch to green cleaning chemicals can help protect the health and safety of building workers and occupants, as well as the maintenance service workers that use them.
- Switching to the use of green cleaning chemicals and janitorial supply products from the traditional cleaning chemicals and services is likely to be less costly when considering life cycle effects. Many traditional cleaning chemicals have been shown to be hazardous to occupants, including lost productivity as well as increased "sick days." Additionally, there are the associated costs of prescription and over-the-counter medicines to cover asthma, respiratory ailments, and other skin irritations.

- Selecting the use of green cleaning chemicals can also have a positive health effect on workers versus long-term exposure effects to traditional cleaning chemicals that might increase the risk of cancer and neurological disorders.
- Green cleaning chemical use can also reduce chemical inhalation exposure which has been shown to be 2-5 times more hazardous and occasionally much higher than outdoor exposure levels. People on average spend about 90 percent of their time in buildings.
- Companies that switch to green chemical use can also help building occupants and workers reduce exposure to contaminants that may be ingested through drinking water and food from cleaning product residues left on food preparation services and poorly cleaned hands.
- Skin absorption of specific traditional cleaning chemicals such as 2-butoxy ethanol is direct and toxic and is of concern to major body organs and the reproductive system.

Case Studies
Metro Health System

In 2002 Metro Health, after an analysis by its supplier Nichols Paper, implemented an extensive and comprehensive GlossTek green cleaning program throughout its Grand Rapids based hospital and healthcare system. One significant and easy change to make was switching to micro-fiber mopping which resulted in less use of water, reduced traditional chemical use, reduced packaging, and less employee injuries due to mopping.

Metro Health was able to reduce their cleaning expenses overall by 21 percent from 2002-2007. The hospital was able to save an estimated $12,000 per year and $61,000 over a five-year period. Metro Health anticipates a 23 percent cost avoidance by implementing green cleaning practices from the onset when they move into their new LEED approved health complex including the use of Green Seal and EcoLogo certified cleaning products.[7]

GlossTek Metro Health Analysis

Area	Discussion
Assumptions	• Two patient rooms @ 115 sq. ft. each • Initial room prep and regular room cleaning the same • Employee cost @ $9/per hour • GlossTek requires 3 patches over 5 years
Initial Application	• GlossTek 100 Kit 1.5 hrs/$242. • One gallon of traditional wax floor finish with dry time between coats .56 hrs/$108.46
Annual Upkeep	• GlossTek patch .75 hrs/$76.25 • One gallon of traditional stripper and one gallon of wax floor finish 2.33 hrs/$199.96 with dry time between coats, spray burnishing and recoat
Overall 5-Year Cost Comparison	• Traditional Wax Floor Finish = $908.30 • lossTek = $318.25 • Cost Savings = $590.05

Source: Metro Health System (http://www.enichols.com/images/stories/pdfdownloads/Case%20Study%20-%20Metro%20Health%20Green%20Cleaning.pdf).

Wyoming Public Schools

Nichols Paper also worked with Wyoming Public Schools, a suburb of Grand Rapids, by recommending switching from hand-stripping their floors to the use of an autoscrubber. Manufactured by Clarke, using what the company calls BOOST technology, the autoscrubber relies on water rather than floor-stripping chemicals and associated labor to prepare floors for polishing. The result was a less than 12-month return on investment along with the reduction of chemical odors, reduced risk of falls, and reduced overall use of chemicals. The savings in labor allowed the school district to reallocate labor to other important projects.[8]

Wyoming Public Schools

School	Historical Product Use	Actual Product Use
Rogers High School (office hall, cafe' hall, cafeteria)	• 60 gallons of product • 80 labor hours	• Zero product use • 10 labor hours
Oriole Park (hallways)	• 40 gallons of product • 120 labor hours	• 12 gallons of stripper • 68 labor hours
West Rogers Lane Park High School	• 40 gallons of product • 140 labor hours	• Zero product use • 22 labor hours
Total	• 140 gallons of product • 340 labor hours	• 12 gallons of stripper • 100 labor hours
Overall Savings		• 240 labor hours reallocated to other projects • 140 gallons of product @ $15/gallon or $2100 in product savings

Source: Wyoming Public Schools (http://www.enichols.com/images/stories/pdfs/wyoming-public-schools.pdf).

Call to Action

- What areas represent the largest consumption of cleaning and maintenance chemicals in company facilities and operations?
- Has the company switched away from petroleum and detergent-based chemicals to green biodegradable chemicals for maintenance and cleaning that offer improved health and safety?
- Does the business use eco-friendly green janitorial paper supplies, disinfectants, and other products for restrooms, break rooms, etc?
- Has the company looked at green cleaning and microfiber equipment for floor strippers and floor waxes?

References

1. Why Green?, http://www.advancedcleaningcontractors.com/, accessed August 2011.
2. Green Chemistry, www.epa.gov/greenchemistry/, accessed August 2011.
3. P.T. Anastas, and J.C. Warner, *Green Chemistry: Theory and Practice*, (Oxford University Press, New York 1998), pg 30. By permission of Oxford University Press.
4. Green Cleaning Chemicals, page 3, http://pdfcast.org/pdf/green-cleaning-chemicals, accessed June 2011.
5. Green Cleaning and LEED for Existing Buildings: Operations and Maintenance, http://www.issa.com//data/File/regulatory/Green%20Cleaning%20and%20LEEDEBOM_11%202%2009.pdf, accessed July 2011.
6. Health and Environmental Benefits of Green Cleaning Products, http://www.ewg.org/files/GreenCleanHealth.pdf.
7. Metro Health System, http://www.enichols.com/images/stories/pdfdownloads/Case%20Study%20-%20Metro%20Health%20Green%20Cleaning.pdf, accessed August 2011.
8. Wyoming Public Schools, http://www.enichols.com/images/stories/pdfs/wyoming-public-schools.pdf, accessed August 2011.

PART FIVE

INFORMATION TECHNOLOGY

Information technology (IT) has always been about the processing, manipulation, movement, dissemination, and storage of information and data. In the past IT was also seen as a cost center. It was usually managed by administration and management as key data and information was required in important areas such as sales, operations, and overall business performance. This information and data was developed and used on a consistent and predictable basis including the generation of monthly internal department reports to ensure that the company was on track. Information and data was also used to monitor performance against tactical and strategic business and organizational plans. Also, there was the ongoing need to develop monthly and quarterly performance and financial reports for internal shareholders regarding overall company performance. Businesses and organizations became comfortable with the use of these IT systems. Over the years these IT systems became legacies within the enterprise operations due to the marketplace requirement for real-time data. However, some businesses and organizations did not appreciate the rapidly changing landscape for information technology demand and use.

During the last few years, the use of the Internet and social media has been transforming our lives on a daily basis. In fact there are some estimates that in the future nearly 80 percent of all information will be accessible via the Internet. Today, it is becoming difficult just to have an e-mail address without using social media outlets like LinkedIn, Twitter, Facebook, and others for the additional communication and reach. We are now being driven by the future knowledge economy. The need for transparency and accountability in sharing information with both internal shareholders and external stakeholders and the global marketplace is also a prerequisite for the knowledge economy. Information must now be shared quicker and faster in more demanding response times. IT is now also being required to provide information and data with increased interaction between departments and with greater flexibility. These new directions for the IT department are also being driven by the demand for a more seamless flow of information and data, reduced transactions costs in the supply chain, and the need for overall greater connectivity and global reach.

The primary sustainable development best practice discussed in this section includes green office procedures and green information technology. Green computing describes how computer resources and accessory products can be more efficiently used and more effectively disposed of using environmental stewardship best practices. IT energy requirements have grown significantly in recent years as IT processing and data storage require cooler operating conditions 24/7. Department heads and purchasing managers can assist their business operations by establishing green office procedures and by purchasing energy efficient processing units, desktop computers, and peripherals.

18. GREEN OFFICE PROCEDURES AND GREEN IT

Introduction

In 2007 Americans threw out 2.25 million tons of discarded TVs, computers, peripherals, mice, keyboards, and cell phones commonly known as "e-waste."[1] Many of these products, while considered outdated, could have been recycled!

Additionally, the average U.S. worker uses approximately 12,000 sheets of paper per year. This equals two reams per month or on average six pages of paper wasted per day. The total cost for these pages wasted by the average U.S. worker is nearly $85.00 per year.[2]

It has also been shown that information technology (IT) data centers consume more energy per square foot than any other part of office buildings.[3]

With these data and statistics, there has been a significant increase in focus on establishing Green Office and Green IT procedures among businesses and organizations. These procedures have been shown to not only reduce environmental impact, but also to reduce GHG emissions, and to save money in a number of areas through Electronic Product Environmental Assessment Tool (EPEAT) purchasing guidelines.

In a recent study by Info-Tech Research Group entitled Greet IT: Why Mid-Size Companies are Investing Now, it was reported that there are a number of primary reasons why companies are implementing green IT procedures.[4] These marketplace drivers are:

- Decreased energy use
- Decreased use of consumables
- Increased features and functionality
- Decreased expenses and investments
- Increased requirements to meet customer demands

Office Depot is featured in the applications section and Deloitte/ Adobe Systems as the case study in this chapter.

Description

What are Green Office Procedures? The U.S. Chamber of Commerce Small Business Nation has coined the term "Go Green." Simply put, going green represents small and easy steps that businesses can take to "conserve energy, reduce pollution, and save money." The opportunities are endless to green your office spaces. These possibilities range from and include adjusting heating and lighting systems, purchasing more efficient Energy Star rated computer equipment, regulating computer monitors, disposing of electronic waste, using green recycled office supply products, and the list goes on.[5]

Green computing is a term used to describe how computer resources can be used more efficiently and effectively and disposed of using environmental stewardship best practices. Purchasing and IT departments can begin by looking at the types of computer and accessory products such as central processing units (CPUs), servers, and peripherals being purchased and whether they are more "environmentally friendly" and efficient than other models available. IT departments can also consider additional options and strategies such as virtualization software, power management programs, and electronic waste recycling procedures. Recently, the government proposed new compliance regulations that would pave the way for the certification of green IT data centers. Some of the preliminary criteria include: using low emission building materials; recycling electronic waste products and materials; and using more energy efficient and alternative energy technologies.[6]

There are many Green Office Procedures, tips, guidelines, and tool kits that have been generated and can act as a preliminary framework for businesses and organization.

An overall green office procedures framework or Green Office Guide[7] would address the following areas with potential strategies and actions:

1. Energy

- Switch, turn off, or power down computers and lights when not in use including sleep mode
- Use programmable thermostats
- Establish centralized printing, fax, and office hub operations
- Upgrade lighting such as with CFLs and T8 lighting systems
- Purchase energy efficient Energy Star equipment
- Conduct an overall baseline energy audit
- Add power strips
- Replace Cathode Ray Tube (CRT) monitors with flat screen monitors
- Keep computer equipment updated
- Use weather stripping and sealants to minimize window heat loss
- Use battery chargers wherever possible

2. Office-events and meetings

- Host "Green meetings" and events to create awareness about conserving resources, encouraging green office practices, and educating attendees
- Go paperless by limiting paper distribution and encouraging electronic reporting
- Reduce travel by hosting meetings and conducting candidate interviews via teleconferencing such as with Skype, ooVoo, and GoToMeeting programs
- Purchase local food where possible and select organic, fair-trade products
- Avoid using disposable food service ware and bottled water, juice, and other beverages

3. Transportation

- Request employees, as well as fleet drivers, to log fuel consumption and miles traveled for overall company and business transportation requirements
- Encourage the use of online calculators to track fuel consumption and convert to GHG emissions generated
- If fleet vehicles are owned, implement idle free policies
- Encourage cycling to work (and trips between facilities) by installing bike tracks and available locker space
- Provide alternative transportation options such as car pooling, car sharing, andimproved access to bus transit

4. Waste

- Provide separate waste bins for paper, plastic, recyclable containers, food, e-waste, etc., including reusable printer cartridges, in break rooms
- Discourage disposable coffee cups and bottled water use by offering reusable coffee mugs and water bottles or containers
- Print smarter and more efficiently by providing 1-2 energy efficient printers for the office and place in a central location: refill cartridges; setup default double-side printing; use misprints as printing drafts; discourage fax use, etc.
- Repair and/or donate old electronics
- Purchase environmentally friendly products for the office, kitchen, bathrooms, break room, etc., that are made from recyclable and/or compostable materials such as paper, plastic, and green cleaning supplies
- Use printing options such as green print or eco-print
- Establish green and sustainable purchasing policies

5. Water

- Educate workers and employees about excess water consumption and the use of nontoxic cleaning chemicals

- Report, repair, and replace leaky faucets, toilets and fixtures
- Collect plants that require less water and that help purify the air
- Install ways to capture rainwater for landscaping purposes
- Install low flush dual system toilets, as well as waterless urinals and low waterflow shower heads
- Turn off faucets completely ensuring no drips

There are a number of potential strategies and actions that can be undertaken by IT departments for green computing.[8] Some of these major areas of considerations include:

- Powering down CPUs, servers, and peripherals when inactive and not in use
- Endeavoring to undertake significant computer related tasks during intensive continuous blocks of time
- Powering up and down energy intensive peripherals such as laser printers according to need and tasks
- Using LCD monitors rather than outdated CRT monitors
- Using notebooks versus desktop computers wherever possible
- Using management software programs with features to turn off hard drives when not in use or inactive
- Minimizing paper use
- Properly recycling of waste paper
- Disposing of e-waste in compliance with local regulations
- Employing alternative energy resources for computers, work stations, networks, and data centers wherever feasible
- Establishing virtual conferencing capabilities and telecommuting strategies

Additionally, many companies today are also looking for additional green IT equipment strategies to increase efficiencies and improve overall IT effectiveness. Some of these strategies include:[9]

- Storage consolidation and server virtualization that allows for fewer devices running with the server room; decreased size of the server room; decreased energy demand to run servers and storage units; and operating server rooms at improved utilization rates
- Desktop virtualization projects resulting in decreased maintenance costs and installing "thin client" machines that reduce energy consumption and overall environmental impact
- Upgrading server rooms and building new server rooms because of overheating issues, capacity constraint, and energy use restrictions
- IT energy management projects that allow for reduced energy use, improved energy efficiency, and decreased power consumption
- Printer consolidation and reduction that enables paper, toner, ink, and energy savings
- Centrally managed PC power management strategies that use software to control energy and power settings
- Cloud computing shared services that provide flexible access to resources while minimizing capital expenditures
- Data center consolidation to increase overall IT efficiency and effectiveness. The Department of Navy has set a goal to reduce its IT budget by 25 percent during the next five years while still maintaining operational readiness and security requirements (www.doncio.navy.mil/TagResults.aspx?ID=102)
- Travel reduction programs such as with telecommuting and teleconferencing capabilities to cut down on cost and GHG emissions
- Disposal of electronics and e-waste and recycling IT equipment

Application

Green office and green IT procedures can be applied to all offices and departments, as well as information technology data centers and departments.

A plan-do-check-act (PDCA) approach and strategy should be undertaken.

1. Establish a "Green Team" comprised of departmental members, as well as other employees and users from other areas. Other suppliers and users in the supply chain should also be considered.

2. Conduct an overall environmental audit in these departmental areas. Some of these areas to be covered include energy use, water consumption, products purchased, waste generated, etc. This information will act as an overall assessment or baseline of information.

3. Analyze overall workflow including policies and procedures that are in place. Where are the bottlenecks? What are the key issues to be addressed?

4. Identify the opportunities. What is the "low hanging" fruit? Where are the major opportunities?

5. Determine the feasibility of addressing these opportunities. Is there a cost? How difficult will it be to address the issue and achieve positive results? What are the needed behavior changes?

6. Prioritize the opportunities and select which strategies and actions should be pursued based upon potential efficiencies and ability to achieve the specific goals and overall objectives.

7. Monitor the data, measure the performance, and report the overall progress.

It should be mentioned that establishing a sustainability champion in each office or departmental area is critical to achieving overall success. The key is to find someone who is passionate and trustworthy, who can implement these best practices on a day-to-day basis, and who can share employee sustainability success stories.

The office supply industry, including Office Depot, Office Max, and Staples, has been paving the way with green office best practices.

Office Depot, for example, has developed the top 20 Ways to Go Green at Work (and Save Money!)[10]

"Office Depot's three environmental aspirations are to 'Buy Green,' 'Be Green' and 'Sell Green.'"

According to the company:

- By "Buying Green," we have achieved the widest "green product assortment" in the office products industry - approximately 3,500 products with recycled content and hundreds more with other environmental benefits.
- By "Being Green," we have reduced our electricity use by over 20 percent and saved at least 21,000 tons of waste from landfills.
- By "Selling Green," we have helped many of our customers reduce the environmental impact of their business.

1. Go for "Greener Options" in the products you buy.

Office Depot offers remanufactured ink and toner cartridges that are less expensive than new cartridges. Energy Star office equipment has also been shown to save up to 75 percent in electricity use.

2. Buy remanufactured ink and toner cartridges.

The cost of Office Depot brand remanufactured ink and toner cartridges is on average 15 percent less than national brand competition and also comes with a 100 percent money back quality guarantee. It has been shown that one returned cartridge keeps approximately 2.5 pounds of metal and plastic out of landfills. Also one remanufactured toner cartridge saves about a half-gallon of oil.

3. Buy high Post-Consumer Recycled Content (PCR) paper.

Office Depot recycled papers have been shown to be just as bright and operate just as effectively in printers and copiers as their non-recycled papers, since they use 35 percent PCR content paper for internal operations. Purchasing recycled paper is a great place to start and begin to pave the way for future use of environmentally friendly products.

4. Develop a green purchasing policy.

Office Depot has established a comprehensive and complex paper purchasing policy, which has many opportunistic options.

5. Buy from companies whose supply chain gives you confidence.

Since the Office Depot environmental paper purchasing policy is one of the most comprehensive in the industry, they can guarantee that the paper you buy from them is from "well-managed forests." They have partnered with three major science-focused environmental groups to implement their policy including: Conservation International, Nature Serve, and The Nature Conservancy.

6. Use Digital Storage Solutions to cut paper and reduce clutter.

Office Depot advocates one 100 Megabyte zip drive can hold the contents of a four-drawer filing cabinet and that one CD-ROM can store nearly a roomful of paper! Zip drives, CD disks, and CD-ROMs are also becoming more convenient and easier to use.

7. Buy Energy Star rated electronic products.

Energy Star computers, printers, and other business machines are now the office norm and standard. They also power down when not in use and can use up to 75 percent less electricity compared to standard models. Energy Star products saved Americans more than $3.5 billion in energy costs by switching to "sleep mode" when not in use.

8. Use compact fluorescent bulbs.

Switching from incandescent bulbs to energy-efficient compact fluorescents offers a significant cost savings opportunity, as well as an efficiency opportunity of up to 75 percent energy savings for Energy Star qualified lights. Compact fluorescents can last over 10 times longer than incandescent bulbs, as well as reduce waste.

9. Invest in modular furniture.

Modular components are an essential platform for an environmentally efficient office design. Purchasing modular furniture can help mix, match, and grow your office today and tomorrow without the need to reinvest in an entirely new design. Modular furniture allows for simplified future purchasing decisions regarding upgrades, as well as reducing overall waste.

10. Use power strips to turn technology off when not in use.

Up to 75 percent of the electricity used to power office equipment may be consumed while the products are turned off! Plugging office equipment into a power strip that can be shut off each day is a simple and efficient way to address the issue.

11. Recycle your empty ink and toner cartridges.

Over 50 percent of all ink and toner cartridges were landfilled in the U.S. in 2005. Office Depot offers money back on certain eligible cartridges. They also send free ink jet and toner cartridge recycling boxes to individuals or organizations for shipment.

12. Recycle your office paper.

It is estimated that only about 50 percent of all the paper used in North America is recycled. Furthermore, there is a growing shortage of paper available for recycled products due to the increasing demand from Asian countries. Paper recycling programs are also considered very effective for both customers and employees, as well as the community at large.

13. Recycle other materials in your office.

Office Depot recycles plastic and glass bottles, aluminum cans, cardboard, computers, and cell phones. Many of the products used by businesses in their office operations can be diverted from landfills, recycled, reused, or donated.

14. Donate unwanted products and furniture.

Office Depot donated over $43 million worth of office supplies to charity through a variety of programs in 2005, including a partnership with Gifts In Kind International. Many major businesses have signed up with Gifts In Kind as it is easy, helps reduce waste, and helps your community!

15. Use daylight rather than office lighting whenever feasible.

Artificial lighting accounts for the equivalent of 25 percent of all electricity generation in the U.S. Lighting also consumes nearly half of all coal burned in the U.S. Just moving a desk toward a window saves money and cuts down electricity use. Natural lighting systems can save up to 40 percent of the electricity used in a typical office building.

16. Turn lights off when leaving your office or conference room.

By walking around any office building you most always will see lights left on in empty offices. A fact is that one 100 watt light bulb left on for one hour every day consumes 36.5 kilowatt hours of energy per year. If you multiply that by the millions of lights left on every day, it's quite obvious that to simply turn lights off when they are not needed represents an easy way to reduce our energy dependency.

17. Buy Renewable Energy Certificates to "offset" your energy use.

Energy generated from renewable sources (such as wind, solar, or geothermal) offers lower greenhouse gas emissions than fossil fuels. Purchasing Renewable Energy Credits can effectively offset some or all of the carbon dioxide your organization emits. Renewable Energy Certificates (REC) costs can vary depending on technology, volume, location, and compliance standards. As of October 2011 nationally sourced voluntary RECs sold for approximately $1 per Mwh.[11]

18. Help customers identify the environmentally preferable options across your product range.

Most companies that sell products have a broad portfolio of green certified products with some products being "greener" than others. Many times customers select green product options vs. traditional product offerings. Companies that promote the greener options in their product range can assist in winning loyalty among their customer base, finding new green customers, and helping reduce their organization's environmental impact.

19. Give reusable mugs instead of other promotional items to customers and prospects.

Just think if one of your customers or prospects buys three cups of coffee every workday for one year; that consumption represents over 600 coffee cups that could have ended up in the trash. If a disposable container were used, replacing that waste by selecting reusable coffee mugs with a company logo for promotional giveaways would help send a strong message. Mugs also tend to be kept and used regularly by recipients. Customers also tend to keep using durable mugs at their desks. Sustainable apparel is another consideration as dress shirts and polo shirts are now made from organic fibers such as organic cotton and bamboo.

20. Remember, it all starts with you and you are the power of one.

Take the lead and encourage others. The positive benefits of your actions will start to multiply if and when more people change to greener office options in their daily work life. You can start by making more personal decisions with the environment in mind and help increase awareness by spreading the word to your co-workers, department, management team, customers, suppliers, and your community network.

Results and Benefits

There are enumerable benefits to green office and green IT procedures and programs. These benefits include a reduction in:

- Electricity used for energy and lighting. It has been shown that power management technologies can deliver energy savings up to 50 percent in desktop PCs, 55 percent in fax machines, 65 percent in laser copiers, and 55 percent in copiers while generating up to 25 percent less heat.[12]
- Primary materials used in product manufacture
- Emissions generated, such as greenhouse gases
- Water consumption
- Hazardous waste generated
- Toxic materials used and generated such as with mercury
- Paper products consumed and used
- Travel costs
- Maintenance and management costs
- Number of servers and desktops used
- Future investments

These overall benefits contribute to significant overall cost savings reflected in the bottom line.[13]

There are many application areas for green IT best practices that businesses can capitalize on. In a report by the Info-Tech Research Group, over 65 percent of the mid-sized companies surveyed had successfully realized one or more of the major benefits of green IT.[4]

Case Study

Deloitte has undertaken an extensive study entitled Green IT: The Fast-track to Enterprise Sustainability concerning information technology (IT), and its importance to environmental impact and overall sustainability. They note that IT represents on average 30-40 percent of an organization's overall energy consumption and that energy consumption consumed by servers, both peripheral and related infrastructure equipment, doubled between 2000 and 2005. Furthermore, low-end servers accounted for 90 percent of the growth.

In the last few years reducing environmental impact has become an imperative for all information technology groups. Environmental sustainability now impacts IT in a number of areas including renewable energy, energy efficiency, energy conservation, climate change, GHG emissions, and green and LEED buildings.

Deloitte has developed best practices and an approach to fast-track the greening of IT in your organization.[14]

Greening Your IT Organization

Project Planning Phases	Implementation Steps	Change Steps
• Develop implementation roadmap • Develop high level environment and sustainability approach • Identify "quick hits" to drive short-term benefit • Review facility inventory and establish high level rationalization targets • Develop ROI model • Define the roadmap, implementation resources, and infrastructure	• Implement short-term/"quick-hit" initiatives • Establish initial business energy and emissions baseline and targets (carbon footprint) • Execute plan for data center footprint reduction (facility optimization) • Execute carbon trading and offset options • Track and measure "green" performance	• Build and execute IT organization awareness, training, and communication plan • Support authorship and publication of annual sustainability and corporate responsibility report • Establish and measure green IT culture

Focus areas are:

- IT Organizational Change (People)
- Green Engineering (Process)
- IT Enablers (Technology)

Deloitte and others point out some of the key strategies for greening the IT of organizations that include the evaluation of:

- System integration software for building and facility operations
- More efficient servers, micro-processors, and storage technologies, such as those with the Energy Star label and new Electronic Product Environmental Assessment Tool (EPEAT) standard managed by the Green Electronic Council
- Chips that run on multiple applications that reduce the number of individual servers that IT needs to display
- Power down technologies for systems when not in use
- More energy efficient work stations
- Establishing more efficient layout systems for racks and servers and improving airflow systems
- Consolidating multiple data centers and reducing data center space utilization
- Virtualization software for optimization

The Deloitte report discusses the efforts of GREEN-IT at Adobe Systems. They advocate that GREEN-IT equals greater profit through renewing IT's overhead costs, specifically in the area of energy use, conservation, and efficiencies.

Adobe has been able to proactively address overall enterprise sustainability with very positive results with a $1.4 million "green" renovation of their San Jose, California, headquarters including:

- 10.5 month payback
- 121 percent ROI
- Saved $1.2 million annually

Additionally Adobe Systems spent $153,095 on a relatively simple "Watt-Stopper" program that established outlets and power strips connected to motion sensors to turn off office equipment in rooms that are not occupied. The ROI on the project was 253 percent.[15]

Call to Action

- Has the company established "green office" procedures?
- Can the business develop and implement an incentivized "green office" awareness/certification program for employees and departments? Who are the department sustainability champions?
- Does the company showcase green office procedures by hosting "green" meetings, webinars, conferences, and programs?
- Does the company purchase "green office" products such as those from Office Depot, Office Max, Staples, etc.?
- Has the company set green computing targets such as power down management programs, virtualization, and electronic waste recycling programs, etc?
- Has the company established office voice communication procedures and programs such as Skype, ooVoo, or GoToMeeting, etc., to cut down on air travel costs and improve overall meeting efficiencies?

References

1. Wastes-Resource Conservation-Wastes and Materials-eCycling, www.epa.gov/osw/conserve/materials/ecycling/faq.htm, accessed August 2011.
2. Office Worker Paper Waste: Create Employee Awareness, http://hr.blr.com/HR-news/HR-Administration/HR-Strategy/Office-Worker-Paper-Waste-Create-Employee-Awarenes, accessed August 2011.
3. What is Green IT?, http://energypriorities.com/entries/2007/06/what_is_green_it_data_centers.php, accessed August 2011.
4. Green IT: Why mid-size companies are investing now, Info-Tech Research Group, www.greenbiz.com/research/report/2009/03/11/green-it-why-mid-size-companies-are-investing-now, page 5.
5. What is Going Green?, http://www.uschambersmallbusinessnation.com/toolkits/guide/P15_1001, accessed August 2011.
6. Green IT, www.webopedia.com/TERM/G/Green_IT.html, accessed August 2011.

7. The Green Office Guide, http://sbinfocanada.about.com/od/environmentbiz/a/greenoffice.htm, accessed August 2011, and Green Office procedures toolkit for Nova Scotia Municipalities.

8. Green Computing, http://searchdatacenter.techtarget.com/definition/green-computing, accessed August 2011.

9. Green IT: Why mid-size companies are investing now, Info-Tech Research Group, www.greenbiz.com/research/report/2009/03/11/green-it-why-mid-size-companies-are-investing-now, page 7.

10. Top 20 Ways to Go Green at Work (and Save Money!), http://www.community.officedepot.com/top20list.asp, accessed August 2011.

11. U.S. Department of Energy, http://apps3.eere.energy.gov/greenpower/markets/certificates.shtml, accessed March 2012.

12. Electronics Guide, http://www.bchydro.com/guides_tips/green-your-home/electronics_guide.html, August 2011.

13. Environmental Benefits of 2007 EPEAT Purchasing, http://www.telecommuting360.com/images/files/file/EnvironmentalBenefits2007ExecSumm.pdf, accessed June 2011.

14. Green IT – The Fast-track to Enterprise Sustainability, http://www.deloitte.com/view/en_US/us/Services/additional-services/sustainability-climate-change/ff962e45b72fb110VgnVCM100000ba42f00aRCRD.htm, accessed June 2011.

15. September 2006, CNN Money, "The Greenest Office in America," http://money.cnn.com/magazines/business2/business2_archive/2006/09/01/8384321/index.htm.

PART SIX

SUPPLY CHAIN MANAGEMENT

Supply chain management has always been a most critical component of any business or enterprise. In the past supply chain management was viewed primarily as "gate to gate" operations. Businesses were focused on inbound raw materials from suppliers that arrived at the "gate" or the manufacturing plant. Once the raw materials were processed and used in production for the manufacture of products, businesses then shifted their attention to the delivery of products to customers as they left the "gate" of the production facilities. With "gate to gate" operations, the key functions that businesses needed to excel in included inbound logistics, receipt of raw materials, manufacture, outbound product distribution, logistics, and packaging. This type of supply chain management fit closely with other "cradle to grave" strategies and approaches in the marketplace.

Today, businesses must look differently at supply chain management strategies. Greater importance needs to be given to more inclusive aspects of the supply chain including: research and development; supplier requirements including material requisition and supplier operations; operations and manufacturing such as inbound logistics and packaging; production; outbound logistics and packaging; product reuse; and disposal. Additional requirements have now surfaced in the need for environmentally friendly or "green" purchasing in order to reduce the overall environmental impact of the businesses' products and services.

There are two important sustainable development best practices that are explored in this section. Both of these practices look at the need and opportunity to minimize and reduce environmental impact, while improving overall economic and social returns. The first is sustainable supply chain management that goes beyond more inclusive supply chain management to also cover customer and consumer product in use and end of life product disassembly, remanufacture, and disposal techniques. Sustainable procurement looks at the purchase of products and materials that have high recycled content, generate low or minimal impact on the environment, are safe for employees to handle and nontoxic for the community at large, can ensure proper working and labor conditions for others, and can adhere to fair trade and enhance overall human rights.

19. SUSTAINABLE SUPPLY CHAIN MANAGEMENT

Introduction

Today every business and organization is focused on its supply chain. Many larger and mid-size businesses outsource a number of their operations, products, and components. Businesses are most concerned about the implications and risks that are also connected and associated with outsourced and overall supply chain management. The United Nations Global Impact group in communication with Business for Social Responsibility (BSR), the corporate responsibility organization, issued a study in 2010 entitled Supply Chain Sustainability — A Practical Guide for Continuous Improvement.[1]

"We live in an increasingly resource aware and resource constrained world. We need to live within our means and not borrow from the future. To build a sustainable tomorrow we need to make our supply chain sustainable today. In fact, I firmly believe that increased sustainability in the supply chain reduces risks and increases profits for all organizations and stakeholders."

—Kris Gopalakrishnan
CEO and Cofounder Infosys

The United Nations states that "supply chain sustainability is the management of environmental, social, and economic impacts and the encouragement of good governance practices, throughout the life cycle of goods and services."

Businesses today should focus not just on what raw materials, products, or components they purchase at a competitive price. They should also look at the companies they purchase from and what are the supply chain management practices and policies these companies have put in place. The opportunity exists today for customers and suppliers to collaborate mutually on improving supply chain management issues, and even with competitors on a broader market focus or industry basis and perspective.

"Business is often taking the initiative to move things forward – focusing only on the business case underplays the value that business is and should be providing in society and with regards to development."
—*Mads Ovlisen,*
Chair of the UN Global Compact Advisory Group
on Supply Chain Sustainability

Whirlpool Corporation is featured in the applications section, and Walmart, the Green Suppliers Network, and Ford Motor Company as case studies in this chapter.

Description

For companies engaged in the global marketplace, sustainable supply chain management is a prerequisite to overall success. Many tier two and three suppliers in the U.S. and Michigan are becoming well aware of these requirements through the purchasing patterns of the automotive and furniture industries.

Tier one furniture producers and suppliers such as American Seating, Haworth, Herman Miller, HON, Irwin Seating, Knoll, Steelcase, and others have set the bar quite high regarding their supply chain management requirements and standards. Their objectives are to ensure that TBL environmental, economic, and social value is created, grown, and sustained for both shareholders and stakeholders involved with manufacturing, selling, distributing, and servicing their products. Companies can ensure their long-term business viability, protect and enhance their brand image, and obtain a social license to operate in other countries by using effective sustainable supply chain management strategies.

Why is sustainable supply chain management so important? It is because sustainable supply chain management can address every stage in the life cycle of a product including all economic, environmental, and social impacts on employees, workers, users, residents, and the overall community in which the business operates.

The product life cycle includes research and development; raw material input such as those materials extracted from the environment; manufacturing; distribution; logistics; end-of-use; recycling; and final disposal.

Traditionally, a supply chain operational focus was known as a gate to gate strategy. This process basically looked at just inbound logistics and how raw materials arrived "at the gate" to product manufacture, and final outbound logistics as the finished product "left at gate." Essentially traditional supply chain operations involved primarily a manufacturing perspective and operations focus.

Sustainable Supply Chain Management

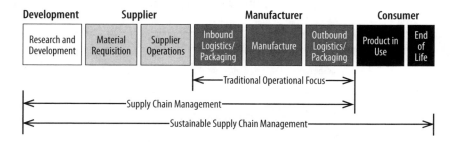

Source: Sustainable Supply Chain Management-How to Manage Triple Value Chains, adapted by Norman Christopher, 2012.

As the supply chain management process developed in the marketplace, next came the need to review material requisition and supplier operations as well as the product manufacture, inbound logistics and packaging, and outbound logistics and packaging. This supply chain management strategy focused not only on business operations, but also on the supplier and where the raw materials were sourced.

Today sustainable supply chain management has evolved into all aspects of the Sustainability TBL from a development, supplier, manufacturer, and consumer vantage point. Consumer aspects of product use, including product take back and product, reassembly, as well as final end-of-life disposal are also included.[2]

Application

Companies, businesses, and suppliers today are developing a common goal and mutual mindset about the importance of sustainable development best practices across all aspects of the supply chain. This cradle to cradle process starts with incoming raw materials from suppliers and includes the sale of finished goods to customers as well as end-of-life product disposals. With many suppliers there are various degrees and approaches of engagement that can be undertaken.

Sustainable Supply Chain Framework

The "What!" ⟶	Stage ⟵	The "Where!"
"Walk the talk"	**Leadership**	• Knowledge sharing with stakeholders, partners, and customers
Get "outside the box" and "raise the bar"	**Innovation**	• Sustainable product and process development best practices
Align with corporate strategy	**Integration**	• Supply chain operations • Procurement • Supplier management • Tactical and strategic plans
Measure and improve results	**Continuous Improvement**	• Supplier encouragement • Pollution prevention • Environmental management systems • Customer demands
Meet or exceed requirements	**Compliance**	• "Price of entry" • A given

Source: Sustainable Supply Chain Framework, source unknown, adapted by Norman Christopher, 2012.

Businesses and organizations can look at a sustainable supply chain framework approach to establishing overall objectives and specific goals or targets for their supply chain.[3] At a baseline level, companies need to ensure compliance and then seek continuous improvement in their supply chain operations. The next phase requires integration and alignment with business and company strategy and vision. Innovation and creativity follows as businesses seek to implement sustainable product and process development best practices. The final stage addresses overall leadership in sustainable supply chain management and sharing knowledge with others, even in some cases the competition.

At a macrolevel, supply chain management engagement can be broad and include setting mutual sustainable development expectations and contractual obligations, as well as asking suppliers to self-assess, audit, and monitor their TBL sustainability performance. At a deeper engagement level, companies and businesses can build trustful working relationships including mutual accountability and responsibility by addressing poor performance, offering training, and providing overall support to improve sustainability performances across all aspects of the supply chain. With a deep supplier engagement, both parties work together to address root causes, improve upon major issues, increase performance, and exhibit industry and market leadership.

The UN in their supply chain sustainability study developed the Ten Principles of the Global Compact and Supply Chain Sustainability.[4]

Source: Supply Chain Sustainability, page 6, accessed August 2011, adapted by Norman Christopher, 2012.

Ten Principles of the Global Compact and Supply Chain Sustainability

The Ten Principles	Relationship to Supply Chain Sustainability
Human Rights Principle 1: Businesses should support and respect the protection of internationally proclaimed human rights; and Principle 2: Make sure that they are not complicit in human rights abuses.	Companies have a responsibility to respect **human rights**. The baseline responsibility is not to infringe on the rights of others. In addition, businesses can take steps to support and promote the realization of human rights, and there are good business reasons to do it.
Labor Principle 3: Businesses should uphold the freedom of association and the effective recognition of the right to collective bargaining; Principle 4: The elimination of all forms of forced and compulsory labor; and Principle 5: The effective abolition of child labor; and Principle 6: The elimination of discrimination in respect of employment and occupation.	**Labor** conditions in offices, in factories, on farms, and at natural resource extraction sites such as mines, particularly in the developing world, often fall significantly below international standards and national regulatory requirements and can lead to serious human rights abuses. Businesses should strive to uphold international labor standards within their supply chains, including the right to freely choose employment, the freedom of children from labor, freedom from discrimination, and the freedom of association and collective bargaining. In addition, workers at times suffer from other labor rights abuses, including excessive work hours, degrading treatment by employers, and inhibited movement. In order to avoid complicity in abuses, businesses should seek to ensure that they do not cause the rights of workers and others affected by their supply chain to be infringed upon, including the right to freedom of movement, freedom from inhumane treatment, the right to equal pay for equal work, and the right to rest and leisure. The rights of all peoples to work in safe and healthy working conditions are critically important as well. Companies can also begin to address human rights (including and beyond labor conditions) alone or by working with partners to promote a broad range of human rights such as gender equality and access to education and health.
Environment Principle 7: Businesses should support a precautionary approach to environmental challenges; Principle 8: Undertake initiatives to promote greater environmental responsibility; and Principle 9: Encourage the development and diffusion of environmentally friendly technologies.	**Environmental** impacts from supply chains are often severe, particularly where environmental regulations are lax, price pressures are significant, and natural resources are (or are perceived to be) abundant. These impacts can include toxic waste, water pollution, loss of biodiversity, deforestation, long-term damage to ecosystems, hazardous air emissions, as well as high greenhouse gas emissions and energy use. Companies should engage with suppliers to improve environmental impacts, by applying the precautionary approach, promoting greater environmental responsibility, and the usage of clean technologies.
Anti-Corruption Principle 10: Businesses should work against corruption in all its forms, including extortion and bribery.	The significant **corruption** risks in the supply chain include procurement fraud and suppliers who engage in corrupt practices involving governments. The direct costs of this corruption are considerable, including product quality, but are often dwarfed by indirect costs related to management time and resources spent dealing with issues such as legal liability and damage to a company's reputation. Companies that engage with their supply chains through meaningful anti-corruption programs can improve product quality, reduce fraud and related costs, enhance their reputations for honest business conduct, improve the environment for business, and create a more sustainable platform for future growth.

Life Cycle Impacts: A Natural Step Case Study

	Raw Materials	Production	Packaging and Distribution	Use and Peripherals	End-of-Life
SC1: Scarce materials taken from the earth	6	5	6	5	2
SC2: Man-made persistent materials	6	2	2	2	2
SC3: Degradation of nature	5	5	6	5	6
SC4: Meeting people's needs	6	5	6	5	2
Key					
1	2	3	4	5	6
Good	Quite Good	Okay	Quite Bad	Bad	Don't Know
All answers positive. System condition met	Mostly positive responses. System condition mostly met	Some positive responses. System condition on the way to being met	Mostly negative responses. System condition mostly not met	All answers negative. System conditions not met	Insufficient knowledge to make reasonable judgment

Source: A Natural Step Case Study, ICI Paints, Bob Willard slide, adapted by Norman Christopher, 2012.

These ten principles deal with major areas such as human rights, labor, the environment, and anti-corruption. By adhering to and embracing these sustainability supply chain guiding principles, businesses and suppliers can become more socially responsible and better global citizens within global, regional, and local communities as evidenced by supporting human rights; eliminating forced child and compulsory labor; supporting a precautionary principle to the environment; promoting environmental stewardship; implementing the use of clean technologies; and working against all forms of corruption.

All of the above principles provide positive impact to the sustainability TBL and can be monitored for performance and progress.

ICI Paint, a global leader in paints and coatings, has also established a Life Cycle Impact Analysis using the Natural Step[5] for their products across the supply chain.

The above life cycle impact analysis allows a company to score itself on overall sustainable supply chain management in five areas including raw materials, production, packaging and distribution, use, and end-of-life. Each of these areas can be measured in the four steps of the overall Natural Step process. There is also a rating system key that ranges from don't know > bad > ok > quite good > good that can establish baseline performance and determine areas of needed performance.

West Michigan based Whirlpool Corporation has had an active environmental stewardship focus that dates back to the 1970s when the company was one of the first to set up an Office of Sustainability that originally focused on product development. In 2003 the company started tracking GHG emissions and by 2008 Whirlpool had nearly 600 products qualifying for the Energy Star lable. In 2005 Whirlpool started to redesign its supply chain and has made continued progress in recent years. By 2009 their supply chain network had 20 plants in North America, 11 in Europe, 3 in Latin America, and 6 in Asia. Their sustainable supply chain platform consisted of the following Initiatives:[7]

- **Environmentally sustainable and cleaner buildings:** With the acquisition of Maytag, Whirlpool consolidated and rationalized buildings and replaced outdated distribution centers with newer energy efficient facilities that contained energy efficient lighting, skylights, motion sensors, etc., to conserve energy and reduce GHG emissions. With the Maytag acquisition, Whirlpool was able to reduce overall factory distribution centers (DCs) by 17 percent, reduce distribution DCs by 33 percent, and reduce local DCs by 32 percent, while adding 10 new energy efficient regional DCs in North America.

- **Cleaner vehicles:** Whirlpool also replaced many of its internal combustion powered clamp trucks with electric units and models. By switching to electric forklift trucks the company also reduces GHG and NO emissions as well.

- **Optimized distribution and logistics:** Whirlpool also is making a concerted effort to ship full truckload quantities of its appliances in a more eco-conscious manner. The company is also now targeting rail transport including the use of intermodal containers to better maximize weight shipments. These efforts have also cut down on GHG emissions.

- **Fuel-saving initiatives:** When rail shipments are not feasible, Whirlpool still has to rely on truck transport. They have initiated several strategies, such as fuel surcharge policies that provide incentives for carriers to implement fuel saving efficiencies. Whirlpool pays a rate of 6 miles per gallon regardless of the truck's actual mileage per gallon. Additionally Whirlpool has implemented technology that helps carriers "triangulate" their shipments and deliveries to assist carriers in bringing back no empty trailers. Moreover, the company has advocated "drop and hook" practices whereby carriers can drop off empty trailers and pick up full loaded trailers from the warehouse. Whirlpool has also joined the SmartWay Transport Partnership in 2007, an initiative started by the EPA to increase energy efficiency while also reducing GHG emissions.

Whirlpool has made a long-term commitment to developing a sustainable supply chain management system. The company is persistent in its monitoring and reporting of the overall results and benefits.

Source: www.dcvelocity.com/print/article/2009010greenlogistics/.

Results and Benefits

There are enumerable benefits to sustainable supply chain management strategies.[6] Many of these benefits can be quantified and qualified using the appropriate sustainability indicators, metrics, and performance measures:

- Increased productivity
- Greater efficiencies
- Higher quality of goods and services such as less repair, longer durability, and less maintenance
- Increased innovation and creativity
- Improved competitive advantage
- Minimized risk and liabilities
- Focused cost savings and avoided costs
- Enhanced brand reputation
- Better customer loyalty
- Implemented international standards and sustainability indexes
- Accountable sustainability reporting

Case Studies

In 2009, Walmart established a Supplier Sustainability Assessment that all suppliers were required to answer and report back to Walmart.[8] Walmart manufactures no products on their own and has committed to a sustainability vision with broad significant impact sustainability goals. In order for Walmart to achieve their stated sustainability goals and milestones, the company had to develop and implement a rigorous and rigid sustainability assessment for all suppliers.

The sustainability assessment is constructed in four primary areas including:

- Energy and climate
- Material efficiency
- Nature and resources
- People and the community

Walmart Sustainability Assessment Questions for Suppliers

Energy and Climate Reduce energy costs and greenhouse gas emissions	1. Have you measured and taken steps to reduce your corporate greenhouse gas emissions? (Y/N) 2. Have you opted to report your greenhouse gas emissions and climate change strategy to the Carbon Disclosure Project (CDP)? (Y/N) 3. What are your total annual greenhouse gas emissions in the most recent year measured? (Enter total metric tons CO_2e, e.g., CDP 2009 Questionnaire, Questions 7-11, Scope 1 and 2 emissions) 4. Have you set publicly available greenhouse gas reduction targets? If yes, what are those targets? (Enter total metric tons and target date, e.g., CDP 2009 Questionnaire, Question 23)
Material Efficiency Reduce waste and enhance quality	5. If measured, please report total amount of solid waste generated from the facilities that produce your product(s) for Walmart for the most recent year measured. (Enter total lbs) 6. Have you set publicly available solid waste reduction targets? If yes, what are those targets? (Enter total lbs and target date) 7. If measured, please report total water use from the facilities that produce your product(s) for Walmart for the most recent year measured. (Enter total gallons) 8. Have you set publicly available water use reduction targets? If yes, what are those targets? (Enter total gallons and target date)
Nature and Resources High quality, responsible sourced raw materials	9. Have you established publicly available sustainability purchasing guidelines for your direct suppliers that address issues such as environmental compliance, employment practices, and product/ingredient safety? (Y/N) 10. Have you obtained 3rd party certifications for any of the products that you sell to Walmart? If so, from the list of certifications below, please select those for which any of your products are, or utilize materials that are, currently certified.
People and Community Vibrant, productive workplaces and communities	11. Do you know the location of 100% of the facilities that produce your products(s)? (Y/N) 12. Before beginning a business relationship with a manufacturing facility, do you evaluate their quality of production and capacity for production? (Y/N) 13. Do you have a process for managing social compliance at the manufacturing level? (Y/N) 14. Do you work with your supply base to resolve issues found during social compliance evaluations and also document specific corrections and improvements? (Y/N) 15. Do you invest in community development activities in the markets you source from and/or operate within? (Y/N)

Source: Sustainability Index, accessed July 2011 Walmart, adapted by Norman Christopher, 2012.

Today many other companies, as well as other industry trade associations, are reviewing this sustainability assessment in regards to their own business operations and overall industry performance.

Another good example is the Green Suppliers Network (GSN) which is a collaboration between the U.S. Environmental Protection Agency (EPA), the Department of Commerce, and large manufacturers in West Michigan. The Green Suppliers Network focuses on sustainability and targets key suppliers to help reduce energy consumption, minimize carbon footprints, increase productivity, and establish creativity and innovation. Some of the West Michigan manufacturers include: Metalworks, Light Corporation, Steelcase Inc., Cascade Engineering, Herman Miller Inc., and DuBois Chemical. [9]

To date the GSN has conducted 162 interviews with the following results:

Lean and Green Opportunities	Savings
Annual Environmental Savings Identified	$35,875,940
Annual Lean Savings Identified	$40,513,447
Other Cost Savings	$1,146,947
Total Annual Potential Impact Identified	$77,536,334
One Time Lean Impact Opportunities	$40,687,072

Environmental Outcomes	Conservation/Reduction
Energy Conserved (MM BTU)	2,957,509
Energy Conserved (KWH)	866,542,434
Water Conserved (gal)	95,712,052
Air Emissions Reduced (lbs)	44,204,941
Solid Waste Reduced (lbs)	10,103,413
Hazardous Waste Reduced (lbs)	270,605

Environmental Outcomes	Conservation/Reduction
Toxic/ Hazardous Chemicals Reduced (lbs)	181,150
Waste Pollution Reduced (gal)	20,898,354

Source: Green Suppliers Network accessed 2011, adapted by Norman Christopher, 2012.

The Ford Motor Company has also taken a sustainability best practices approach to their supply chain management activities. The basis of their work with supply centers around the Ford Code of Human Rights, Basic Working Conditions, and Corporate Responsibility which was formally adopted in 2003.[10] In 2010 Ford's annual purchases were $65 billion and in 2011 they grew to $75 billion.

Ford has a three-pronged approach to supplier engagement in sustainability issues such as human rights, working conditions, and corporate responsibility:

- Build capabilities at individual supplier facilities such as assessment, training, and remediation programs
- Engage with strategic suppliers regarding corporate alignment and enhancement activities
- Collaborate with peers in the automotive industry such as the Automotive Industry Action Group (AIAG) on a broad range of sustainability platforms and developing common approaches

The Ford results to date have been impressive:

- More than 1,750 Ford suppliers have been trained on human rights and environmental sustainability issues
- $6.14 billion of goods and services were purchased from approximately 400 minority or woman owned suppliers in 2011
- 128 suppliers representing roughly 60 percent of annual purchases regarding GHG emissions were surveyed with an 86 percent response rate. Over 50 percent reported their GHG emission publicly

Call to Action

- Has the company determined and addressed the "Triple Bottom Line" of environmental, social, and economic impact in the various stages of the business supply chain?
- How does the business look at its supply chain–from a traditional operational focus, supply chain management perspective, or a sustainable "Triple Bottom Line" supply chain management strategy?
- Has the company engaged with any of its suppliers regarding improved supply chain management strategies? What are the specific areas of concern and opportunities?
- What are the key life cycle impacts to be addressed in the supply chain from raw materials purchased to end-of-life product disposal?

References

1. Supply Chain Sustainability, www.unglobalcompact.org/docs/news_events/8.1/Supply_Chain_Sustainability.pdf, accessed August 2011.
2. Adapted from Sustainable Supply Chain Management-How to Manage Triple Value Chains, www.triple-innova.de/images/stories/publikationen/triple%20innova%20scmbrochure.pdf, accessed August 2011.
3. Adapted from Sustainable Supply Chain Framework, source unknown.
4. Supply Chain Sustainability, page 6, www.unglobalcompact.org/docs/news_events/8.1/Supply_Chain_Sustainability.pdf, accessed August 2011.
5. A Natural Step Case Study, ICI Paints, Bob Willard slide, Life Cycle Impact.
6. http://www.triple-innova.de/images/stories/publikationen/triple%20innova%20scmbrochure.pdf, accessed August 2011, adapted by Norman Christopher.
7. The Greening of Whirlpool's Supply Chain, *DC Velocity* magazine, January 2009, http://www.dcvelocity.com/articles/20090101greenlogistics/, accessed June 2012.
8. Walmart Sustainability Index, http://walmartstores.com/sustainability/9292.aspx, accessed July 2011.
9. Green Suppliers Network, Results, www.greensuppliers.gov/results/index.html, accessed August 2011.
10. Ford Motor, Sustainability 2011/12, http://corporate.ford.com/microsites/sustainability-report-2011-12.

20. SUSTAINABLE PROCUREMENT

Introduction

For decades many companies have thought about their purchasing function as being tasked with acquiring raw materials, along with needed goods and services for company and business operations while achieving the "best deal at the fairest price." In order to obtain the "best deal at the lowest price" companies needed to negotiate relentlessly, leverage purchase volumes, and buy through consortium strategies often with long-term contracts. In some cases companies even developed hedging purchase strategies for key raw materials due to anticipated significant price fluctuations and predictable shortages.

Today, many companies and businesses have begun to adapt sustainable procurement, sustainable purchasing practices, or environmentally preferred purchasing policies to help protect the environment, as well as meet organizational needs with competitively priced raw materials, finished goods, and services.

Sustainable procurement policies and procedures are applicable to all organizations, businesses, and enterprises including those from within the public, private, academic, service, or municipal sectors. Today, organizations are finding that they can achieve strategic goals, as well as fulfill obligations and responsibilities to improve upon environmental, economic, and social impacts with sustainable procurement best practices.

The case studies in this chapter include the West Michigan Sustainable Purchasing Consortium and Grand Valley State University.

Description

Environmentally Preferable Purchasing (EPP) is defined as "those products or services that have a lesser or reduced effect on human health and the environment when compared with competing products and services that have the same purpose."[1]

Sustainable procurement encompasses purchasing guidelines and procedures that address and integrate all aspects of the TBL including involvement in the protection of the environment, quality of life improvement through social responsibility, support of energy and resource conservation, optimization of cost efficiencies, and improvement of quality of goods and services.

Sustainable purchasing therefore addresses:[2]

- Economic considerations including the best value for the price, quality, availability, and functionality of the product or service.
- Environmental aspects and characteristics, such as green procurement, green label and certification, restoration and remediation of the environment, life cycle analysis, and cradle to cradle processes.
- Social implications including purchasing decisions that help reduce or eliminate poverty, improve working and labor conditions, adhere to fair trade, and advance human rights.

In today's marketplace, global sustainability impact issues, especially those in emerging, developing, and third world countries, are driving companies to think differently and change their purchasing strategies regarding sourcing raw materials, products, services, components, and assemblies.

Some businesses might expect that the organization would sacrifice or give something up by adhering to green procurement and sustainable purchasing requirements. A defined strategy that phases in sustainability and green procurement requirements in bids, contracts, and requests for quotations (RFQs) should be developed and implemented to maximize bottom line results.

An appropriate place for a business to start is to assess sustainability throughout the procurement cycle. The Waste & Resources Action Programme in the United Kingdom government established a guide entitled Sustainable procurement—making it happen.[3]

Sustainable Procurement Strategy Approach

Source: Sustainable procurement – Making it Happen, adapted by Norman Christopher, 2012.

By establishing reviews or gates after each phase of the procurement cycle, sustainability issues and concerns such as those with environmental, social, and economic impact can be monitored, addressed, and evaluated. The company can then decide on how best to implement green and sustainable procurement best practices across its business operations moving forward.

Application

The key in establishing a successful green purchasing and sustainable procurement policy is the ability to develop a deep dialogue and conversation with suppliers about new marketplace procurement requirements including an environmental impact of the business and its supply chain partners.

What are the steps a business can take to implement sustainable procurement best practices?[4]

Step 1: Map future procurements: Determine potential label and warranty claim issues that may affect your products, and if your green and environmentally-friendly purchasing guidelines would help provide a positive impact.

Step 2: Identify the most important categories of procurement for targeted action, using a risk-based approach and strategy.

Step 3: Develop a clear plan for reducing environmental impacts, with targets that will enable monitoring of progress and performance.

Step 4: Within each business unit that should respond, make a designated individual responsible for looking at future contracts with regard to a selected category for "greening" (for example, construction projects).

Step 5: Set up an early dialogue with the supplier base on future requirements, including environmental performance. In parallel, acknowledge your policy on sustainable procurement to vendors and supply chain partners.

Step 6: Performance requirement definitions should be developed and implemented to encourage suppliers to come forward with more sustainable product options.

There are various impacts of environmental and social conditions that can be addressed by sustainable procurement.

Green Purchasing and Sustainable Procurement

Areas	Example
Minimizing Impacts of the Supply Chain	• Social; e.g., socio-economic • Environmental; e.g., eco-efficiency
Minimizing Impacts of the Product/Service	• Waste and water minimization • Energy savings • Air pollution and emissions reduction
Purchasing Resource Efficient Products	• Recycled content products • Energy efficient equipment and vehicles • Reduced material content products

These primary areas include: minimizing detrimental social and environmental impacts in the supply chain; minimizing impacts of the product or service, such as with waste minimization and renewable energy use; and buying more resource efficient products such as those with higher recycled content, greater fuel efficiency, and improved energy performance as well as overall eco-efficiencies.

There are a number of products that are now subject to mandatory environmentally preferable purchasing (EPP) requirements. These products include:

- Recycled content products
- Alternative fuel vehicles and alternative fuels
- Energy efficiency and Energy Star products
- Bio-based products
- Non-ozone depleting substances
- EPA priority chemicals

Sustainable purchasing guidelines have now been established by the Federal Government's Green Procurement Preference Program.[5] In addition, the U.S. Environmental Protection Agency (EPA), U.S. Department of Energy (DOE), and the U.S. Department of Agriculture (USDA) have developed a Green Products Compilation (GPC) covering 18 different categories.[6]

Listed below are some of the sustainable purchasing practices that a company can put in place along with some of the basic sustainable and green products that can be targeted for procurement.[7]

- Building construction interior, and furnishing products including timber or wood from Forest Stewardship Certified (FSC) and Sustainable Forest Industry (SFI) suppliers
- Organic, locally farmed fresh produce that meets sustainable agriculture requirements
- Products packaged in recyclable, reusable, and returnable containers
- Rechargeable batteries
- Energy Star equipment products such as PCs, laptops, printers, scanners, faxes, copiers, and monitors
- Biodegradable cleaning products made from green or sustainable chemistry, such as phosphate free detergents, CFC free aerosols, and vegetable oil based products
- High recycled content office supply products, such as paper, printer cartridges, etc.
- High recycled oil content or vegetable oil based lubricants and greases

What then are some of the products that can be purchased today that contain the highest percentage of recycled or recovered materials? Examples include:

- Construction products such as building insulation
- Landscaping materials including compost made from food waste and other recyclables
- Non-paper office products such as binders, pens, pencils, and paper clips
- Paper products including copier paper, tissue paper, and packaging

- Park and recreation materials such as running tracks and sports fields made from crumb rubber, and fencing from recycled plastics
- Transportation products such as traffic cones and barricades
- Vehicle products including lubricants, coolants, and retread tires
- Miscellaneous products such as mats manufactured from recycled rubber, carpet tiles, and pallets

What then are the right questions to consider before purchasing a product?[8]

- Where and how was the product manufactured? What were the labor conditions during manufacture?
- Is the product less hazardous than others?
- Is it reusable and more durable?
- Is it made from recycled materials? Is the product made from virgin materials really needed? Is the recycled version just as good?
- What happens to the product at the end of its useful life? Can it be recycled? Will the manufacturer take the product back? Does it require special disposal techniques?
- Does the product conserve energy or water? Did the product take less embodied energy and water to produce than others?
- Is the product made from bio-based or plant-based raw materials? Is it biodegradable?
- Does the product meet a green or sustainability standard or certification?
- Does the product have reduced or recycled content packaging?
- What is the total cost of ownership for the product?
- Does the product have a positive social impact consideration?

Results and Benefits

Why is environmentally preferable purchasing and sustainable procurement important to a company and its business operations? Sustainable procurement can:

- Provide a significant positive impact on the environment as well as having tangible social and economic benefits as well
- Reduce company risk and exposure concerns
- Minimize further environmental degradation
- Encourage the development and sale of more sustainable ethically manufactured products made from clean technologies
- Enhance the growth of local communities and overall improved labor and working conditions if the product was made in developing or third world countries
- Identify less hazardous products that can reduce regulatory compliance liability, lower disposal costs, while improving overall worker safety
- Create eco-efficiencies and cost savings through the purchase and use of energy efficient and water conserving products
- Use reusable, refillable, more durable, easily repairable products that create less waste and are more cost effective in the long run
- Purchase products that are manufactured locally so that an additional 30 cents on every dollar is kept in the local area versus similar products purchased that are manufactured outside the local area

Case Study

The Responsible Purchasing Network (RPN) is an international network of buyers dedicated to socially responsible and environmentally sustainable purchasing. In 2006, to establish a regional responsible purchasing network, Delta Institute and Sustainable Research Group (SRG) spearheaded the West Michigan Sustainable Purchasing

Consortium (WMSPC) to provide West Michigan businesses the opportunities to easily purchase environmentally preferable products at cost-competitive prices, as compared to traditional products.[9] Its goals include improving regional environmental quality and steward-ship, growing local economies, and increasing social responsibility particularly for those in the West Michigan area. Other key members include the City of Grand Rapids, Steelcase, Grand Valley State University, and the Van Andel Institute.

The organization's first cooperative purchasing project organized a contract that would save its members money on recycled content copy paper. Between October 2008 and May 2009, members purchased 103,705 pounds of recycled content paper. These purchases helped save hundreds of trees and kept tens of thousands of pounds of emissions and solid waste out of the environment.

After collaborative input, the requisite contract specifications for this paper included:

- Green Seal label
- Minimum 30 percent post-consumer content
- Chlorine free
- Jam-free guarantee
- Locally sourced
- Fixed price for one year

Between October 1, 2008 and May 12, 2009, WMSPC members purchased 89,505 pounds of 30 percent post-consumer content (PCC) paper and 14,200 pounds of 100 percent PCC paper with the following benefits and savings:

Using the Paper Calculator and figures from the EPA, compared to the same purchase volume made from virgin forest resources, WMSPC purchases saved:

- 70 tons of wood or 531 trees
- 192,934 gallons of water or 6,890 loads of laundry in a high efficiency washing machine

- 371,000,000 BTUs energy or four average size homes powered for a year
- 42,652 pounds of greenhouse gas emissions or 13 cars off the road for a year
- 22,498 pounds of solid waste or one garbage truck full of trash

Source: Environmental impact estimates were made using the Environmental Paper Network Paper Calculator. For more information visit www.papercalculator.org.

WMSPC determined paper provided a good opportunity for success in launching the consortium because it is relatively simple to swap one kind of paper for another. Other products, such as janitorial supplies and de-icing chemicals, would require more collaboration between end-users and purchasing departments as the environmentally preferable products in these categories require application techniques that differ from conventional products.

"Cooperative green purchasing saves money and reduces environmental impacts. We are proud of the action WMSPC members are taking to improve our local watershed."

—*Mary Ellen Mika, WMSPC Co-chair, Steelcase*

Over the past five years Grand Valley State University has also begun to formalize local green and sustainable procurement practices.

In the 2008 GVSU Sustainability Indicator Report[10] green and sustainability procurement included the following categories:

- Recycled content products
- Environmentally preferable products and services
- Bio-based products
- Energy and water efficient products
- Alternate fuel vehicles
- Products using renewable energy
- Alternatives to hazardous or toxic chemicals

The total amount of purchased green and sustainable products and services totaled $42.6 million and was broken down as follows:

Construction and Renovation	$39,447,085
IT Equipment	1,294,833
Office Supplies and Equipment	844,591
Janitorial Supplies and Equipment	434,880
Recycled Paper products	405,891
Travel and Entertainment	95,315
Ground Supplies and Equipment	81,321
Branded Specialties	47,222
Miscellaneous	30,157
Total	$42,634,073

Source: GVSU, Sustainability Indicator Report, 2008, adapted by Norman Christopher, 2012.

Additionally minority vendor purchases totaled over $8.4 million in 2008 as well.

Call To Action

- Does the company have an established "environmentally preferable green purchasing product policy" (EPP)?
- Has the company addressed a sustainable product and services procurement policy that factors in economic, social, and environmental implications and impacts?
- Does the company address either green or sustainable procurement into "request for quotation" or "request for proposal" (RFQ or RFP) or bids?

- Does the company pursue sustainability grants on its own or in partnership with others that embrace green and sustainable purchasing guidelines?
- In what product area could the company begin to purchase environmentally preferred products (e.g., office supply, office furnishings, and accessories? local food? green cleaning? etc.).

References

1. Environmentally Preferable Purchasing, www.epa.gov/epp/pubs/about/about.htm, accessed June 2011.
2. What is Sustainable Procurement, http://beta.ungm.org/SustainableProcurement/default.aspx, accessed August 2011.
3. Sustainable procurement – making it happen, page 9, www.idea.gov.uk/idk/aio/69979, accessed August 2011.
4. Sustainable procurement – making it happen, page 5, www.idea.gov.uk/idk/aio/69979, accessed August 2011.
5. Green Procurement & Federal Policy, www.aqd.nbc.gov/GreenProcurement.aspx, August 2011.
6. http://www.gsa.gov/portal/content/198257, accessed July 2012.
7. Adapted from Green Living, http://www.brighthub.com/environment/green-living/articles/82195.aspx, www.brighthub.com/environment/green-living/articles/127578.aspx, accessed June 2011.
8. Wastes — Resource Conservation Comprehensive Procurement Guidelines, www.epa.gov/epawaste/conserve/tools/cpg/products/index.htm, accessed July 2011.
9. Adapted from: TerraChoice, http://terrachoice.com/2010/01/08/a-look-back-at-2009/, accessed August 2011.
10. RPN Case Study: Buying Green Paper on Cooperative Contracts, www.responsiblepurchasing.org/includes/cooperative_contracts.pdf, accessed August 2011.
11. Grand Valley State University, 2008 Sustainability Indicator Report, http://www.gvsu.edu/cms3/assets/1ACDDEF0-A15A-67B1-F268BE06B2416593/documents/2008/2008-sustainability-indicator-report.pdf, accessed August 2011.

PART SEVEN

FINANCE AND ACCOUNTING

Businesses will not make any significant business decisions without first obtaining the approval from the finance and accounting department. What do the "numbers" say? Having their sign-off and approval is critical for any business project or activity to move forward. Many times, however, these decisions are made on short-term horizons and payback periods to ensure optimum business performance. Are there accounting procedures that can address sustainable development projects? Can these sustainable accounting procedures create additional value for the company?

Traditionally, finance and accounting has been a very tactical function. In the past, finance and accounting was viewed as a closely held and associated department that always reported to top management. Many times finance and accounting generated reports on a monthly and quarterly basis for executive management, shareholders, and board members. "Closing the books" was a term that all department heads and managers were familiar with as all transactions were needed to be finalized at the end of each month. These types of reports were transaction based and usually confidential in nature and not widely disseminated.

Today, finance and accounting has taken on a much different role. The function is now being viewed as a strategic asset for business or enterprise. New software systems are now available for finance and accounting departments to use. Several of these new systems include Enterprise Resource Planning (ERP) systems that enable businesses and organizations to better coordinate and link all departments in resource planning and Enterprise Risk Management (ERM) systems that allow companies and organizations to better manage risk and improve their overall business decisions. Finance and accounting along with IT departments must be adaptable, flexible, and proactive today in support of top management. But more importantly, the finance and accounting function is now being called on to create additional value for the business or enterprise, not just keep tabs on what is being spent and how many sales are being generated.

There are several key applied sustainability development best practices that are now available for businesses to implement. First is sustainability accounting that now enables companies to generate both environmental and social profit and loss statements, not just traditional company profit and loss (P&L) statements. Next is the increasingly important area of value creation. Understanding all hidden costs is critical for businesses. An important principle of value creation is to minimize total costs as well as accrue total savings. More importantly, the reinvestment of these accrued savings helps make sustainability sustainable in the future. Sustainability risk management looks at risk management from a broad and comprehensive aspect including environmental, supply chain, product and technology, litigation, reputation, and physical risk perspectives. Because of the increasing demand for companies to be more transparent, open, and accountable to both shareholders and stakeholders, many companies now issue sustainability, social responsibility, or corporate responsibility reports that openly report the company's environmental, social, economic, and community impact. Most of these reports are issued on an annual basis.

21. SUSTAINABILITY ACCOUNTING

Introduction

Today, businesses and organizations are required to manage and report on more and more of their operations, both internally and externally. Many of these reporting procedures and compliance requests are the result of transparency issues, as well as the need to specifically monitor the environmental, social, and economic sustainable development impacts of their business operations. Companies and enterprises are being driven by their customers to communicate more information about their overall operations and become more open in their disclosures and reporting.

What then is sustainable accounting? The working definition of sustainable accounting is: "The generation analysis and use of monitored environment and socially related information in order to improve corporate environmental, social, and economic performance."[1]

A more complete definition should really be "sustainable financial accounting" since it focuses only on monitored performance and results and is differentiated from other broader forms of sustainability TBL reporting which include other metrics and measurements.

The case study in this chapter includes the Dow Chemical Company.

Description

Sustainable financial accounting management is a growing area of importance for businesses and organizations as TBL focus is now being given to overall assets, risks, liabilities, efficiencies, and value creation regarding economic, environmental, and social impact and performance. Some of these important accounting and reporting areas that involve sustainable development best practices include:

- Environmental risks and liabilities
- Greenhouse gas emissions inventory and reporting
- Short-term eco-efficiencies
- Long-term creation of value
- Socially responsible investing (SRI)
- Environmental return on investment (EROI)
- Social return on investment (SROI)
- Environmental and social project accounting
- Corporate Social Responsibility (CSR)
- Sustainability reporting, such as with the Global Reporting Initiative (GRI) guidelines

Companies and businesses are now faced with how to manage sustainability internally within operations of their organizations, as well as how to account for and report on sustainable development progress externally among shareholders and community stakeholders.

Paulina Arroyo, a PhD student at HEC Montreal, provided an abstract on the three dimensions of a sustainable management accounting system including a conceptual framework.[2]

The conceptual framework for a sustainable accounting system can be envisioned in the following context:

The firm or company addresses specific sustainability issues and concerns through the use of the values and guiding principles that they have established. Management sets strategic sustainability goals for its stakeholders to be achieved based upon its capabilities and competencies. Competitive strategies and actions are also developed. TBL sustainability results and progress is then monitored within the sustainable management accounting (SMA) system. Financial performance, such as economic value added (EVA), return on investment (ROI), and return on capital employed (ROCE) are reported back internally to management.

Today, many companies also develop a TBL sustainability report based on social and environmental, as well as economic performance. Multinational companies usually develop this report according to Global Reporting Initiative (GRI) protocol. This report is made available to both internal shareholders as well as external stakeholders. The SMA system has become a critical resource in the development of these internal and external sustainability accounting and reporting functions through data management systems and the use of sustainability performance measurements and metrics.

Sustainable Accounting System: Conceptual Framework

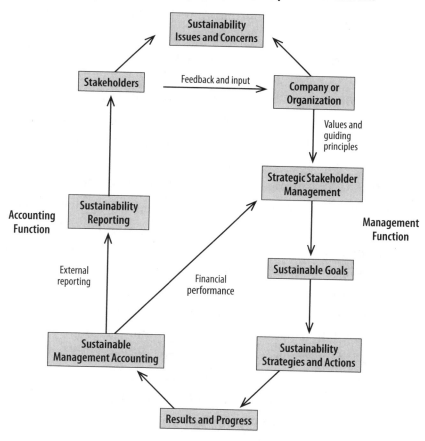

Source: The Three Dimensions of a Sustainable Management Accounting System, http://www2.hec.ca/en/cicma/communications/conferences, August 2011, adapted by Norman Christopher, 2012.

As we have already emphasized, sustainable development project activities, strategies and actions encompass environmental and social impacts as well as overall economic performance. Therefore, environmental and social impacts must be incorporated into costing systems, capital budgeting systems, and performance measurement systems. The degree to which a company or business implements sustainable development management, accounting, and performance systems, is really dependent upon the overall use of applied sustainable development best practices. In order to maximize returns and performance with sustainable development best practices, businesses should look to generate both short-term efficiencies, as well as long-term value creation which include avoided costs, and reduced risks and liabilities.

The importance of accounting from a TBL sustainability perspective, however, cannot be overlooked. These sustainability accounting procedures can ensure transparency about social, environmental, and social impacts; consistency in terms of indicators and performance measurements that are used; improved decision making for management teams; and participation and empowerment of organization departments and employees.

A four step systems process that uses life cycle analysis (LCA) can be utilized to help account for and report the performance of sustainable development best practices.[3]

1. Define the cost objectives and targets as being a discrete project using TBL economic, social, and environmental impact.
2. Specify the project scope including parameters and boundaries to track TBL impacts over full-life cycles including disposal and End-of-Life (EoL).
3. Identify all impacts of the project including cost objectives and targets. These targets would include economic, environmental, and social TBL impacts, including metrics such as resource use, energy intensity, embedded water content, etc.

4. Monetize the project across all areas of the TBL to capture both short-term efficiencies and long-term value for the overall project.

It should be noted, however, that there are a number of hidden costs associated with both environmental and social cost structures.[4] Take for example hidden costs contained in environmental accounting and reporting. Some of these hidden and external costs for environmental projects and operations could include:

- Value of lost inputs and thruputs
- Incremental cost of substitutes
- Environmental cost associated with intermediates
- Environmental product specifications
- Water and power for consumption
- Use of on-site power generation
- Cost of environmental labeling
- Take back of used packaging or recycled materials
- Compliance monitoring requirements and reporting systems
- Environmental related maintenance of equipment
- Legal expenses
- Permitting time and fees
- Environmental training and development
- Environmental driven research and development
- Non-product outputs
- Process penalties and shut downs
- Depreciation
- Environmental auditing

Application

Tracking down and reporting on these hidden and external costs will enable companies to better develop a total cost analysis for specific products and core technology platforms. How then can a company or business develop environmental or social financial statements that take into account environmental and social costs as well as environmental and social benefits? Pro forma environmental and social performance statements can be established for company projects. These financial statements are in essence cost/benefit analyses. Sigma in the U.K. developed project accounting formats for both environmental and social sustainability.[5]

Pro Forma Environmental Financial Statement

Item	Description	Amount ($)
1	**Environmental Costs** **Operating expenditures:** Staff costs and proportion of personnel costs allocated to environmental management; staff training and development	
2	**Suppliers:** Environmentally related operational costs	
3	**Regulatory:** Includes federal, state, and local compliance fees; waste management fees, land fill costs; air emission changes	
4	**Other:** Includes contributions to environmental organizations	
5	**Capital Expenditure – Depreciation** "End of pipe" costs and Integrated capital expenditures	
	Total Environmental Costs	
6	**Environmental Benefits** **Revenue Generated:** Revenue from recycled waste; additional revenue from environmental price premium; additional business generated due to environmental reputations; additional revenue generated from DfE products, etc.	
7	**Cost Savings:** Reduced waste disposal costs; energy conservation savings; packaging cost reductions; recycled product savings	
8	**Regulatory Costs Avoided:** Landfill savings; waste effluent savings; penalties/fines avoided etc.	
9	**Grants/Subsidies Received:** Enhanced capital for energy efficiency, waste minimization, etc.	
	Total Environmental Benefits	
	Net Environmental Costs/Benefits	

Source: The Sigma Guidelines-Toolkit, adapted by Norman Christopher, 2012.

A Pro Forma Social Financial Statement could be developed as follows:

Item	Description	Amount $
1	**Social Costs** **Operating expenditures:** Staff costs and proportion of personnel costs allocated to socially related activities; staff training and development	
2	Suppliers: Socially related operational costs including additional cost of social/ethical specification on products or suppliers	
3	Regulatory: Federal, state, local, and socially related taxes and penalties and fines for non-compliance such as insurance contributions; health and safety fines, etc.	
4	Community: Contributions to community activities such as grants and in-kind contributions, etc.	
5	**Capital Expenditure – Depreciation** Socially related investments including health and safety; staff welfare and recreation facilities, etc.	
	Total Social Costs	
	Social Benefits	
6	**Revenue Generated:** Additional revenue from social/ethical price premium; additional business generated due to social/ethical reputation	
7	**Cost Savings:** Savings from low staff turnover; savings from reduced insurance due to improved health and safety record; increased staff productivity and morale	
8	**Regulatory Costs Avoided:** Penalties/fines avoided	
9	**Grants/subsidies received:** Revenues received and recognitions for the organization and individuals; grants for disability access, etc.	
	Total Social Benefits	
	Net Social Costs/Benefits	

Source: The Sigma Guidelines-Toolkit, adapted by Norman Christopher, 2012.

Businesses and organizations can generate both "pro forma environmental financial statements" and "pro forma social financial statements" for sustainable development best practice project activities. Through the use of the pro forma financial statements, businesses can account for specific sustainable development costs, monitor overall project progress, and report performance and overall project success to internal shareholders and external stakeholders. Many times cost saving efficiencies and value created from sustainable development projects are then reinvested into additional projects that meet similar criteria.

Results and Benefits

Sustainability Finance Accounting

There are a number of related benefits for companies and businesses that implement sustainability finance accounting best practices.[6] These benefits and opportunities include:

- Collecting information and data on environmental and social sustainability related costs and expenditures, then linking these costs to financial statements.
- Providing environmental and social sustainability pro forma financial statements that highlight net benefits, short-term efficiencies and long-term value created by implementing these projects.
- Illustrating that TBL economic, environmental, and social costs, budgets and expenditures can decrease over time by using sustainable development best practices.
- Highlighting social and environmental risks linked to financial performance that can be minimized and mitigated by implementing sustainable development best practices.
- Identifying stakeholder relationships in the supply chain that present sustainability risks as well as sustainability benefits.
- Encouraging the development of trustful working relationships and partnerships among shareholder and stakeholder organizations.
- Improving investor returns as well as shareholder and stakeholder value.

- Becoming a more responsible corporate citizen in the community by addressing key TBL environmental, economic, and social sustainability issues with a holistic systems approach.

Sustainability finance accounting is still a relatively new financial accounting methodology. One of the more significant challenges is to be able to appropriately measure and document the short-term and long-term effects of sustainability on both shareholder and stakeholder returns. However, with the use of sustainability financial accounting, businesses and organizations are able to reduce environmental impact, address social responsibility issues, while being able to achieve improved financial performance. The keys to success include the use of life cycle analysis (LCA) and total cost accounting measures and techniques.

Case Study

The Environmental Accounting Project was developed by the EPA in 2000 and focused on the lean and green supply chain. The project established a practical guide for materials managers and supply chain managers to reduce costs and improve financial performance. The guide was known as *The Lean and Green Supply Chain: A Guide for Materials Managers and Supply Chain Managers to Reduce Costs and Improve Environmental Performance.*[7]

Many companies, both large and small in size, found that pursuing environmental accounting procedures, or what is now known as "green accounting," created significant cost savings through lean and green opportunities across the supply chain. Additionally these companies were also able to increase their competitiveness.

These environmental accounting activities were able to enhance performance in a number of areas such as:[8]

- Reducing the amount of waste of maintenance, repair, and operating (MRO) materials through improved inventory management control
- Decreasing scrap material costs and losses
- Lowering training and development costs relating to hazardous and toxic materials, as well as introducing new procedures and processes
- Decreasing the use of hazardous and toxic materials through more efficient materials and tracking procedures
- Decreasing the use of paints, solvents, and other chemicals used in the supply chain
- Recovering and reusing valuable materials through effective product take back programs

Back in 2000 a number of companies had already been able to quantify some of these benefits:

- General Motors had adopted reusable containers programs and reduced disposal costs by $12 million.
- Commonwealth Edison, a major utility, had been able to realize $25 million in financial benefits through more efficient and effective resource management utilization.
- Anderson Corporation, a major supplier of windows, achieved internal rates of return (IRR) of greater than 50 percent for their sustainability projects.

In the mid-1990s, Dow Chemical was facing a decision regarding a polymer based coating material "DuraGen," a name given to the case study. During the manufacture of this product, two volatile organic components (VOCs) were released. Dow was concerned about the generation of waste as well as pending regulations about the Clean Air Act and needed to refine their accounting practices to determine whether to further upgrade the production unit or shut down the operation.[9]

Standard cost information about the product determined that 32 percent of manufacturing costs were found to be in the conventional environmental category and focused mainly on waste disposal and treatment.

The accounting system at that time was determined to be comprehensive and the corporate policy was to trace all costs, including environmental expenditures. However, it was determined that out-of-pocket/controllable and historical/noncontrollable costs were not generated in the reporting process. Different costs were pooled and then allocated.

However, upon further investigation it was determined that the direct variable costs for DuraGen were approximately 40 percent and the indirect variable costs, mainly utilities, were approximately 10 percent. Furthermore, there were significant other costs including solvent recovery, the use of a proprietary reactant, as well as research and development (R&D) and maintenance costs that would actually increase the range of total environmental costs for DuraGen up to 20 percent.

Summary of Environmental Costs for DuraGen

Cost Item	Estimated Environmental Percentage	Environmental Cost as a Percentage of Total
Wastewater treatment	100	2.2
Water waste	100	0.6
Solids (wastewater)	100	0.1
Rubbish to pit	100	0.2
Incinerator (liquids)	100	<0.1
Incinerator (solids)	100	0.1
Nonhazardous landfill	100	<0.1
Depreciation	0-10	0-0.6
Totals		3.2-3.8
Other Potentially Relevant Costs		
Solvent	0-100	0-1.0
Proprietary reactant	0-100	0-14.9
Maintenance	0-100	0-10.9
R&D	0-100	0-1.3

Source: Green Ledgers Case Studies in Corporate Environmental Accounting, The World Resources Institute 1995, adapted by Norman Christopher, 2012.

The EPA in 1995 also developed an introduction to "Environmental Accounting as a business management tool." They tested a number of examples of environmental costs that could be incurred by firms and broke them down by category.[10]

The following chart describes many of the associated costs that should be evaluated to fully represent a total cost analysis for a sustainable development project.

Potential Hidden Costs

Regulatory Costs	Upfront Costs	Conventional Costs	Back-End Costs	Voluntary Costs
• Notification	• Site studies	• Capital equipment	• Closure/	• Community relations
• Reporting	• Site preparation	• Materials	decommissioning	• Monitoring/testing
• Monitoring/testing	• Permitting	• Labor	• Disposal of	• Training
• Studies/modeling	• R&D	• Supplies	inventory	• Audits
• Remediation	• Engineering/	• Utilities	• Post-closure care	• Qualifying suppliers
• Record keeping	procurement	• Structures	• Site survey	• Reports; e.g.,
• Plans	• Installation	• Salvage value		environmental
• Training				• Insurance
• Inspections				• Planning
• Manifesting				• Feasibility studies
• Labeling				• Remediation
• Preparedness				• Recycling
• Protective equipment				• Environmental
• Medical surveillance				studies
• Environmental				• R&D
insurance				• Habitat/ecosystem
• Financial assurance				• Protection
• Pollution control				• Landscaping
• Spill response				• Financial support
• Storm water				
management				
• Waste management				
• Taxes/fees				

Contingent Costs	Image and Relationship Costs
• Future compliance costs • Penalties/fines • Response to future • Releases • Remediation • Property damage • Personal injury damage • Legal expense • Natural resources damages • Economic loss damages	• Corporate image • Relationship with customers • Relationship with investors • Relationship with insurers • Relationship with staff • Relationship with suppliers • Relationship with lenders • Relationship with community • Relationship with regulators

Source: An Introduction to Environmental Accounting As a Business Management Tool: Key Concepts and Terms, adapted by Norman Christopher 2012.

Call to Action

- Has the company ever developed an environmental P&L statement for an important environmental project or program?
- Has the company ever developed a social P&L statement for an important social responsibility project?
- Does the business look to integrate sustainability accounting into its management function to improve overall decision making for the company?
- Does the company incorporate life cycle analysis (LCA) and total cost accounting principles into its business operations?

References

1. The Sigma Guidelines–Toolkit, http://ojs.acadiau.ca/index.php/ASAC/article/viewFile/948/825, accessed August 2011.
2. The Three Dimensions of a Sustainable Management Accounting System, http://www2.hec.ca/en/cicma/communications/conferences paulina_arroyo_actecolloque_10-11avri08_Sprott%20Doctoral%20Symposium.pdf, accessed August 2011.
3. Accounting for sustainable development performance adapted from: http://www.cimaglobal.com/Documents/Thought_leadership_docs/Tech_ressum_accounting_for_sustainable_development_performance_Jan2007.pdf.

4. Green Ledgers: Case Studies in Corporate Environmental Accounting, page 21, http://pdf.wri.org/greenledgers_bw.pdf, accessed August 2011.

5. The Sigma Guidelines-Toolkit, www.projectsigma.co.uk/toolkit/SigmaSustainabilityAccounting.pdf, accessed August 2011.

6. Adapted from: Sustainability Accounting, http://www.constructingexcellence.org.uk/pdf/fact_sheet/sus_accounting.pdf, accessed August 2011.

7. The Lean and Green Supply Chain: A Practical Guide for Materials Managers and Supply Chain Managers to Reduce Costs and Improve Environmental Performance, US EPA and Office of Pollution Prevention and Toxics, EPA 742-R-00-001; January 2000, accessed August 2011.

8. The Lean and Green Supply Chain: A Practical Guide for Materials Managers and Supply Chain Managers to Reduce Costs and Improve Environmental Performance, page 31-33, http://www.epa.gov/oppt/library/pubs/archive/acct-archive/pubs/lean.pdf.

9. Green Ledgers Case Studies in Corporate Environmental Accounting, The World Resources Institute, 1995.

10. An Introduction to Environmental Accounting As a Business Management Tool: Key Concepts and Terms, page 9, www.greenbiz.com/sites/default/files/document/016F13759.pef, accessed August 2011.

22. SUSTAINABILITY VALUE CREATION

Introduction

For many companies managing business operations has been a difficult challenge on a day-by-day and month-by-month basis. In essence, the challenge in running a successful business has been one of getting beyond mere existence and overall survival of the fittest. The keys to the success of companies and businesses who have weathered the storm has been how they have retooled their processes. Their business operations are more lean and fit. Now these companies can look to the future for improved performance through increased efficiencies and value creation as the economy begins to rebound.

Sustainable value creation is the ability of a business or company to deliver shareholder value with above average returns and performance using a balanced portfolio approach with a consistency of purpose over a longer period or time frame. If businesses are able to create sustainability value, their overall economic, environmental, and social impact will benefit over the short- and long-term as well.

Dupont is featured in the applications section, BHP Billiton, Steelcase, and Comerica Bank are the case studies for this chapter.

Description

One of the first strategic approaches to develop longer-term sustainability performance and value creation was the use of the Balanced Scorecard. This scorecard was briefly mentioned in a previous chapter.[1]

The Balanced Scorecard concept established the ability for companies to integrate and promulgate objectives, measures, targets, and initiatives across four key areas including financial, internal business processes or operations, learning and growth, and customers.

305

By monitoring and measuring data in these areas, businesses were able to improve their operations and overall business performance.

Balanced Scorecard

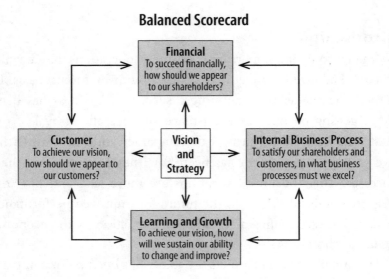

Source: R. Kaplan and D. Norton 1992 the Balanced Scorecard measures that drive performance Harvard Business Review: Jan-February, pages 71-79, adapted Norman Christopher, 2012.

Over time, the Balanced Scorecard has enabled companies to be introspective and discerning while assessing and reflecting upon their overall vision and mission, as well as their business operations:

- How should we define successful economic, environmental, and social performance to our internal shareholders and external stakeholders?
- What sustainable development best practices should we embed into the organization and excel at?
- How can sustainability be used to change and improve our organization or company?
- How can sustainable development best practices be used to improve upon brand image and reputation to gain more customers and increase sales?

How then is sustainable value creation any different than a Balanced Scorecard? Value creation takes into account both sustainability efficiencies and sustainability effectiveness over the short and longer-term. Value creation accounts for cost savings as well as avoided costs, along with risk mitigation. Jay Carney in his book *Gaining and Sustaining Competitive Advantage* highlighted a number of opportunities where sustainable value creation goals and strategies can be developed.[2]

Industry Structure and Strategic Operations

Industry Structure	Opportunities

Fragmented industry	• Consolidation:
	  - Discover new economies of scale
	  - Alter ownership structure

Emerging industry	• First-mover advantages:
	  - Technological leadership
	  - Preemption of strategically valuable assets
	  - Creation of customer switching costs

Mature industry	• Product refinement • Investment in service quality • Process innovation
Declining industry	• Leadership strategy • Niche strategy • Harvest strategy • Divestment strategy
International industry	• Multinational opportunities • Global opportunities • Transnational opportunities
Network industry	• First-mover advantages • Winner-takes-all strategies
Hyper-competitive industry	• Flexibility • Proactive disruption

Source: Jay B. Carney, Gaining and Sustaining Competitive Advantage, adapted by Norman Christopher, 2012.

Creating sustainable value can be developed as a strategy over any stage of an industry or business life cycle whether it is emerging, growing, maturing, or declining as well as whether the industry or market is fragmented, international or global, or highly competitive in nature.

How then can a company create value for its goods and services regardless of the life cycle stage of the industry or business?

Where are the opportunities for companies to create additional value for their product goods and services?

- Avoid costs
- Accrue savings
- Gain higher productivity
- Achieve better quality
- Minimize waste
- Obtain higher durability
- Develop less liabilities
- Make improved decisions
- Create local jobs
- Decrease consumption
- Improve assets productivity
- Reuse materials and recycle
- Improve safety
- Improve toxicity
- Increase local economic development
- Reinvest cost savings and efficiencies

As can be seen, there are a number of opportunistic sustainable development best practices that can be implemented across all TBL impact areas.

Some of these sustainable development best practices create "tangible" long-term TBL value and benefits that can be quantified such as: increased asset productivity; avoided costs; increased worker productivity; less defects and waste; decreased consumption and overall resource recovery.

However, there are also other "intangible" TBL values and benefits that are more difficult to quantify and qualify when using sustainable development best practices. Examples of this type of value that could be created through the use of applied sustainability best practices include: positive employee morale, risk avoidance, and the ability to make improved management decisions. Employee morale might be determined through the use of employee surveys. Risk avoidance could be determined by looking at a project area and generating the costs and liability issues as if the risk actually took place. The same analysis might be undertaken for making a management decision using sustainable development best practices and comparing a previous management decision that was made that did not use these practices.

Application

How then can a company apply sustainable value to its overall vision, mission and strategy? [3]

The first step is to rethink the source of growth. DuPont, once known primarily as a producer of basic and traditional chemicals, is now known as a life sciences company based on clean and green renewable technologies that embrace sustainable development best practices. They have transformed their company and, in doing so, helped the overall chemical industry reposition itself for leadership in the future. Dupont is also a charter or founding member of the World Business Council on Sustainable Development and the U.S. Climate Action Partnership (www.dupont.com/our_company).

DuPont reached a decision point that they had been following a traditional growth model typical of the chemical industry. Strategies of liability and cost reductions, portfolio changes, acquisitions, product development, and globalization had only achieved incremental modest growth.

Value and Growth

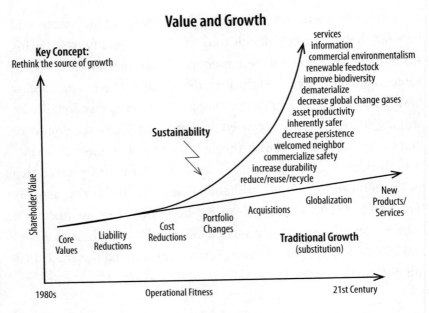

Source: Greg Rubin, Global Business Manager, Dupont, adapted by Norman Christopher, 2012.

For the 21st century DuPont desired a higher growth model that would generate improved operational fitness and increased shareholder value. They made the decision to implement sustainable development best practices to achieve value and growth, as well as establish transformational changes and the need for new leadership.

Many of their strategies were modeled after life cycle analysis (LCA), design for the environment (DfE), green chemistry, clean technologies, and renewable energy technology platforms. Using this highly innovative approach, DuPont has set in place a transformational change model to create future long-term sustainable value.

Creating long-term sustainable value for a company and its business operations requires commitment, dedication, and resiliency. The Boston Consulting Group in 2009 released their report Searching for Sustainability Value Creation in an Era of Diminished Expectations.[4]

The report highlighted several critical factors that will help ensure success for businesses over the long-term. The first is to set a goal to be a market leader in a fast growing profitable segment of the new, green and clean sustainability economy. Secondly, relatively stable businesses can generate a great deal of cash in the short-term that will help create above average sustainable value creation with only modest revenue growth. This cash can be reinvested into new sustainable development projects. Third, many companies today have essentially played out their hand and find few opportunities to grow with adequate returns. Though they are always tweaking and refining existing products and services, it usually results only in small incremental returns. As a result, companies must be willing to weed out those business operations that are cash consumers and unlikely to grow, resulting in poor competitive positioning, and divest or harvest them. At the same time companies must be willing to license new technologies and acquire new businesses that complement existing business operations and are built upon the company's core competencies. Assets to be licensed or acquired should be evaluated in terms of green and clean technologies that are dynamic, disruptive, and offer rapid change. Fourth, companies must manage their businesses as an overall value portfolio by setting specific accountable goals for their businesses over a 3-5 year time horizon, ensuring that business operations know what phase such as a growth, cash or financing, or turnaround they are in, and establishing the appropriate performance metrics for each business model phase.

Another area to be reviewed by a business is the pricing strategy for its products and services. Companies can also achieve additional value for their products and services ensuring they are priced correctly and not subject to common mistakes and flaws.[5] Some of these pricing best practices include:

- Base your pricing on the customer's perception of value, not on costs to develop them. When prices are established on the perceived value of a product or service, sales growth can be achieved with maximized cash generation and profits. In today's marketplace, many customers will base their purchasing decision on perceived value not just on price. Perceived value can be determined by the quality and durability of the product, after-sales service and technical support, social responsibility efforts of the company, the shopping or buying experience, and many more determinants.
- Do not base prices on the "overall marketplace" as companies will begin to see the commoditization of their goods and services by their customer base.
- Do not try to set the same profit margin across different product lines as different customers will determine different perceived value for the same product. Each product's price is a reflection of what that customer is willing to pay.
- Remember to segment your customers through packaging, delivery, and service options in order to realize and capture the additional value that is created for these offerings.
- Alter your prices to changing market conditions, changes in costs, customer needs and wants, and the overall dynamic competitive environment. Be knowledgeable about the market you serve and be willing to change your pricing strategy as necessary.
- Provide incentives for your sales people based on contribution maximization and strategic objectives, not on revenue generated. Selling lower price products always leaves "something on the table."
- Anticipate your competitor's reaction to a price change before implementing the change and thereby avoiding a price war.

Tracking historical price moves by competitors within an industry or market can help with this analysis.

- Invest resources in your pricing practices including the use of real time data, updated procedures, and enterprise system technologies.
- Ensure the development and implementation of internal procedures and controls to optimize pricing strategies including data analysis and review on a consistent basis.
- Spend the proportionate amount of the time on the most profitable customers, not necessarily on those customers that require the most attention. Remember the 80-20 rule. Eighty percent of your sales will come from 20 percent of your customers.

Source: Dennis E. Brown, Atenga, Inc., Ten Common Mistakes Companies Make in Pricing their Products and Services, March 2012, adapted by Norman Christopher, 2012.

Results and Benefits

Creating long-term sustainable value is the preeminent goal for any company or business. Sustainable value creation can provide optimal performance at multiple management dimensions and levels, including both shareholder and stakeholder organizations. Therefore sustainable value creation cannot be viewed by management as just a linear dimensional process.

Stuart Hart and Mark Milstein in their article Creating Sustainable Value provided several frameworks that companies and businesses can utilize to maximize payoffs and reap returns for shareholders and stakeholders. They identified four key areas of potential shareholder value over the short- and long-term as well as internally and externally including cost and risk reduction, reputation and legitimacy, innovation and repositioning, and growth path and trajectory.[6]

Key Dimensions of Shareholder Value

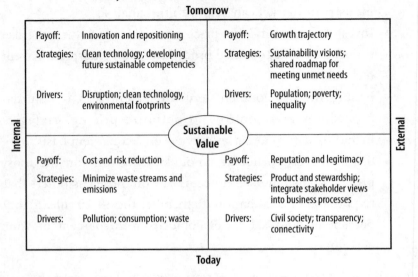

Source: Stuart L. Hart and Mark B. Milstein, Creating Sustainable Value Academy of Management Executive, 2003 Vol. 17. No.2, adapted by Norman Christopher, 2012.

Hart and Milstein described a number of strategies that businesses and companies can develop to maximize the understanding of short-term efficiencies and long-term value. Internally most companies today are being driven by ways to reduce consumption, generate less waste, and minimize pollution. Strategies include generating as little waste and emissions from operations as feasible, while using less resources and materials. The payoff is eco-cost efficiencies and overall risk reduction.

Next most companies today are facing external transparency, civic engagement, and customer buying behavior changes in the markets they serve. Strategies of product stewardship and improved brand and company identity are being developed through the integration of shareholder and stakeholder input. The resulting payoff is improved overall company legitimacy and reputation, such as with more transparent product labeling and community engagement.

However, most companies and organizations are also being challenged by future growth and profitability concerns for their business operations. Key drivers include the need to reduce carbon footprints and their environmental impact from overall operations, as well as the ability to access new disruptive technologies that would enable competitive strengthening and repositioning in the marketplace. As a result companies and businesses internally are assessing their future capabilities, determining and developing their sustainability competencies, and evaluating and pursuing clean technologies. The resulting payoffs include the ability for the company to innovate, reengineer, and reposition their business operations into higher growth and higher market segments of the new, green, clean, and sustainability economy.

And finally some companies are pursuing a long-term sustainability vision for their organization that will enable their businesses to externally capitalize on sustainability opportunities tomorrow and in the future globally, regionally, and locally. In West Michigan, companies such as Steelcase, Herman Miller, Haworth, and other Business and Institutional Furniture Manufacturers Association (BIFMA) members, as well as Cascade Engineering, Amway, and others are good examples. These companies and organizations are being driven by global, international, and domestic sustainable supply chain management issues and opportunities that address social impact issues such as inequity, social justice, and worker rights. The long-term payoffs for these companies and businesses are that they will be seen as socially responsible companies and corporate citizenship leaders with an increased desire by shareholders and stakeholders for doing right as well. Many of these companies are now finding realistic business opportunities serving markets and customers at the "Base of the Pyramid," where billions of people live on less than $5 per day.[7]

Case Studies

BHP Billiton has developed their Business Case for Sustainable Development. They have incorporated a vision of excellence for sustainability including achieving superior performance in financial returns; meeting community, employee, and stakeholders' expectations; and improving health, safety, and the environment. [8]

Sustainability Value Added

If we get management of these right...
• Community Development
• Cultural Heritage
• Product Stewardship
• Depletion of Natural Resources
• Ambient Pollution
• Greenhouse Gas Emissions
• Water
• Biodiversity
• Land
• National Economic Impacts
• Global Economic Impacts
• Liabilities Post-Closure (Environmental/Social)
• Local Economic Impacts
• Fatalities/Injuries
• Employee Relations
• Short- and Long-Term Costs of Injuries/Illnesses
• Occupational Health Exposures
• Employee Skills and Morale
• Human Rights
• Community Health Impacts
• Access to Land and Resources

We can then deliver…
• Increased long-term shareholder returns
• Improved attraction to and retention of work force
• Improved work force morale and productivity
• Security of operations
• Improved license to operate and grow
• Enhanced brand recognition/reputation
• Enhanced stakeholder trust
• Self-sustaining communities
• Improved standards of living
• Improved operational performance and efficiency
• Enhancement of biodiversity
• Reduced business risk
• Improved access to and lower cost of capital
• Better ability to strategically plan for the longer term
• Enhanced economic contribution

Source: BHP Billiton HSEC Full Report 2004, adapted by Norman Christopher, 2012.

Strategic Value Positioning for Sustainability

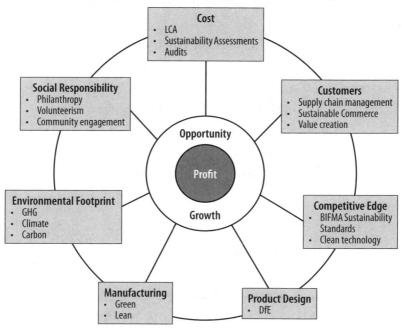

Source: David Rinard for Steelcase, adapted by Norman Christopher, 2012.

BHP Billiton, one of the premier mining companies, has set high expectations for sustainable development value creation that addresses all aspects of the "Triple Bottom Line" (TBL).

Steelcase, one of the leading furniture manufacturers, has established a strategic value positioning for sustainability that focuses on opportunity, growth, and profitability. TBL sustainable development best practices are embedded in cost structures, purchasing, supply chain management, product design manufacturing, and corporate social responsibility.

Over the long-term Steelcase expects sustainable value creation to be reflected in a competitive advantage, additional sustainable commerce with existing and new customers, increased community engagement, and reduced environmental impact.[8]

Comerica Bank has also followed the Stuart Hart and Mark Milstein model for "Creating Sustainable Value." The bank has two primary objectives:

1. To integrate sustainability into their overall business strategies and bank operations that create sustainable value for all their stakeholders

2. To achieve consistent progress in their environmental, social, governance (ESG) performance and business results by managing risks and liabilities while proactively pursuing growth and revenue opportunities created by sustainability change forces

The Comerica Bank Value Creation roadmap[10] focuses on:
- cost and risk reduction
- reputation, brand, and legitimacy
- innovation concerning skills, capabilities, products, and services
- green and new economy revenue opportunities

Comerica Value Creation Road Map

Tomorrow

Innovation: Skills, Products and Services	Green Economy Revenue Opportunities
• Green Economy Training Programs • Employee Sustainability Awareness Training Programs • Energy and Eco-Technology Market Assessments • Green Banking Products and Services	• Renewable Energy and Clean Technology • Energy Efficient Buildings • Smart Grid Technologies • Bio and Sustainable Materials • Alternative Vehicle Technologies • Carbon Capture and Storage • Water Resources Management
Cost & Risk Reduction	**Reputation, Brand & Legitimacy**
• Energy Efficiency • Reduction of GHG Emissions • Reduction of Water and Paper Used • Waste Minimization • Reduction of Corporate Travel • Technology Optimization • Management of Carbon Risk in Lending	• Annual Sustainability Reporting • Carbon Disclosure Project Reporting • Environmental Policy Statement and Commitments • Sustainability Governance Structures • Stakeholder Engagement Processes • LEED Certified (Green) Banking Centers

Internal Focus (left axis) — *External Focus* (right axis)

Today

Source: Comerica Bank 2010 Sustainability Report, adapted by Norman Christopher, 2012.

Call to Action

- Has the company run its business using a "Balanced Scorecard" approach?
- Does the company know how to create additional value for its goods and services?
- What are the sustainability strategies the company can take to increase value and growth for its business?
- What are the important sustainability strategic values for repositioning the business?
- What assets can the business leverage to increase sustainable value creation?

References

1. R. Kaplan and D. Norton, The Balanced Scorecard Measures that Drive Performance, *Harvard Business Revenue*, Jan-Feb 1992, pages 71-79.

2. Jay B. Carney, *Gaining and Sustaining Competitive Advantage* (Pearson Education, 2001).

3. Source: DuPont slide, adapted by Norman Christopher 2012.

4. Searching for Sustainability Value Creation in an Era of Diminished Expectations, http://www.bcg.com/documents/file31738.pdf, accessed August 2011.

5. Dennis E. Brown, Atenga, Inc., Ten Common Mistakes Companies Make in Pricing their Products and Services, http://atenga.com/whitepapers/top-10-pricing-mistakes-most-companies-make, accessed March 2012.

6. Creating Sustainable Value, page 57, http://e4sw.org/papers/Hart_Milstein.pdf, accessed August 2011.

7. Creating Sustainable Value, page 60, http://e4sw.org/papers/Hart_Milstein.pdf, accessed August 2011.

8. Our Approach to Sustainable Development-The Business Case, http://sustainability.bhpbilliton.com/2004/repository/sustainabilityBHPBilliton/ourApproach/businessCase.asp, accessed August 2011.

9. David Rinard Steelcase slide, adapted by Norman Christopher 2012.

10. Comerica Bank Sustainability Report, 2010, http://www.comerica.com/about-us/community-involvement/Pages/sustainability.aspx.

23. SUSTAINABILITY RISK MANAGEMENT

Introduction

Looking back on environmental disasters that many can still relate to, the Exxon Valdez oil spill in 1989 was catastrophic in terms of environmental damage, disruption to local businesses, and adverse effects to the local economy. The same can be said about the BP oil rig disaster of 2010 in the Gulf of Mexico. Most people have also seen a number of additional environmental sustainability risks and hazards associated with the use of asbestos, chlorine containing compounds, lead, and the resultant deforestations, air pollution, acid rain, eutrophication, and biodiversity loss. Some of these environmental sustainability risks are natural occurring, such as with hurricanes and earthquakes. However, many others are "man-made" or induced. There are also social sustainability hazards that arise when companies allow the practice of unfair, inequitable treatment of foreign worker's families and communities in the production and supply of components, products, and services in their supply chain management practices.

Could some of these social and environmental sustainability risks be anticipated or prevented?

Could contingency plans have been developed around sustainability risk management?[1]

The Dow Chemical Company is the case study in this chapter.

Description

There have been two significant environmental disasters and spills both associated with oil exploration and transport. These "spills" caused great harm to the environment, as well as loss of life.

In March 1989, the Exxon Valdez ran aground in Alaska on the Bligh Reef spilling hundreds of thousands of gallons of crude oil. In August 2008 Exxon agreed to pay 75 percent of the $507.5 million damages ruling and in 2009 a federal ruling ordered Exxon to pay an additional $480 million in interest on the delayed punitive damage awards. At the time the Exxon Valdez spill was the 54th largest in history.[2]

In April 2010 BP announced that an oil spill gusher was occurring in the Gulf of Mexico stemming from an oil rig explosion that killed 17 men working on the platform. "One year after the explosion on the Deep Water Horizon, the costs of the human and environment disaster are still being counted."[3] BP put aside $41billion in 2010 to pay for the spill which was 2.5 times their 2009 profit. In one of the largest anticipated fines to be levied by the U.S. EPA, BP could be fined between $1,100 and $4,300 per barrel of oil spilled.

On a social sustainability issue, in 2006 a Pennsylvania jury ruled that Walmart must pay $74.87million in damages to current and former Pennsylvania employees for forcing them to work during rest breaks and "off the clock" times.[4]

Exxon, BP, and Walmart were corporations that were fined. Other corporations such as Nike, who outsourced some of their operations to sweat shops, and Boise Cascade, who practiced cutting down old growth trees, endured boycotts and suffered other legal setbacks. Could any of these occurrences been avoided and managed differently?

Would an in-depth risk assessment have provided any insights to management to help them make better decisions? Today, sustainability risk assessments have become an important management tool for businesses and companies to practice. Sustainability risk management can address many sustainability issues besides social justice issues, and toxic and hazardous waste. These risks can include supply chain, reputational, and physical sustainability risks as well.[5]

Business operations can endure major setbacks with these risks if they are not properly addressed and managed.

Risk Management Examples
Environmental Risks • Toxic and hazardous materials and components • Brownfield and Renaissance Zone development
Supply Chain Risks • Suppliers of raw materials and components • Global network
Product and Technology Risks • Toxic and hazardous materials and products • Emissions such as greenhouse gases
Litigation Risks • Environmental exposure • Shareholder lawsuits
Reputational Risks • Negative brand image • Consumer and shareholder backlash and boycotts
Physical Risk • Changing climate and environmental conditions • Higher insurance premiums

Source: HBR on Green Business Strategy.

Risk options should be analyzed for all business operations and new business opportunities and their potential financial impact determined. What strategy should a business pursue? A business can overlook potential liabilities and be subject to total risk exposure. A company might reduce and mitigate risk to some degree. Another option might be to reduce overall risk exposure. A fourth option might be to avoid risk entirely. All of these options have financial implications. A company must first address their overall risk tolerance as well as try to mitigate, reduce, or avoid risk if at all possible in their business operations as well as with suppliers, shareholders, stakeholders, customers, and the overall community.

How then should companies address and manage risk? In their report Sustainability-Beyond Enterprise Risk Management

(ERM), the leading risk management insurer, Aon Corporation, acknowledges that with sustainability companies can look at risk in a broader and deeper perspective rather than just with Enterprise Resource Management. This new framework can include environmental, social, as well as economic, strategic, and operational considerations and impacts.[6]

Traditional Enterprise Risk Framework
vs
Aon's Business Sustainability Platform

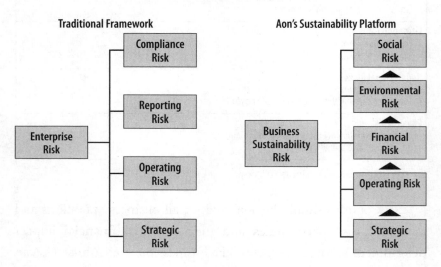

Source: Aon, Sustainability-Beyond Risk Management, adapted by Norman Christopher, 2012.

Traditionally many companies have approached risk using an ERM approach. ERM entails looking at risk from compliance, reporting, operating, and strategic perspectives. Key questions to address involve determining what is the overall management risk appetite? What are the guiding principles that shape management decision making? Next, management needs to ensure that company objectives align with the company mission and are consistent. How will the company manage risk and what are the contingency plans? What resources will be required and deployed? What policies and procedures have been established to effectively deal with the risk? How will communications and information be disseminated amongst shareholders, stakeholders, suppliers, customers, employees, and the communities in which they serve? What ongoing monitoring activities, assessments, and third-party audits are taking place within the organization?

How then is a business sustainability risk framework different? In essence, a business sustainability risk framework builds upon the ERM approach and provides an expanded perspective and view for management. Business sustainability risk allows companies and businesses to proactively look at issues that could significantly impact the organization in the future including social, environmental, financial, operating, and strategic risks.

Some of these future concerns, exposures, and risks could come from a number of TBL areas.

Examples of Potential Environmental, Social, and Economic Risks

Environmental	Social	Economic
• Climate change	• Social justice	• Debt
• Resource depletion	• Worker rights	• Fiscal obligations
• Pollution (air, water, land)	• Diversity	• Tarnished reputation
• Land use	• Health and wellness	• Reduced work force and loss of jobs
• Biodiversity	• Health and safety	

Application

Business Sustainability Risk Management (BSRM) essentially adds two new components of environmental and social risk assessment and provides management with a new tool and capability. BSRM allows management to incorporate both existing as well as future anticipated risk assessments in order to develop better overall scenario and contingency planning. While ERM may involve use of existing tracked data, BSRM may require the development of additional databases and information to be tracked and monitored as well. BSRM has been shown to be compatible and complimentary with all aspects of business operations: [7]

The overall goal of utilizing business sustainability risk management is to improve the overall TBL economic, environmental, and social performance of a company or business.

John Elkington in his book *Cannibals with Forks* first articulated this fully developed Triple Bottom Line (TBL) concept.

- TBL = Financial Performance (F) + Environmental Performance (E) + Social Justice (SJ)
- TBL = F - risk costs of E - risk costs of SJ
- Maximize TBL by reducing risk costs of E & SJ

Source: John Elkington, *Cannibals with Forks*, 1999, adapted by Norman Christopher, 2012.

Overall financial performance is determined by subtracting risk costs associated with social and environmental performance. This performance equals the TBL. In order to maximize the TBL, an organization should focus on reducing the environmental and social risks through BSRM.

Results and Benefits

Bob Willard in his book *The Sustainability Advantage* identified and validated the benefits of sustainability risk management best practices.[8]

Lower market risk such as less chance, risk, or possibility of:

- Regulatory ban
- Reduced demand for core products

- Poor product quality
- Reduced product acceptance

Lower balance sheet risk including:
- Reduced remediation liabilities
- Lower insurance premiums due to lower underwriting losses
- Less chance of reduced property values

Lower operating risk such as:
- Reduced costs for environmental spills and clean ups
- Lower risks regarding worker safety
- Less cost burden for process changes and upgrades
- Less environmental impact with product usage

Lower capital risk cost including:
- Less product redesign and reformulation
- Lower cost substitutions in order to meet new industry standards, certifications, and compliance
- Lower waste and pollution control expenses

Lower overall sustainability risk through a displaced process including:
- Less competitive disadvantage in the marketplace
- Less cost burden for product recalls
- Less tax exposure

BSRM has also demonstrated similar results and benefits:
- Reputation and image where greater than 25 percent of company's reputation is based on social and environmental performance
- Differentiated and value added products and services in the market place such as those built on design for the environment (DfE)

- Improved productivity through use of less energy and materials
- Greater transparency through improved trust and adherence to regulatory compliance
- Decreased supply chain costs through support of sustainability standards and certifications
- Access to greater forms of capital with the use of sustainable development best practices

Overall reduced risk means improvement to the TBL as well as access to easier financing and improved reputation and image for the company and its operations.

Case Study

The Dow Chemical Company recently undertook an in-depth analysis of overall supply chain management risk due to their increased global outsourcing, global procurement, and global manufacturing. The recent oil spills in the Gulf of Mexico paints a vivid picture for their concerns. Dow believed that improved risk mitigation would lead to better overall security.[9]

Concerns were expressed for worker health and safety along the supply chain as well as "at-risk" communities. Environmental regulations and compliance needed to be met but many times there was inconsistency with compliance and regulations across state, national, and country lines. Issues to be addressed also included the need to improve environmental sustainability and reduce overall environmental impacts without adversely affecting the bottom line. Additionally, could these social and environmental concerns and costs be shared across the supply chain?

Dow Chemical has developed and undertaken a comprehensive ERM using a sustainable approach. Dow Chemical focused on transportation which is a key component of the chemical industry. The risk associated with transportation of chemicals is inherently greater than with other industries. Dow also wanted to utilize the most effective technology (MET) and loss prevention principles (LPP) in developing this risk management process which also included assessments, audits, reviews, and reporting of overall supply chain operations.

Dow partnered with many other companies including Union Pacific to create TRANSCAER (Transportation Community Awareness and Emergency Response) which is a national voluntary organization that provides free safety training for Community Emergency Response Teams (CERT) nationally. There are over 160,000 miles of railroad tracks in the U.S. TRANSCAER partners are already designing the next generation tank car, developing GPS tracking satellite systems and sensors, and deploying radio frequency identification technology (RFID). Suppliers, customers, and supply chain partners are now realizing better overall safety in their operations, improved customer satisfaction, better supply chain security, and better inventory management. With their experience to date, Dow chemical believes it can achieve the following results using sustainable supply chain risk mitigation:

- 50 percent improvement in response time to identify, evaluate, and resolve in-transit problems of chemicals transportation
- 20 percent reduction in excess chemical product safety stock inventories
- 20 percent reduction in container fleets
- Up to 90 percent improvement in reliable, on-time delivery vendors
- Elimination of or advanced detection and warning of chemical product theft
- Elimination of historical 10 to 15 percent human error rates associated with manual entry of supply chain data

Call to Action

- What are the most critical risk management areas for the company and its operations?
- What are the greatest areas of potential liabilities to the business and company?
- Has the company reduced its exposure to the environmental risk and business?
- Does the company practice a traditional enterprise risk or sustainability risk management framework?
- How does the company manage uncertainty in business operations?
- How does the company become familiar with risk management best practices at the management, advisory team, and/or board level?

References

1. Don R. Anderson, The Critical importance of Sustainability Risk Management, Risk Management, April 1, 2006.
2. Exxon Valdez, http://en.wikipedia.org/wiki/Exxon_Valdez, accessed August 2011.
3. Counting the Cost of the BP Disaster One Year On, http://www.bbc.co.uk/news/business-13120605, accessed August 2011.
4. Pennsylvania Jury Fines Wal-Mart $78 Million, http://www.msnbc.msn.com/id/15251910/ns/business-us_business/t/pennsylvania-jury-fines-wal-mart-million/, accessed August 2011.
5. Harvard Business Review on Green Business Strategy, Harvard Business School Press, 2007.
6. Sustainability—Beyond Enterprise Risk Management, http://www.aon.com/about-aon/intellectual-capital/attachments/risk-services/sustainability_beyond_enterprise_risk_management.pdf, accessed August 2011.
7. John Elkington, *Cannibals with Forks* (Wiley, 1999).
8. Bob Willard, *The Sustainability Advantage* (New Society, 2002).
9. Sustainability Initiatives at Dow Chemical, http://www.supplychainbrain.com/content/nc/general-scm/environmental/single-article-page/article/sustainability-initiatives-at-dow-chemical-1/, accessed August 2011.

24. EXTERNAL SUSTAINABILITY REPORTING

Introduction

It has always been stated that what you don't monitor or measure, you don't manage or report. If a company or business implements sustainability finance accounting, value creation, and risk management best practices and has already established a "Balanced Scorecard," it most likely will be able to develop and produce a sustainability report as well.

Business owners in today's marketplace are also challenged by new reporting requirements that are being requested by customers and stakeholders to ensure transparency and provide timely and accurate reporting of overall sustainability performance.

A sustainability report can be considered as an extension or expanded version of sustainability finance accounting. It usually takes the form of a TBL format where sustainability performance measurements or metrics are provided for economic, social, and environmental impact areas. The report is primarily developed for external use. The contents of the report can include progress made, or not made, toward stated sustainability goals, milestones, commitments, or initiatives. Sustainability reporting allows businesses, companies, and organizations to share and tell their sustainability story and overall journey. The report, when done properly, can help address shareholder and stakeholder expectations, as well as position the organization as a good corporate citizen in the community.

Sustainability reporting comes in many different types and formats. Some of these sustainability reports are known as Corporate Social Responsibility (CSR); Corporate or Global Citizenship; Corporate Sustainability; Environmental Social Governance (ESG); and TBL Sustainability Indicator Reports that cover "people, planets, profits or economy, environment, and equity" impacts.

The case studies in this chapter include Fifth Third Bank, Dow Chemical, and Dow Corning.

Description

Financial reporting, such as cash flow and profit and loss statements, only focus and capture a portion of the organization's overall risks and potential value creation. Many times financial accounting reports do not suffice. Companies are now being requested to disclose their environmental and social performance as well as economic returns, especially for their global operations.

As a result an increasing number of companies have chosen to develop sustainability reports, mostly on a voluntary basis. The issued sustainability report can be developed in different format styles and with varying degrees of reporting depth. Many companies and businesses with global operations have been able to standardize their sustainability reporting by using the Global Reporting Initiative (GRI) format.

Other companies have begun to develop and generate "Triple Bottom Line" (TBL) sustainability reports as well. TBL sustainability reporting is becoming a standardized reporting process for many global, international, and multinational companies and organizations. Several well-known iconic brand name companies are leading the way such as Nike, Johnson & Johnson, Proctor & Gamble, Baxter International, and General Electric. Each of these companies issue annual sustainability reports based on the "Triple Bottom Line." Global commerce has also raised social justice and other issues such as fair trade, employee health concerns, toxic materials exposure, and overall poor quality products that have been outsourced and manufactured in emerging countries. Transparent sustainability reporting will help address many of these issues and concerns, depending upon the reporting format and performance metrics used.

For many companies the sustainability reporting process has become a complementary fit and extension of the organizational management processes that are already in place. As the business continues to implement sustainable development best practices, this overlap and extension becomes more evident. The World Business Council for Sustainable Development in 2002 issued a report entitled "Sustainable Development Reporting: Striking the Balance" that established a sustainability reporting process and framework.[1]

Sustainability Reporting Process

Drivers
Business Case
Commitment
Approach

5 Review and Learning

1 Objectives

4 Follow-up and Approval

2 Planning

3 Activities

Management Process

Sustainability Reporting Process

3 Construction of the Report

2 Planning

4 Distributing the Report

1 Objectives

5 Collecting and Analyzing Feedback

Source: World Business Council for Sustainable Development, 2002, adapted by Norman Christopher, 2012.

The sustainability reporting process is integrated within the management process and driven by commitment, marketplace driving forces, and the competitive business environment.

As can be seen, the management process follows the "plan-do-check-act" (PDCA) approach, but many times management processes are only seen as internal yardsticks. The Sustainability Reporting process also follows a similar PDCA approach. Sustainability reporting tracks and monitors TBL impacts and provides an opportunity for the company to report more in-depth performance metrics both internally to shareholders as well as externally to community stakeholders that also view the company as a responsible citizen in the community and region.

Today, sustainability reporting has seen a shift from focusing not only on environmental performance but to a more inclusive and integrative approach that includes economic and social performance as well. This TBL perspective provides additional insight for both the company's shareholders and community stakeholders regarding the company's overall performance and impact. Samples of sustainability reports (using different sustainability reporting frameworks from many global, multinational, and international companies) can now be found at:

- Global Reporting Initiative (www.grireporting.org)
- Corporate Register Reporting (www.corporaterigister.com)
- Corporate Social Responsibility Newswire (www.csr.com/reports)

Application

When it comes to monitoring and measuring sustainable development best practices, it is suggested that a business or a company develop a "starter" TBL sustainability report with key performance metrics.

Measuring Sustainability Performance—Impact Area Examples

Environmental Stewardship	Economic Vitality	Social Responsibility
• Energy consumption • Water consumption • Climate mitigation • Waste minimization • Materials usage • Emissions reduction (e.g., carbon, hazardous waste, toxic release inventory (TRI))	• Taxes paid • Productivity rates (e.g., sales per employee) • Amount of local "green" and (EPP) purchasing • Cost control measures (e.g., cost per employee) • Revenues from new or improved sustainable development or DfE designed products • Standardized level wages vs. minimum wages	• Cash and in kind contributions • Employee volunteer hours • Number and amount of citations/fines • Lost time rates • Employee health and safety incidents • Breaches of ethical behavior • Collaborations and partnerships to improve industry environmental and/or social outcomes

Source: Cascade Engineering, www.cascadeng.com/sustainability, adapted by Norman Christopher, 2012.

The "starter" sustainability report can be generated and established by selecting a balanced number of corresponding key performance metrics or measurements that cover the TBL including environmental stewardship, economic vitality, and social responsibility. These external reports are usually generated and reported with transparency on an annual basis.

Cascade Engineering is a well-known and well-recognized business in West Michigan. Fred Keller is President and Chairman of the Board. Keller is considered to be one of the most influential and important business leaders in sustainable development nationally, as well as in Michigan. Cascade Engineering has approximately $250 million in sales and has developed, embedded, and utilized sustainability best practices to transform their business model, which had been geared mainly toward the automotive industry. Since 2006, Cascade has developed an annual TBL sustainability report.

Their most recent annual scorecard provides very favorable sustainability performance results with Cascade posting impressive results in:

- Lowering accident and incident rates
- Reducing lost work time
- Reducing Greenhouse Gas (GHG) emissions
- Using increasing amounts of recycled materials
- Reducing water consumption
- Reducing their waste to landfill costs

Results and Benefits

Sustainability reporting can be looked at as a management tool, or as an accountability tool.[2] By generating sustainability reporting as a composite tool for shareholders and stakeholders, there are a number of mutual benefits:

- There is growing evidence that overall financial performance is improved.
- Internal shareholders and external stakeholders, collaborations, working relationships, and partnerships are enhanced and developed.
- Risks and liabilities are reduced and overall risk management improved.
- Investor relationships can be grown among individuals, banks, and other institutions.
- New product, market, and business opportunities can be pursued.
- Company or business reputation and image is enhanced and more visible.
- The company or business can compete more effectively locally, regionally, nationally, and globally.
- Business leadership in various markets and industries is evidenced by the increasing number of firms that issue sustainability reports.
- Value channels and sustainability supply chain requirements can be met more effectively and efficiently.

- The ability to benchmark world class leaders in sustainable development best practices is now more readily accessible.
- The company or business can become more proactive in addressing market, business, and industry needs and requirements.
- The company or business can attract and retain employees more effectively.
- Company and business management can make a greater commitment to leadership and more effective executive decision making.

However, the overriding primary value that sustainability reporting provides is the transparency it generates among shareholders, stakeholders, consumers, and interest groups. It has been reported that an estimated 80-90 percent of all multinational corporations report some sustainability data without adhering to any formal guidelines.[3]

There are also a number of issues or obstacles for businesses to sustainability reporting moving forward. First of all there are up-front costs mainly in terms of time, and commitment but also with possible consulting fees to develop such a report – especially the first one. The resource costs and time commitment may be seen as prohibitive, especially for Small to Medium-size Enterprises (SMEs) versus large multinational or global corporations. However, as these up-front costs begin to decrease over time, sustainability reporting becomes more cost effective as in-house systems for data collection and monitoring become established. Secondly, although the GRI is recognized as the "gold standard" in sustainability reporting, there aren't any universal and especially national sustainability reporting frameworks and models that have been well tested with consensus. Several other important factors can also adversely impact sustainability reporting. These include lack of commitment from top management, as well as the short-term thinking by financial analysts who are only concerned about the next quarter's business report. However, even given these issues and concerns, sustainability reporting is becoming more evident among small- to medium-size businesses and enterprises.

Case Studies

Fifth Third Bank completed its second Corporate Social Responsibility Report in 2010. In essence this report covered all aspects of the TBL and can be considered an overall sustainability report as well.[4] Highlights include:

Economic
Financial Improvement
- Since its inception in 2000, over 6,000 students have graduated from the Fifth Third Young Banker's Club for 5th graders.
- Over 11,000 student workbooks and 87 teacher kits were handed out on Dave Ramsey's Foundation Personal Finance in 12 states.
- Since its inception in 2007, over $2.3 billion bank owned mortgage loans have been modified through the "You have options" program.
- Nearly 22,000 people attended free E-Bus events with 2,154 taking one-on-one credit counseling sessions.

Fair and Responsible Lending
- The Fifth Third Community Development Corporations (CDC) invested $2.54 million in affordable housing and new market tax credits.
- Received a "satisfactory" rating under obligations to the Community Reinvestment Act (CRA).

Social

Philanthropy and Volunteerism

- Made $2.6 million in grants in support of health and human services, education, community development, and the arts.
- Provided $7 million in support to the United Way through affiliates and employees.
- Donated 17 one-time scholarships of $2,500 at an institute of higher learning.
- Acted as a trustee for over 70 private foundations.
- The North Carolina affiliate donated over 1,000 volunteer hours for 40 different organizations.

Diversity and Inclusion

- Employs over 21,000 with respect and inclusion as a core value of the company.
- 92 percent of employees participated in an engagement survey with a mean of 4.13 on a 5 point scale.
- Was one of 29 companies to earn the Gallup's 2011 Great Workplace awards.

Environmental

Environmental Sustainability

- Reduced electricity consumption by 12 percent or 27.5 million kWh relative to 2007 baseline.
- Reduced natural gas consumption by 39 percent or 183,500 million BTU relative to 2007 baseline.
- Reduced GHG emissions by 16 percent or 26,000 MT CO_2E relative to 2007 baseline.
- Purchased renewable energy certificates (RECs) equivalent to 2 percent of projected electricity consumption.
- Reduced paper usage by 300 tons.
- Recycled 1,954 tons of paper and 63 tons of cardboard.

Also, Dow Chemical's 2015 Sustainability Goals reports show its progress on:

- Sustainable chemistry
- Climate change
- Clean power
- Energy efficiency and conservation
- Product safety leadership
- Community success
- Human health and the environment
- The percentage of sales from Highly Advantaged sustainable chemistry performance products increased from 3.4 percent in 2009 to 4.3 percent in 2010
- Measured in BTUs per pound of product, Dow's manufacturing intensity has improved more than 40 percent since 1999, saving the company a cumulative total of $24 billion and 5,200 trillion BTU's
- Since 1990 Dow has avoided over 200 million metric tons of GHG emissions
- In 2011 there were 411 Product Safety Assessments (PSAs) undertaken. PSAs now cover over 75 percent of Dow's product sales revenues
- Dow currently generates over 215 megawatts of clean energy which represents over half of its target of 400 megawatts of clean power by 2025
- At the end of 2011, Dow's injury and illness severity rate was 1.09 per 200,000 hours of work, a 23 percent improvement over 2010
- Dow experienced 262 Primary Contaminant incidents in 2011 and has a stated goal of having 130 or fewer incidents which represents a 90 percent reduction from 2005
- The company also has a stated goal of achieving individual community acceptance ratings for 100 percent of Dow sites where there is a major presence[5]

In addition, Dow Corning issues a quarterly report that focuses on the TBL areas of sustainability as well.[6] These areas include:

- Employee health and safety
- Energy efficiency
- Process safety
- Green House Gas (GHG) emission performance
- Waste reduction and value recovery
- Financial performance

In 2005 the corporation set four aggressive environment, health, and safety sustainability goals covering a five year period including:

- Reducing GHG emissions through energy efficiency projects, use of renewable energy, and overall carbon sequestration efforts
- Improving employee and overall process safety through an aggressive reduction of occupational injuries, illnesses, and incidents
- Reduction of the overall environmental impact of processes, products, and technology
- Pursuit of zero waste and emissions through waste reduction, conversion, recycle, reuse, and recovery

How is Dow Corning's sustainability performance? As of 3Q11 their report indicates:

- A reduction of 30 percent in GHG per kilogram of product versus a goal of 20 percent
- A total occupational injury and illness rate of 1.11 versus 1.47 in 3Q10
- A process incident rate of 1.97 versus 1.99 in 3Q10

Dow Corning follows triple bottom line sustainability through their "prosperity, planet, and people" programs and initiatives. For example, Dow Corning supports "prosperity" by assisting textile producers in finding new eco-efficient solutions. For "people," they believe in their employees being sources of new creative and innovative ideas, becoming active members of the community, and pursing safety as one of their core values. For the "planet," Dow Corning supports Responsible Care and eco-innovation programs.

Call to Action

- Has the company ever produced an accountability or sustainability report for both shareholders and stakeholders?
- Is the company prepared to become more transparent in the reporting of its business operations and results?
- Can the company prepare, develop, and issue a "starter" sustainability report?
- What are the steps the company can take to integrate sustainability reporting into its overall management process?

References

1. Sustainable Development Reporting—Striking the Balance, *World Business Council for Sustainable Development*, 2002, page 33.
2. Adapted from: The Benefits of Sustainability Reporting, http://souleconomy.com/the-benefits-of-sustainability-reporting/, accessed August 2011; and Karen J. Jonowski and Kathleen Giligod, Trends in Sustainability Reporting: A Close up Look at Bay Area Companies, Eco-Strategy Group, April 2010.
3. Fifth Third Bank, Corporate Social Responsibility Report, www.53.com/CSRR, accessed August 2011.
4. How Many Corporations Issue Sustainability Reports?, http://www.quora.com/How-many-corporations-issue-sustainability-reports, accessed March 2012.
5. Dow Chemical 2015 Sustainability Goals, www.dow.com/sustainability/pdf/Q4_Sustainability_Report.pdf, accessed September 2012.
6. Dow Corning, www.dowcorning.com/sustainability, accessed April 2012.

CONCLUSION

Demystifying Sustainability: A Practical Guidebook for Business Leaders and Managers has been designed and developed for managers and executives of enterprises, organizations, and businesses who share the following belief. They want to improve and grow their enterprises while decreasing their environmental impact, while also creating additional economic impact, and improving the social impact of their respective organizations and the communities in which they operate and serve.

This guide is about processes and tools that can be used to renew and improve organizational performance. "RE" is about doing things over again and doing things anew. That is what sustainable development is all about – continuously investing, continuously improving, and continuously learning about applied new best practices.

Businesses can REDESIGN their systems by implementing design for the environment (DfE), total cost accounting, and life cycle analysis (LCA) processes. All of these new systems and processes are focused on "cradle to cradle" not "cradle to grave" approaches. Cradle to cradle strategies involve interdisciplinary holistic systems thinking and connections. Using these approaches, organizations can develop new creative, innovative, and entrepreneurial strategies and action plans that will position their businesses more competitively in the marketplace.

Organizations can RESTORE the land and properties on which their facilities operate by focusing on environmental stewardship areas of importance. Businesses can implement Environmental

Management Systems (EMS) to ensure that their operations do not impact the environment in a detrimental way, such as through air, water, and waste pollution sources. EMS is designed for companies to plan-do-check-act on a consistent and regular basis. Organizations can also develop climate action plans to help mitigate carbon generation, as well as to help adapt and reduce their impact to climate change.

Enterprises can also REBUILD their facilities, using natural landscaping and improved land use. Their operations and corporate locations can benefit by using Green and LEED building standards and certifications. LEED building design and construction standards are available for both existing buildings (EB) as well as new construction (NC). By building to LEED standards, organizations can also obtain LEED certification ratings for their buildings that range from LEED certified, to silver, to gold, and to platinum levels. LEED buildings can generate substantial energy and water savings that typically range from 25-35 percent over similar buildings. The cost for LEED buildings that obtain LEED certified or LEED silver status also do not usually cost more than other similar building construction. Additionally, green and LEED buildings also provide a more healthy and productive workplace for the building occupants.

Organizations and businesses that REDUCE or minimize their waste can find substantial savings and efficiencies. One simple approach is to recycle waste materials such as paper, metal, plastic, cardboard, food, and even electronic waste. Many of these recycled materials can be sold as scrap materials and generate a side-stream or by-product waste income. Recycled metals today are especially in high demand, as commodity costs have risen. Many times these waste stream materials can be REWORKED and REPROCESSED and used as raw materials in manufacturing processes. By REUSING waste materials, enterprises can realize significant cost savings, as well as potentially improve upon or reduce their environmental impact or environmental footprint.

By implementing sustainable development best practices, organizations and businesses can REINVEST their cost savings into other sustainable development projects and opportunities. Sustainable development best practices can generate efficiencies and cost savings in the short-term, as well as create accrued cost avoidance, reduced risk, and tangible and intangible value in the long-term. These cost benefit strategies will enable businesses to "sustain sustainability" throughout the tactical and strategic plans for their organizations.

Enterprises can also REWARD their employees for implementing sustainable development best practices through recognition and incentive programs. One of the most effective approaches for organizations to take to communicate sustainable development is to highlight "sustainability stories" as told by their employees. Workers learn best from other workers!

Management of businesses and organizations can also become role models for their enterprise and their employees. They can REVEAL their integrity and accountability through their actions with both internal shareholders and external stakeholders.

Businesses, organizations, and enterprises need to embrace transparency in their operational performance both to their internal shareholders as well as to their external community stakeholders. One approach is to reveal their integrity and transparency through periodic sustainability reports. These reports are usually issued annually and report progress on the "TBL" using key environmental, economic, and social performance indicators and metrics. These sustainability reports help establish credibility and accountability for organizations, as well as improve overall brand image.

Overall by implementing sustainable development best practices, managers can RECREATE, REFRESH, and REVIVE the overall performance of their organizations. The improvement can be realized in the performance of the work force, as well as the "TBL" of environmental, economic, and social progress and performance of their company and business operations.

The MIT Sloan Management Review in conjunction with the Boston Consulting Group issued a research report in the winter of 2011 entitled "Sustainability: The Embracers Take Advantage." Over 3,000 business executives were interviewed during the economic downturn of 2009 and 2010. The results of the study are very revealing:

- "Sustainability spending has survived the downturn with almost 60 percent saying that their investment increased in 2010."
- "All companies, both embracers and cautious adopters, see the benefits of strategies such as improved resource efficiency and waste management."
- "Companies across all industries agree that acting on sustainability is essential to remaining competitive."
- "All companies recognize the brand-building benefits of developing a reputation for being sustainability-driven. This benefit was rated greatest by all respondents."

From this study, as well as the many others, businesses, organizations, and enterprises can all recognize that sustainable development best practices have gained worldwide use and support. These practices are here to stay globally, nationally, regionally, as well as locally here in West Michigan. The benefits and results are real and tangible!

I wish you all great success on your sustainability journey. Stay the course!

Best!

Norman Christopher
Grand Valley State University

ACKNOWLEDGMENTS

Encouragement is What We all Need!

As I look back on this Practical Guide and its development, I have been encouraged by so many people of distinction and influence along the way. I have spent my professional career in business until my most recent years at Grand Valley State University. During my career in business, I have been afforded the opportunity to serve in many various and different management capacities, beginning as a salesman and concluding as a president. I have always been interested in applying business best practices, raising the bar, and improving performance. I was always most curious about learning what works and why. There has also been a desire to learn more about creative, innovative, and entrepreneurial business development strategies and approaches. *Sustainability Demystified!: A Practical Guide for Business Leaders and Managers* is about those best practices that businesses can apply now to improve performance today as well as in the future. Many thanks and heartfelt appreciation goes out to the following:

- Roy Kesting, an Olin Corporation business unit executive, for encouraging me to start a business while having a full time position, to obtain my MBA, and to attend the Program for Management Development at Harvard.
- Fred DiMaria, a business consultant, for helping me to learn about business consultancy services and how to effectively deliver projects on time that meet client expectations.
- John Senz, a Lubrizol Corporation company president, for supporting transformational business development capital

projects and assisting me in the implementation of business development strategic plans.

- Dick Garner, past CEO at Haviland Enterprises for helping me to learn about and manage a family owned business.
- John Logie, a previous mayor of Grand Rapids, for welcoming my wife and I to the Grand Rapids area and helping me to feel at home in new surroundings.
- John Canepa, the past President of Old Kent Bank in Grand Rapids, for encouraging me to remain in the Grand Rapids area and continue to serve the local community.
- John Jackoboice, past president of Monarch Hydraulics, for spending countless hours with me to mutually learn about sustainable development best practices, as well as coaching and mentoring me on my professional journey.
- Tim Schad, previous vice president of administration at Grand Valley State University, for hiring me as a business consultant and helping me to start my rewarding career at GVSU.
- Stuart Hart, author of Capitalism at the Crossroads, for allowing me to join the Base of the Pyramid Learning Laboratory at Cornell University and opening doors to network among other leading recognized sustainability practitioners.
- President Tom Haas of Grand Valley State University for placing confidence in me and empowering our Sustainability Initiative, as well as embracing sustainability as a core value at the university.
- Dean James Williams of the Seidman College of Business at Grand Valley State University for allowing me to develop and teach sustainability courses at Grand Valley in the Masters in Business Administration program.
- Dr. Jaideep Motwani, chair of the Management Department at the Seidman College of Business at Grand Valley State

University for supporting the development of the Practical Guide and progressing the development of an MBA program with an Emphasis in Sustainability.

- Wendy Wenner, past dean of the Brooks College of Interdisciplinary Studies at Grand Valley State University for her support in guiding the Sustainability Initiative, formalizing my current position, and chairing the Sustainable Community Development Initiative Advisory Council.
- Mayor George Heartwell of Grand Rapids for being a sustainability visionary and leader for our city and community, a close friend, and a fellow fly fisherman.
- Fred Keller, chairman and president of Cascade Engineering for the encouragement and support in the pursuit of excellence and leadership in sustainable development best practices on a personal, community, and regional basis.
- Bob Willard, author of *The Sustainability Advantage*, who provided observations and perspectives on the framework for this book, asked all the tough questions about being a writer and author, and encouraged me to stay the course to complete it!
- Sukhmani Singh, Manprit Kaur, Chris Richter, and Andrea Marz, students at Grand Valley State University, who helped provide administrative support during various stages of this work.
- Vern Jones and Dirk Wierenga of Principia Media, for their friendship, support, and partnership in the editing, publishing, and printing of the book. Thanks!
- My wife Anita and our family for their encouragement and support for allowing me to spend the required time to write and publish this Practical Guide.
- To the many others that I have not mentioned who have been instrumental, supportive, encouraging, and helpful

with this book and my career, as well as the many others not mentioned who have been using applied sustainability best practices in their companies and organizations.

"With men it is impossible, but not with God, for with God all things are possible"

Mark 10:27 (NKJV)

"Let a man so consider us, as servants of Christ and stewards of the mysteries of God. Moreover it is required in stewards that they be found faithful."

I Corinthians 4: 1-2 (NKJV)

Norman Christopher
August 10, 2012

APPENDIX A

Selected Business Resources

1. American Sustainable Business Council (www.asbcouncil.org). The mission of this organization and website is to disseminate information about public policies that ensure a vibrant, just, and sustainable economy.

2. Center for Sustainability (www.centerforsustainability.org). A web-based clearing house of information for consumers, businesses, non-profit organizations, government agencies including sustainability programs, conferences, workshops and publications.

3. CERES (www.ceres.org). Founded the Global Reporting Initiative. The mission of this broad based coalition group of public and private organizations is to embed sustainability guiding principles into day-to-day business practices and to address sustainability.

4. Clean Energy Coalition (www.cec-mi.org). This website provides information about consuming less energy and using more renewable energy in Michigan across our communities and structures.

5. Environmental Protection E-News (www.1105media.com). The Environmental Protection E-News on this website is a solution resource for managing air, water, energy, and waste issues.

6. Fivewinds International (www.fivewinds.com) is an experienced management consulting firm in sustainability with

available best practices, tools, and processes. White papers are also available.

7. Global Reporting Initiative (www.globalreporting.org). The "GRI" is a multi-stakeholders group that develops and disseminates global applicable and acceptable sustainability reporting guidelines and performance reporting.

8. Goodguide (www.goodguide.com). Goodguide provides information on healthy, safe, and green products using expert ratings for popular food, household chemicals, personal care, and other products.

9. Great Lakes Renewable Energy Association (www.glrea. org). The GLREA is an organization that educates, advocates, promotes, and publicly demonstrates renewable energy technologies in the Great Lakes region.

10. Green Biz (www.greenbiz.com). Green Biz provides green business news and tools focused on sustainability success including resource efficiency, CSR, environmental and green jobs, supply chain, and marketing, etc.

11. Green Economy Post (http://greeneconomypost.com). This information and updated resources website provides ongoing information on green jobs and careers, business sustainability, police, green business, and other opportunities.

12. Green Guide for Healthcare (www.gghc.org). This clearinghouse is a best practices website for creating high performance for the health care industry, operations, buildings, and healing environments.

13. International Society of Sustainability Professional (www. sustainabilityprofessionals.org). This website is for sustainability professionals and practitioners dealing with conferences, best practices, book reviews, and training opportunities for those who are trying to make sustainability a standard practice.

14. Local First (www.localfirst.com). This website offers sustainability related events, activities, workshops, and networking for small to medium-sized local industrial and retail businesses in West Michigan with a focus on local purchasing and sustainability.

15. Local Harvest (www.localharvest.org) is America's #1 organic and local food website that maintains an ongoing list of local food sources.

16. Michigan Small Business and Technology Development Center (www.misbtdc.org). This organization offers training and development resources and best practices including consulting for small businesses.

17. Michigan State University, Land Policy Institute (http://www.landpolicy.msu.edu). This information source deals with land policy and sustainability related news, conferences, white papers, and other research journal articles. There also are many forums related to land use, economic development, and sustainability.

18. Natural Logic (www.natlogic.com). This website is a strategic advisor to the sustainable economy and offers regular updates in a number of areas to help companies and governments design, implement, and measure profitable sustainability strategies.

19. On Sustainability (www.onsustainability.com). This website provides sustainability news relating to municipalities, cities, and communities as well as conferences and events. It also includes a scholarly journal.

20. Sustainability (www.sustainability.com). This website is a think tank that provides the latest information on sustainability surveys and challenges as well as topics of interest to help transform business leadership on sustainability. A library of resources is also available.

21. EDC, the official magazine for the LEED professional (www. edcmag.com). This website that features an on-line magazine, feature, products for manufacturing and facility managers across the education, retail, industrial, and government sectors.

22. Sustainable Grand Rapids (www.sustainablegr.com). This City of Grand Rapids website provides updated sustainability articles, conferences, events, and sustainability newsletters, concerning business, academic institutions, non-profits, and communities in Grand Rapids and the surrounding area.

23. Sustainable Industries (www.sustainableindustries.com). This website is a portal for updated sustainable business related information on a variety of industries such as green building, clean energy and technologies, food, finance, transportation, and education including a monthly publication and best practices guide.

24. Sustainability Journal (http://www.liebertpub.com/sus). The Sustainability Journal of Record, is an online publication regarding sustainability topics of interest, articles, alerts, and news.

25. Sustainability-Reports (www.sustainability-reports.com). This portal offers sustainability reports from global and international companies all over the world by sector and country.

26. Sustainability Source (www.ene.com). This website from Ecology and the Environment provides multidisciplinary expertise, ideas, innovation, and technology to improve performance through sustainable solutions.

27. Sustainability Watch (www.ebscohost.com). This website provides summaries on over 2,000 sustainability related topics and best practices including sustainability trends and change forces, as well as databases and other resources.

28. Tree Hugger (www.treehugger.com). This website features aesthetic prospectives on sustainable design, green new, and solutions.
29. Waste News (www.wasterecylingnews.com). This website provides up-to-date news on waste and recycling initiatives.
30. Water and Wastewater News (www.eponline.com). This environmental protection website provides solution resources for managing air, water, energy, and waste issues.
31. World Business Council for Sustainable Development (www.wbcsd.org). Over 2,000 international firms have joined this coalition with a commitment to "triple bottom line" sustainability. The website also offers a "How to Report" guide and many sustainable development resources and best practices for change.

APPENDIX B

Listing of Acronyms

~	Approximately
AASHE	Association for Advancement of Sustainability in Higher Education
ACUPCC	American College & University Presidents' Climate Commitment
AIA	American Institute of Architects
AIAG	Automotive Industry Action Group
ANSI	American National Standards Institute
ASTM	formerly American Society for Testing and Materials
BIFMA	The Business and Institutional Furniture Manufacturers Association
BLS	Bureau of Labor Standards
BSR	Business for Social Responsibility
CCAR	California Climate Action Registry
CCP	"Clean" Cities for Climate Protection
CERT	Community Emergency Resource Team
CFL	Compact Florescent Lightbulbs
CHP	Combined Heat and Power
CPUs	Central Processing Units
CO_2	Carbon Dioxide
CRT	Cathode Ray Tube
CSP	Community Sustainability Partnership
CSR	Corporate Social Responsibility

DfD	Design for Disassembly
DfE	Design for Environment
DfL	Design for Life
DfS	Design for Sustainability
DOC	Department of Commerce
DOE	Department of Energy
EoL	End of Life
EMS	Environmental Management System
EPA	Environmental Protection Agency
EPEAT	Electronic Product Environmental Assessment Tool
EPP	Environmentally Preferred Purchasing
EQAT	Environmental Quality Action Team
ERM	Enterprise Risk Management
EROI	Environmental Return on Investment
ERP	Enterprise Resource Planning
ESG	Environmental Social Governance
EVA	Economic Value Added
FSC	Forest Stewardship Certified
GBCI	Green Building Certification Institute
GDM	Gross Domestic Product
GE	General Electric
GHG	Green House Gas
GPC	Green Products Compilation
GRAM	Grand Rapids Art Museum
GRCC	Grand Rapids Community College
GRPS	Grand Rapids Public Schools
GSN	Green Suppliers Network
GVSU	Grand Valley State University
ICCF	Inner City Christian Federation
ICLEI	International Council for Local Environmental Initiatives
ILBI	International Living Building Institute

KWH	Kilowatt Hours
LCA	Life Cycle Analysis
LED	Light Emitting Diode
LEED	Leading Environmental and Energy Design
LOHAS	Lifestyle of Health and Sustainability
LPP	Loss Prevention Principles
MDEQ	Michigan Department of Environmental Quality
MEDC	Michigan Economic Development Corporation
MET	Most Effective Technology
MML	Michigan Municipal League
MMTC	Michigan Manufacturing Technology Center
MRO	Maintenance, Repair, and Operations
NGO	Non-Government Organization
NMI	Natural Marketing Institute
PCR	Post-Consumer Recycled Content
RCRA	Resource Conservation and Recovery Act
RECs	Renewable Energy Credits
RFID	Radio Frequency Identification Technology
RFQ	Request for Quotations
ROA	Return on Assets
ROCE	Return on Capital Employed
ROE	Return on Equity
ROI	Return on Investment
RPN	Responsible Purchasing Network
SAG	Self-Assessment Guide
SCORE	Sustainability Competency and Opportunity Rating Evaluation
SFI	Sustainable Forest Initiative
SMA	Sustainable Management Accounting
SME	Small and Medium-size Enterprise
SPE	Society of Plastic Engineers

SRG	Sustainable Research Group
SRI	Socially Responsible Investing
SROI	Social Return on Investment
STARS	Sustainability Tracking Assessment Reporting System
SWOT	Strengths, Weaknesses, Opportunities, Threats
TBL	Triple Bottom Line
TRI	Toxic Release Inventory
USDA	United States Drug Administration
USGBC	U.S. Green Building Council
VOCs	Volatile organic compounds
WBCSD	World Business Council on Sustainable Development
WMEAC	West Michigan Environmental Action Council
WMSA	West Michigan Strategic Alliance
WMSBF	West Michigan Sustainable Business Forum
WMSPC	West Michigan Sustainable Purchasing Consortium

INDEX

ABOUT THE AUTHOR

Norman Christopher is currently the Executive Director of Sustainability at Grand Valley State University. Prior to joining GVSU in 2004, he served in many management capacities in the chemical industry including sales, product, marketing, general, and executive management positions including Chief Operating Officer, President, and Chief Executive Officer. He helped improve the performance of the Dow Chemical Company, Olin Corporation, Lubrizol Corporation, and Haviland Enterprises.

During the last eight years, Norman has been actively developing, applying, and supporting the growth of sustainable development best practices on a local, regional, and national level.

Currently, Norman serves on a number of boards, advisory groups, and committees including:

- The City of Grand Rapids Sustainability Team
- The Grand Rapids Community Sustainability Partnership Leadership Team
- The Michigan Chemical Council Advisory Board
- The Business and Institutional Furniture Manufacturers Association Sustainability Assessment E-3 Joint Committee
- The Seeds of Promise Board
- The Department of Commerce Environmental Technologies Trade Advisory Committee
- GVSU's Sustainable Community Development Initiative Advisory Council

Norman also teaches several MBA courses in sustainability at the Seidman College of Business at GVSU. In the recent years GVSU has received national and global recognition for its sustainability activities and programs by a number of college guides including the Princeton Review, Kaplan, Peterson, Sustainable Endowment Institute, and the Sierra Club. More information can be found at www.gvsu.edu/sustainability.

Norman is married to his wife Anita and lives in Ada, Michigan. They have two children and four grandchildren.